Morality and Foreign Policy

Other books by Kenneth W. Thompson

Principles and Problems of International Politics   1950
Man and Modern Society   1953
Christian Ethics and the Dilemmas of Foreign Policy   1959
Political Realism and the Crisis of World Politics   1960
American Diplomacy and Emergent Patterns   1962
Foreign Policies in a World of Change   1963
The Moral Issue in Statecraft   1966
Higher Education for National Development   1972
Foreign Assistance: A View from the Private Sector   1972
Reconstituting the Human Community   1972
Understanding World Politics   1975
World Politics   1976
Higher Education and Social Change   1976
Changing Times   1976
Truth and Tragedy   1977
Ethics and Foreign Policy: An Essay on Major Approaches   1977
Interpreters and Critics of the Cold War   1978
Foreign Policy and the Democratic Process   1978
Ethics, Functionalism, and Power in International Politics   1979
Masters of International Thought   1980

❖ Morality and Foreign Policy

Kenneth W. Thompson

43-751

LOUISIANA STATE UNIVERSITY PRESS
Baton Rouge and London

Design: Joanna Hill
Typeface: VIP Baskerville
Composition: LSU Press
Printing: Thomson-Shore, Inc.
Binding: John H. Dekker, Inc.

LIBRARY OF CONGRESS CATALOGING IN PUBLICATION DATA

Thompson, Kenneth W   1921–
    Morality and foreign policy.

    Includes bibliographical references and index.
    1. United States—Foreign relations—Moral and
religious aspects. 2. International relations—Moral
and religious aspects. I. Title.
JX1417.T49   172'.4   79–23211
ISBN 0-8071-0656-9 (cloth)
ISBN 0-8071-1007-8 (paper)

Louisiana Paperback Edition, 1982

To Hans J. Morgenthau

Contents

Acknowledgments

Acknowledgment of all the encouragement and help received in a project extending over several years is bound to be incomplete. For thoughts about morality and foreign policy, plainly there is no beginning and no end. For me, the subject took on its first importance in a family setting where no issue was discussed more consistently than that of right and wrong. Fortunately, it was an issue for both my mother and my father, for whom inquiry was more appropriate than dogmatism. I must acknowledge, therefore, my first debt to parents who taught by example open-mindedness and free discussion of the great themes of justice and freedom, virtue and self-interest, good and evil. Acknowledgments that are inclusive, as this example illustrates, go back to the formative years of my life.

On a more immediate level, I must also thank my secretary, Kathryn Wiencek, who has assisted in the final stages of preparation of the manuscript; Frances Lackey of the Center for Advanced Studies at the University of Virginia, who edited, proofread, and typed first drafts of the manuscript with patience, good humor, high intelligence, and sound judgment; Maebelle L. Morris, who also assisted me at the center with great energy and skill; and Dean W. Dexter Whitehead, director of the center, who made possible two years of free and productive research and thought for which I shall always be most grateful.

I also want to thank my wife, Beverly C. Thompson, who put aside many of her own personal interests and plans to enable me to go forward with this work.

Modified versions of some of the sections in this book have appeared in the *New Oxford Review, Orbis, Review of Politics, Journal of Politics, Common Ground*, and in my book *Herbert Butterfield: The Ethics of History and Politics*, published by the University Press of America.

Introduction

A treatise on morality and foreign policy runs the risk of either over-stating or underestimating the influence of the former on the latter. Nations, like individuals, are endlessly tempted to claim that they are more moral than they are. National self-righteousness has run like a red skein through much of American diplomatic history. Doctrines such as no entangling alliances, manifest destiny, and Wilsonianism all rested at their center on a rather extravagant estimate of the American national character and American foreign policy. An opposite error, and one to which Americans are especially inclined, is the cynicism that de-rives from failure to take the harsh imperatives of international politics in stride. Once committed to great power politics or to fighting a war for the unconditional surrender of an implacable foe, American lead-ers have thrown caution to the winds and have tended to make an abso-lute out of such imperatives as force and power. They have stayed out of wars until the eleventh hour, but once engaged they have sought to-tal victory. From having nothing to do with the world, Americans have fashioned a policy of having everything to do with it—but on their own terms.

Anxiety, which has been the root cause of personal and group inse-curity in other cultures, may partially explain the sharp and dramatic turns from moralism to cynicism and back in American foreign policy. Some, though not all, of our early American diplomats felt out of place in the courts of late eighteenth- and nineteenth-century European states. They poured ridicule on their European counterparts, particularly for their exaggerated attention to protocol and diplomatic ritual. More than once, an American government has sent its envoys to negotiate peace with nothing that resembled a plan for settlement of territorial disputes, and they have often failed to define terms they were prepared to accept and defend.

Before we can talk about what is morally right for states, we must come face to face with the security-power dilemma. Like individuals, nations are anxious and insecure, seek influence and power to check threats against them, and often become caught up in a profound moral and political predicament. Because they cannot defend their acts solely in terms of political interests, they cover the nakedness of their fears and dreams of expansionism by moral statements and ideological rationalizations. Yet their righteousness as they seek to convey it to the rest of the world is usually more than "a tissue of lies and self-deceptions." It may often express honest intent, and moral statements by men and nations can indeed express genuine commitments and deeply held beliefs. The classical critics are sometimes right in asserting that statesmen and political leaders do in fact say what they mean and strive to instruct the people in what is right.

Yet the rationalists obscure political reality when they ignore the self-justifying nature of much political discourse. The function served by political rationalization ought not to lie beyond the understanding of political scientists or observers of the political scene. Surely it has its counterpart in the habits of the child who accuses his sibling of having prompted the current aggression. Whatever the requirements of legitimate self-defense, conflicts are heightened and struggles made more irreconcilable by the altogether understandable human tendency to excuse and accuse, to justify and condemn, and to build nearly impregnable moral defenses around every human response and action.

Any study of morality and foreign policy that overlooks the moral predicament and ignores the fact that human conflict has roots in the security-power dilemma may be momentarily persuasive. It may satisfy the moral instincts that are as integral to human life as the will to dominate or control another, however one explains their origins. Yet approaches of this type do nothing to clarify or bridge the immense gulf between moral pronouncements and human conduct. They tell us nothing about the harsh choices with which men are continuously confronted, and they leave unexamined the place of hypocrisy in everyday human life. We must try to answer the question, unanswerable as it may be for every person or nation: "Why do I find moral reasons for acts that at best are amoral and that stem from the inescapable network of circumstances in which I find myself and which I try to explain to myself and to others?" If hypocrisy is no more than a strategy called into play by each person to cover his tracks, as it were, this leads to one view of the nature of man. If, however, as the noted theologian Reinhold Niebuhr argued, hypocrisy is the tribute vice pays to virtue, political and moral theorists take on a further responsibility. That responsibility, briefly, is the examination of the relationship between morals and politics or between moral principles and national interests.

What follows is an inquiry into such a relationship, with emphasis on international politics. It draws on a respected and enduring body of political and moral thought. It pits opposing viewpoints against one another. It strives, within the limits of my knowledge and experience, to be concrete; all too frequently moral philosophers try to escape the world of experience by building what they hope are secure and imposing edifices of thought that are far removed from the arena of public and scholarly debate. I admit that I have followed certain routes—at various forks in the road of long-standing historic debates—that some readers will reject. Strongly held assumptions and underlying premises guide each of us to the positions we ultimately take. If, through this work, the main lines of the debate are crystallized and defined a little more sharply than in the past, my effort will have been worthwhile.

Morality and Foreign Policy

What Ethics and Foreign Policy Are Not

The first requirement of philosophy, William James once wrote, is to make "an unusually stubborn attempt to think clearly." It might be said that thinking about norms and values requires the same discipline. A normative approach to politics or foreign policy subsumes more than law or policy, though norms may include both law and values. Normative approaches may include well-defined systems of thought, such as natural law systems and codes of practice; but they may also be seen as more flexible precepts and guidelines, including moral maxims. Thinking clearly about norms means establishing principles of inclusion and exclusion that are helpful in delineating the boundaries of ethics and foreign policy.

It is easier to say what ethics and foreign policy are not than to draw precise definitions or make unqualified affirmative statements. We may sharpen our focus on the subject by excluding certain trends of thought and practice, by defining what the subject is not. Especially in the second half of the 1970s, in the post-Watergate era, *morality* has become a word possessing all the most positive connotations. It has tended to become a repository for all manner of political and intellectual movements and their favorite creedal notions. Morality has become a meeting place for many diverse schools of thought including those who have seen the nineteenth-century idea of progress shattered and destroyed by the cruelty and barbarism of the twentieth century. For Populists it has meant resisting the persistent hold that men of wealth and power retain over much of American society. Morality to the captains of American capitalism has meant the free enterprise system. Socialists have maintained that no one could be morally concerned unless he were a Socialist. Those who speak in the United Nations for "the Party of liberty," to use the words of New York's junior senator, Daniel Patrick Moynihan, have assumed that morality and freedom are identical, whereas Communists in that same and other international forums have maintained that their party is the only moral one because it alone is concerned with basic human needs.

Either all these claims are supportable or none of them can be defended. Or the spokesmen for these differing views may sometimes be right and at other times may be engaging in political rhetoric. To say that none are always right or that none have enunciated universal moral principles is not to assert that each is equally true or false. At the level of proximate moral reasoning, one may be more right than another. Thus Americans see in freedom a substantially more valid moral principle than, for example, in Hitler's claim that the cause of national socialism was pure and exemplary and the destruction of civilized life was justified because of the Nazi quest for a society of *übermensch* (supermen).

Behind every effort to identify and exhaust the definition of *morality* by equating the word with the theory and practice of individual political movements is almost always a considerable degree of Manicheanism —that portrayal of the world as made up of good and evil people and governments. Many contemporary young people, encouraged no doubt by the steady flow of popular television programs and movies, view the world as being composed of the good guys and the bad guys. They see good pioneers and settlers and bad Indians; "cops and robbers"; Americans and foreigners; peace-loving and aggressor nations; God-fearing, honest people and criminals (the Mafia is only the most recent embodiment of criminals); and responsible Englishmen or Nordics and sinister East Europeans. For some this simplistic worldview may survive a lifetime of experience. There are always sufficient lawbreakers among blacks or any other minority groups to support the all-too-persistent dictum that whites obey the law and blacks thwart its observance. If educated people question these popularly held views, there seem everywhere to be unthinking people who cling to the stereotypes and emotionally charged attitudes that have become a part of group mythology.

Another characteristic of popular discussions of morality stems from the illusion that merely invoking morality can provide a guarantee to solving moral problems. For some, including "lapsed Christians" or defectors from other religious groups, the word is seen as equivalent to the deed. To invoke moral principles is to dispense with civil practice; to affirm the good is to follow it. But, as history attests, an astounding amount of political corruption and individual duplicity has followed in the wake of noble declarations. Political cynicism covers its deeds with garments of virtue. The watchword of corrupt politicians has always been, "Make the worst appear the better cause." Even where the shortfall from high proclamations has been less dramatic, observers note an obvious gulf between the two. There is no reason to disparage moral approaches just because morality and moral principles have become battle cries for aspiring or beleaguered politicians. There is, however, good reason to explore more fully the nature and content of positions men take on morality and politics and foreign policy. More specifically, there is good and sufficient reason for asking what ethics and foreign policy are not, for testing the definitions and formulations that are advanced and clearing away the underbrush of the claims and counterclaims offered on the subject. In a series of propositions, then, I would hope to suggest, without elaborate historical and logical documentation at this point, what ethics and foreign policy are not:

To begin, we must acknowledge that to declare an interest in ethics and foreign policy is not to proclaim the triumph of good over evil, virtue over vice, or justice over injustice. In certain respects, indeed, it is to infer the opposite. If statesmen were on the point of attaining wholly moral and righteous foreign policies, if the standard, however defined, had become the practice, the whole discussion would be less urgent than serious thinkers have declared that it is. One purpose of a norm is to make clear the inevitable tension between ideals and reality.

To assess and explore principles of ethics and foreign policy is not to proclaim the transformation of the historic patterns of politics or international relations. The main shortcoming of moralists is to suppose that having pronounced noble aims, the world will then change to fit these aims. It is one thing to proclaim that national purposes are receding as the basis for the foreign policies of nations and the common aims of mankind are taking their place. It is quite another thing to believe that uttering such words will transform reality.

The quest for ethical principles in foreign policy, some writers notwithstanding, is not grounds for promising a science of right and wrong. Some self-styled scientists of international relations make the claim that through their methods of study "human nature will be restored to the universe of science." Scientific laws employ abstract concepts such as force and mass, which can be used to account for physical behavior. "Valuational or ethical behavior also involves bodies—in this case, human beings—and an explanation or assessment of this behavior should be given in terms that are as related to human beings as are the explanations of physics with respect to physical objects." Even when the social scientist Morton Kaplan acknowledges that ethical theories may not yet have attained the full status of natural science, he argues that, unless ethics becomes a science, the subject will remain shrouded in "an impenetrable veil of ignorance." Lacking a scientific basis, "valuation behavior will remain a mystery." Given large-scale scientific effort, that mystery need be no more than a few system theories away, nourished by a few million dollars and brought to light by the discovery of "what type of fact a value is. . . . We determine hot and cold by touch but temperature by means of a thermometer and on the basis of an 'absolute scale.'"[1] It will become obvious that I categorically reject the view that science offers the only route to ethical understanding and the dispelling of ignorance.

Ethics is not social reformism—neither progressivism or populism, the social gospel or other prevailing movements for social and moral change, even though these approaches have often originated from deep concern with right and wrong, justice or injustice. The danger of social reform, however noble its moral purposes, lies in the fact that failure can bring disillusionment, despair, and social apathy. To say we will give the system just one more chance confronts the political actors with a terrible dilemma when goals are not realized. It invites quietism, withdrawal, and resignation at the end of a thwarted reform movement. The consequences of failure may usher in a new situation worsened by the retreat of men of goodwill upon whose continuing efforts society's improvement may depend.

Ethics is not political evangelism or personal or national self-righteousness. These avenues more often herald the end of the political process, when compromise and adjustment become impossible.

Ethics is not the discovery of absolute truth by a single social discipline. Good government in the 1930s was promised by the champions of public administration. By the 1950s and 1960s, new administrative systems had been adopted for good and bad ends. It is now clear that administration cannot be divorced from politics and ethics.

Ethics is not the attainment of a certain stage of development in the historical process representing the end of history (Georg Hegel) or the withering away of the state (Karl Marx).

Ethics is not the judgment of all history and politics from one secure vantage point wherein right and wrong are finally determined.

Ethics is not single-factor analysis or politics in which right and wrong are determined by devotion to a single goal, such as liberty or equality or social justice. In this approach rests the fallacy of almost every community movement that attempts to settle once and for all what is good and bad, right and wrong in politics. Such approaches are not so much wrong as insufficient. Some recent invitations for me to speak on ethics and society may illustrate my point. A business group asks me to discuss ethics and politics and sends along a proposed outline suggesting that I analyze ethics and the free enterprise system. One of the war colleges invites me to lecture on ethics and foreign policy—and the defense of freedom. A student group proposes that I address them on ethics and the new politics. What is common to each of the groups is the assumption that their particular concern and goal (usually singular) provides the answer to all the dilemmas and problems of life and politics.

Ethics is not to be defined as giving iniquitous leaders and governments one more chance to behave virtuously. Regardless of the moral factors involved, ending the Vietnam war, backing the United Nations or the League of Nations, or making a commitment to international law is not synonymous with ethics.

Ethics seldom if ever can be equated with a single national or political goal. Human rights, collective security, and the outlawing of war have been equated with morality and right in successive periods of American diplomacy. At its best, this approach is too narrow, too exclusive. Ethics for a given era is both more and less than a proposed policy or slogan, and the prudent observer has reason to reserve judgment when individual policies are defended in ethical terms.

Ethics is not the universalizing of a single electoral process or constitutional formula, however worthy. Yet public debate has tended to focus precisely on such questions as free elections in repressed countries, public diplomacy, or free trade.

Ethics is not necessarily majority rule or *vox populi*, however appealing and satisfying this may appear to democratic people in resolving ethical dilemmas. Whenever a government or its leaders are unable to choose what is right, a natural tendency is to let the majority decide. In the aftermath of the 1930s, we know that a majority can be as unjust and tyrannical as an authoritarian ruler. Who, looking back on American history, can say the majority is always right? Or who would ignore the death-dealing evils perpetrated in part by the manipulated majorities who supported Adolf Hitler and Jospeh Stalin?

Ethics is not ideological rationalizing or, in Max Weber's sociology, covering our acts with a tissue of excuses and moral justifications as a means of reinforcing political strength.

Ethics is not the divine right of kings and rulers, of business or labor, of old people or youth, of left or right—indeed, of any group. In every historical epoch, various groups have sought the public trust, have often secured it, and have ultimately fallen short of the ethics that were proclaimed.

Ethics is not trusting the "people," for the people too may be wrong and do wrong. Inescapably, we must ask, "Who are the people?" And how are they to decide on the cruise missile and the backfire bomber, on alternative energy sources, or on the landing rights of supersonic airplanes? What evidence is there that the people are always right? Edmund Burke, in his letter to the electors of Bristol, endeavored to illuminate the problem, and his statement on representative government has come down through the ages as a classic formulation. He asked the electors to trust him in areas in which he had more information to do what the people would do if they possessed similar information. For a complex technological society, it is scarcely enough to say, "Trust the people."

Ethics is not following a blueprint, a rigid code, the wisdom of the ancients or, for that matter, of the moderns. In the era of Robert Maynard Hutchins, I taught in the social science program at the University of Chicago. What corrupted an otherwise rich and engaging curriculum was the tendency of students and professors to ask: What would Plato have said about the long ballot, the referendum and recall, or proportional representation? Paul Tillich repeatedly warned his students at Union Theological Seminary in New York and others around the world: "Ethics is not slavish conformity to any rigid code."

Ethics is not the right of the strongest; yet neither are the weak always right. As Thucydides wrote in his history of the Peloponnesian War, it is likely, as in the Athenian reply to the delegation of Melos, that the strong impose their will on the weak in the name of justice. However, not only does power corrupt; impotence can breed irresponsibility.

Ethics must not be seen as the values of the victors alone. Hitler was partly right in his appeals against an unjust status quo following World War I, claiming the British and French were like country gentlemen who by theft and deceit had acquired their estates and were condemning others who were merely following the same path they had trod. Hitler's arguments in no way justify the barbarism of his politics, but they point up a factor that is sometimes overlooked in moralistic writings. Older men and women who have long since sown their wild oats become unbearably virtuous in judging the young. The haves lack the basis for dealing justly with the have-nots, the privileged with the underprivileged, or the advantaged with the disadvantaged.

Ethics and foreign policy do not mean the disappearance of tragedy. Moralists and religious people are too often tempted to make a success story out of their faith. No one, and least of all religious leaders, can guarantee prosperity and success, even though some early religious movements in the United States tried to give assurance that outer signs of well-being pointed to inner virtue. Reinhold Niebuhr told of two men, one who tithed from his youth and became a very wealthy man, always attributing his wealth to his observance of a religious norm. The other man, Adam Denger, who employed the young Niebuhr in his grocery store in Lincoln, Illinois, extended credit to unemployed miners who left Lincoln without paying their debts. Niebuhr's biographer, June

Bingham, wrote that "Mr. Denger kept believing that God would protect him if he did what was right. But God let Adam Denger go bank-
rupt and his young assistant grew up to preach against sentimentality
and reliance on special providence."[2] In such preaching against sentimentality, Niebuhr often chose as his text: "For He makes his sun rise
on the evil and the good and sends rain on the just and unjust." Nothing
in the approach to morality and foreign policy espoused in this study
assures that the virtuous will be successful or that those who seek righteousness will inherit riches and wealth. Indeed it is a corruption of
moral reasoning to hold out the promise that the good man and the virtuous nation are always triumphant. Religious people too often lobby in
the courts of the Almighty, citing their piety or goodness as proof that
they deserve special favors. There is a tragic element in human relations;
and the intricate balancing of harmony and disharmony in the social
order is at war with any too-simple notion that those who are good and
virtuous are foreordained by God to inherit prosperity and success.

Moral Maxims in Statecraft

International politics, more than municipal or national politics, is resistant to the binding force of laws and norms, in part because of the
weight of national sovereignty. For nations within international society,
confronted with rules and standards, a host of necessities and forces intervene. Even when such binding provisions as compulsory jurisdiction
are written into international agreements and treaties, such agreements
require ratification by a nation's political bodies. The jurisdiction of international legal bodies is therefore subject to exceptions demanded
both by national legislative bodies and national negotiators. Lawmaking
bodies on the international scene lack sanctions; international legislative bodies are not subject to the political processes whereby a minority can fairly rapidly become a majority, thus bringing about peaceful
change. National governments and policy makers are responsive to
public opinion that is primarily national. At the same time, nations live
in the shadow of war and, in our time, in the terrifying shadow of total
war. Doubts continue to be expressed as to whether international law
is law at all; questions are posed about international norms, and uncertainty surrounds broad areas of international practice regarding
whether international agreements will be observed.

Taken together, all these characteristics of the living international system drive statesmen toward considerably more flexible rules and norms that, for the purpose of discussion, may be called moral maxims. States live, therefore, in a world not devoid of norms, but one in which moral principles are observed less faithfully than in smaller, more intimate communities. A brief review of these so-called moral maxims may help to define and delineate the status of international morality.

First, agreements between major powers in international relations often take the form of tacit agreements, not solemn contracts bound by the force of law. Sovereign governments in certain relationships cannot afford to acknowledge the constraints under which they operate. If a proud public were asked to approve limitations on power, say, in relations between the Soviet Union and the United States, the people might turn against their leaders. Any American president who too openly confessed limits on American actions in Eastern Europe would suffer defeat at the polls, in part because of the capacity of certain ethnic groups to rally support against what would be portrayed as political defeatism. Moderates within a democratic state are especially vulnerable to jingoist attacks on their patriotism. Those who propose compromise with an adversary are likely to be condemned for their weakness. At the height of the Cold War, no criticism was more devastating than to be called "soft on communism." The word *appeasement*, whose origins go back to the concept of legitimate accommodation, has acquired an almost wholly negative connotation. Thus nations turn to unwritten agreements, to tacit understandings, and to practices in foreign policy that give others a more predictable basis for understanding the rules of the game.

Second, international cooperation quite frequently has a functional rather than a political base. Cooperation on social and economic issues and in such specific and urgent problem-solving concerns as world hunger and environmental deterioration is one or more steps removed from the pressures of national sovereignty. Functionalism as an approach to international cooperation undergirds the search for global response to critical human needs. International conferences are designed, at least in the first instance, to provide forums for the discussion of unsolved problems. Subsequent efforts are aimed at achieving continuity through new worldwide social and economic instrumentalities, such as the United Nations Environmental Program headquartered at Nairobi, Kenya. Functionalism presupposes the indirect rather than direct approach to problems of international politics. Nations with special interests tackle a mutually recognized problem, hoping both for its resolution and for spillover into other areas of international cooperation on politically more sensitive issues. The underlying theory is roughly analogous to the concept, well known in educational circles, of hoping that young people who achieve self-confidence and self-discipline through pursuing studies in one area will carry their skills and enhanced motivation into other spheres. Functionalism approaches the problems of international relations, not through a direct attack on sovereignty, but by seeking its erosion through subtle changes in and flexibility regarding custom and usage. It aims to transform international society by building a network of interlocking social and economic relationships among peoples and states.

Third, international norms for mankind are formed, C. Wilfred Jenks has argued, through the gradual evolving of a common law of mankind. This view sees norms as less a matter of formal law in the strict legal sense than as precepts and practice broadening out from precedent to precedent. It sees social standards as unfolding from problem to problem. It assumes that international structures will be fragmentary, not unified. The common law depends on national societies learning to cooperate in sectors of international society as professional and interest groups within national communities work out new international arrangements. Jenks, who was for three decades a major force in the International Labor Organization (ILO), predictably pointed to cooperation among labor and management representatives, as well as government officials within the organization.

What Are Moral Maxims?

Moral maxims provide signposts and rough guidelines for people and nations to follow as they seek to do right. They are less binding than laws, less authoritative than the fixed rules of a moral code. Penalties and rewards are not attached explicitly to such guidelines. Not necessarily a part of a comprehensive moral system, these guidelines have about them more a literary than a scientific quality. Few who articulate such maxims enter into a debate over whether they are objective or subjective in character. Rather, such spokesmen recognize that maxims partake of native lore and the homespun wisdom of statecraft. There is no pretense that everyone follows the maxims. In the era of classical diplomacy, moral maxims were part of the School of the Statesmen.

One group of moral maxims, therefore, that deserves consideration is the one that surrounds traditional diplomacy. The most cynical definition of diplomacy was summarized by British Ambassador Sir Henry

Wotton who identified "an ambassador as an honest man who is sent to lie abroad for the good of his country." This definition is made up of three ingredients: a concept of the role of lying in diplomacy, an implication that privately the ambassador is an honest man but publicly he is something else, and an acceptance of the inevitability of the "official lie." Lying in diplomacy and politics has always been a troublesome problem. Morality in diplomacy, if it means anything, does not mean incessantly proclaiming one's virtues. As Sir Harold Nicolson wrote: "The worst kind of diplomatists are missionaries, fanatics and lawyers; the best kind are the reasonable and human skeptics. Thus it is not religion which has been the main formative influence in diplomatic theory; it is common sense."[3] Niccolo Machiavelli went further than Nicolson in arguing that the character of international relations sets limits to truth telling. The debate over Machiavelli's intention has centered on whether his aim was to warn against the dangers of weak government or to appeal for an acceptance of a thoroughgoing cynicism in politics. "You must know," he wrote, "that there are two methods of fighting, the one by law, the other by force; the first method is that of men, the second of beasts; but as the first method is often insufficient one must have recourse to the second." Politics, including international politics because of the power struggle involved, is never far from the possible use of coercion and force. Therefore Machiavelli could write:

> How laudable it is for a prince to keep good faith and live with integrity, and not with astuteness, everyone knows. Still the experience of our time shows those princes to have done great things who have had little regard for good faith, and have been able by astuteness to confuse men's brains and have ultimately overcome those who made loyalty their foundations. . . . Therefore, a prudent ruler ought not to keep faith when by doing so it would be against his interest, and when the reasons which made him bind himself no longer exist. If men were all good, this precept would not be a good one, but as they are bad, and would not observe faith with you, so you are not bound to keep faith with them.[4]

Truth telling in diplomacy is limited by the fact that diplomacy is not a system of moral philosophy; it is the application of intelligence and tact, as Sir Ernest Satow maintained, "to the conduct of official relations between independent states."[5] Diplomacy has many strands: Roman law and the memory of a once-powerful universal state, the Byzantine tradition of ingenuity, diplomacy as an adjunct to the military-feudal caste, the papal idea of a world discipline resting on religious sanctions, and mercantile diplomacy governed by a process of reasonable bargaining between men. At its center, Nicholson has explained, diplomacy is caught up in a struggle between two tendencies: the feudal and the bourgeois or the warrior-heroic and the mercantile-shopkeeper models of diplomacy. The first of these tendencies regards diplomacy as war by other means; the second sees diplomacy as an aid to peaceful commerce. For the first, negotiations resemble a military campaign. Its purpose is victory, and anything short of total victory is considered defeat. Its strategy is to outflank, to occupy strategic positions before undertaking any further advance, to weaken the enemy by attacks behind his lines, and to use surprise attacks, intimidation, ruthlessness. In such a system, the pursuit of trust and fair dealing is not very apparent. A concession is not a means of settlement, but an evidence of weakness and retreat. Opposed to the feudal or warrior form of diplomacy is the civilian, commercial, or mercantile type, which is based on the premise that compromise among rivals is better than destruction, that negotiation is the quest for mutual understanding. National honor must yield to national honesty. National prestige must not stand in the way of a sound business deal.

Each of these theories of diplomacy has strengths and weaknesses. Each has its own peculiar dangers and illusions. The greatest hazard is failure of the one to understand the deeply rooted unchanging assumptions of the other. One believes too much in the ability of force to produce what it wishes. The other gives too much stress to the possibility of building confidence. Yet the development of successful diplomacy depends more on the contrast between the two and the problems involved in their interaction than on the pursuit of any ascertainable standards of moral values. Down to the present, whether in negotiating armaments agreements or the end of a state of war, the controlling factor is always the interconnection of the two types as each is practiced by the diplomats of rival states.

Thus the context of diplomacy, its major characteristics and constraints, and the operative influence of its two rival forms influence both the conduct of negotiations and the role of morality. It is obvious that important differences exist between eighteenth- and twentieth-century diplomacy. The former is diplomacy between monarchs or the members of an aristocratic elite. The latter involves envoys of the people. One was more likely to engage the efforts of professionals, the other of amateurs. Whatever the differences, diplomacy still requires a certain human equation. Thus Nicolson wrote of the twentieth-century diplomat that, as with his predecessors, what is needed is "a man of experience, integrity and intelligence, a man, above all, who is not swayed by emotion or prejudice, who is profoundly modest in all his dealings, who is guided only by a sense of public duty, and who understands the perils of cleverness and the virtues of reason, moderation, discretion and tact." Having formulated in comprehensive terms a moral maxim that necessarily can be realized only by the exceptional diplomatist, Nicolson wryly adds: "Mere clerks are not expected to exhibit all these difficult qualities at once."[6] But regardless of whether clerks or popular diplomatists can attain such levels of moral excellence, the guideposts have been staked out and the standards set.

Nor is Nicolson alone in having offered a set of guidelines for the ideal diplomat. Whatever the pressures may be on the personal morality of the representatives of one state to another, the need for truthfulness, precision, loyalty, calmness, and modesty are recited by nearly every major writer on the subject. On truthfulness, we have the word of M. de Callières that "a lie always leaves in its wake a drop of poison." On precision, successive diplomatic authorities have insisted that diplomatic agreements must be registered in hard print. Diplomacy is a written rather than a verbal art. An attitude of calmness is proposed—*pas trop de zèle* (never too much enthusiasm)—in the conduct of diplomacy. The diplomat must strive to be patient, perservering, and good-tempered. In diplomacy, as in sailing, the wind is bound to be contrary, and one has to tack to get into port. Modesty is urged over vanity. Once a diplomat takes to boasting of his victories in negotiations, he has sealed the fate of such negotiations because no representative of another state can afford to acknowledge defeat. Empathy and imagination are essential, for nothing is more difficult than putting oneself in another's shoes and gauging thereby the effects of one's own representations or proposals. Loyalty is indispensable, but a loyalty balancing one's ultimate commitment to his native country with respect and openness to the country with which negotiations are carried on.

In summary, all the best writings on diplomacy couple an emphasis upon the *raison d'état* with an enumeration of the human qualities of the good diplomat. The authors of such works not only set forth moral maxims, but give examples of the ways in which celebrated diplomatists have dealt with their problems. Morality flows from such maxims and the personalities of those who best exemplify them.[7]

Moral Maxims of Peace

Peace and its maintenance is also assumed to depend on a collection of moral maxims. The father of Sir Harold Nicolson, Sir Arthur Nicolson, whose career is chronicled in the son's *Portrait of a Diplomatist*, wrote as World War I neared its end: "I am always in favour of Bismarck's policy not to exact conditions which will compel your former adversary to await his time for revenge." Later Sir Arthur wrote: "A peace to be durable—though nothing in this world is durable or permanent—should, so far as human foresight can provide, be moderate and just." He was appalled by the Treaty of Versailles, which forced Germany to admit responsibility for the war. "I cannot understand it," he said in words that echo those of Edmund Burke; "you cannot impose a moral judgment on a whole people."[8]

A peace that is punitive and unjust merely plants the seeds of another war. Following World War I, the settlement that so troubled Sir Arthur provided Hitler's justification for claiming that Germany had been the victim of a conspiracy against its very survival. The psychological wounds Germans suffered in being excluded from social meeting places (such as golf courses) contributed to their willingness to strike back against the West. The nature of the peace provided political capital that extremists could organize into a massive propaganda campaign. Following World War II, the Allies, despite proposals to the contrary such as the Morgenthau Plan, had learned a lesson from the high cost of the Versailles peace. That lesson rested primarily on the moral maxim set forth with such clarity by Sir Arthur Nicolson and Edmund Burke.

The Diplomatist as a Man of Virtue and Goodness

Finally, certain qualities inherent in the individual leader can be described in the language of moral maxims even though fixed rules and laws of human conduct may lie beyond sound analysis. Sir Harold Nicolson caught the spirit of the diplomatist as a man of virtue and goodness in this portrait of his father, and what he had to say of one man offers signposts for a more universal statement:

> With all his gentleness, all his simplicity, he contrived to impose his personality so that in a company of several people it was of *his* presence that one remained aware, and to *him* that one naturally deferred. He might sit silent in his armchair, watching, trying to hear—for he was growing deaf—but one could never forget that

he was there. This quality must be due, one inevitably thought, to something essential in the man himself. What, I used to wonder, is at the root of one's deference, respect and affection? For, in spite of his irreproachable manners and his charm, he is aloof, slightly unreal, removed from life by reason of his age, his disabilities, and the absent-mindedness which comes over him as he grows tired. But the answer was not hard to find. It is not often that one meets a man whose absolute goodness and integrity proclaim themselves in the first glance of his eyes . . . not often that one feels compelled to acknowledge the moral attributes as the basis of a personal impression.[9]

Somehow morality in the end must be made incarnate; it can never be considered apart from man. Yet even the best of characterizations, like Harold Nicolson's of his father, leaves an element of mystery, something unexplainable, to be inferred from experience and impressions. At my mother's death at age ninety-five, I tried to enumerate the virtues that had made her, for those who knew her well, a great lady. I tried to account for all she had accomplished as concert pianist, organist, teacher, devoted wife, and loving mother. I described her hard work, patience and sympathy, trust and determination, courage and unforgettable example. But I was forced to conclude: "She did all this despite uncertain health and an indifferent diet. She never put herself first. She wasn't socially active. There was an unexplainable mystery about her effectiveness. She was always present when needed."[10]

It is possible perhaps to sketch the broad outlines of the life of a good person. It may also be possible to offer a few moral maxims about peace and truth telling in international politics. From the vantage point of this study, though, we must begin the search for the norms of international politics in guideposts of this almost ineffable kind rather than in rigid codes, broad multilateral declarations or pacts, or binding rules and precepts. For, it is not in slavish conformity to some rigid code, but in maxims lived out in practice that morality is achieved and made incarnate.

The Moral Problem in Foreign Policy

There would be no moral problem in politics or foreign policy if the actors involved perceived one another's interests and goals in the same way. There would be no moral problem in foreign policy if the nations of the world had more or less convergent interests. Or, stated broadly, there could be no moral problem in foreign policy or politics, or in individual life for that matter, if everyone were pursuing one goal or interest and one only. None of these conditions, however, obtain in life, in politics, in foreign policy; and this is the source of the profound moral problem that lies at the heart of the human condition. The threefold nature of the elements making up this problem require early attention in any discussion of normative approaches.

Perception and Misperception

Perception and misperception shape every approach to reality. They determine what men see; they form the main ingredients of choice and action. Thus in *King Richard the Second* (II, ii, 18), Shakespeare tells of "perspectives, which when rightly gaz'd upon / show nothing but confusion, ey'd awry / Distinguish form." A philosophical perspective helps us to see one reality, theology another, and science a third. Objectivity and subjectivity of outlook provide different pictures of the world, as in Søren Kierkegaard's affirmation that "the passion of the infinite is precisely subjectivity, and thus subjectivity becomes the truth." We speak of reality, but reality is many-sided and profound. Its perception is not merely a result of farsightedness or myopia; it is also a matter of the observer's position or his angle of vision, as every law student knows after mock trial training asks him to describe what transpired before his eyes.

In foreign policy, reality takes root in certain objective circumstances. The perception of objective reality is influenced by myriad factors that inevitably shape an observer's vision. The first task of diplomacy, we know, is to cultivate the art of putting oneself in someone else's shoes. At one point in my life, I worked for a foreign assistance agency. A wise and perceptive colleague who had met a far larger number of applicants asking for assistance counseled his younger associates: "Try to imagine how this conversation is sounding on the other side of the desk."

There is something enormously pretentious about individuals and nations claiming that they can fully grasp and comprehend one another's hopes, fears, and goals. At every stage in life and in all human communities, a sensitive person is made conscious of the profound nature of the problem. A great gulf separates the generations; and, as men grow in understanding, the gulf and the conditions that affect it deepens. As we pass from one stage of life to another, we sense how ill-founded our perception has been, how deep is the misperception that separates us from one another. The state of our independence or dependence affects the way we look at the world. Who has not noted the difference between the perceptions of the driver of a car and those of its passengers? Bodily health and human vitality mold perception. So does the consciousness of being strong or weak. Deeply rooted human values bred in the marrow of one's bones are a determinant compared with values one has memorized. Knowledge of being at the beginning of life with too much time on one's hands as contrasted with having come to life's end with too little time remaining shapes and affects one's perception. Nearness or remoteness from death casts differing shadows on life, as anyone who has tasted death in the passing of a loved one knows only too well.

What is true of individuals is true *a fortiori* of nations. Young and old nations see the world through different eyes, as do great powers and the powerless nations of the world. The ground on which we stand, our capacity as a citizen or a nation, influences our perspective and likewise influences politics and policies and governs our moral sense. Isocrates, writing in the fourth century B.C., urged his contemporaries to "test justice when a man is in want, temperance when he is in power, continence when he is in the prime of youth."

Whatever the differences that may exist, modern man prefers to view such differences in capacity and circumstance as not much more than slight deviations from a norm. Western liberal and progressive thought and, even more, the Socialist or Marxist perspectives lead men to suppose that the gulf separating mankind at various stages of existence is rapidly narrowing if not closing. Nothing could be further from the truth. History offers abundant evidence that certain differences lie in the very nature of things. As such, they profoundly and unalterably affect perception. These differences include age, class, wealth, social status, and power, to say nothing of religious, political, economic, ethnic, and national outlooks. For nations in particular, such differences constitute the single greatest source of perception and misperception. They are organic and historical, not accidental. They have roots in a nation's tradition and culture. For Americans, a comparatively successful attempt to connect, couple, and reconcile religion and liberty has roots in the flight of the colonists from religious oppression. In Russia, acceptance of and resignation to oppression by the state goes back to an era of tsarist tyranny. A host of factors combine to influence a nation's perception of the world: its economic needs, geographic position, military threats, sense of security and insecurity, memories of invasions, history of war, political persecution, present stage of development, natural resources, political ideology, economic condition, and national character and morale.

It is as illusory to ignore the fundamental differences among nations as it is to disregard individual human differences. Out of these differences, a vast array of perceptions and misperceptions flows. Morality, including common norms and standards, is affected by such perceptions. No purpose is served by urging initiative on the poor man or responsibility on the weak nation if the gulf separating them from others is too great. Many of the epic tragedies of war and human suffering take root in misperception. By act of resolve and will, the moralist no less than the cynic must seek to come to terms with this reality.

Interests

The interests of the individual or the nation-state are seldom if ever determined by whim or caprice. They have an objective basis. The words *self-interest* or *national interest* are too easily used; they roll from the lips of pundits and propagandists. Most writers claim that there either is or is not a national interest undergirding the conduct of a state in foreign policy. Observers maintain that such interests either are or are not persistent forces. Whether we like it or not, the truth is that a given set of needs and requirements lies at the roots of survival for every political group. Some see such interests as archaisms and exhort national leaders never to be anxious over their survival. The individual can sometimes dare to lose himself in order to save himself, but the responsible national leader pledged by his oath of office to preserve the union can rarely indulge himself thus. His first duty is to safeguard his people. Should he fail, the people will turn him out, if the crisis has not deepened into national suicide or disaster. There is also inherent contradiction in some of the preachments of critics of the national interest. For themselves, these critics proclaim national independence and for the world, national self-determination, yet they resent its actual practice by others.

Similar concerns exist for every minority group. Older people urge youth to be independent but grow restive over the consequences. Every newly independent minority group following its own course is condemned if its group resolve brings it into conflict with the ruling group. Shakespeare warned that when society taught its underprivileged people to speak, it ought not be surprised if they cursed society. Within integrated societies, each emerging minority seeks protection under the law. It looks to the constitutional system and the goodwill of the majority for its right to overcome, and perhaps become, the new majority.

The life of the nation-state is infinitely more precarious. Nations are much closer to knowing the sense of powerlessness that the isolated individual feels in a vast impersonal mass society. Nations, particularly the weak ones, feel isolated in an unfriendly world. Life for such nations is more comparable to the anonymous life in a great city than to the friendly ties and primary relations of a once-simple rural village. Each holds to its own turf, partially protected by alliances in the United Nations. Misery loves company, but there is something a little pathetic about weak nations cleaving together behind meaningless voting majorities within an international organization. They glorify such practices with symbols and certain ostensibly universal legitimacy myths set forth in international charters and covenants. The truth cannot for long escape them. Nations are and will remain unequal. In the end they survive or are destroyed by their own will.

State interests that are linked to national survival are in fact more durable than liberal rationalists acknowledge. These interests are changeable, but persistent. The Monroe Doctrine laid down for the United States in 1823 was based on certain rational calculations of threats to the nation's existence. Those threats are to this day being defined and redefined; the political alignments and power constellations that pose the threat and throw up countervailing power to meet the threat are under continuous scrutiny. Although the enemy is not always the same, it was the Monroe Doctrine which decreed that the United States would not and could not tolerate Soviet missile bases in Cuba; but without the overwhelming atomic superiority of America, Washington's ultimatum to Moscow would have been ineffective. Britain for centuries resisted any and every threat to the balance of power in Europe. For Russia, control of Poland, in Stalin's words, "was a matter of life and death."

Any approach to moral reasoning in foreign policy that fails to take national interests into account or that presupposes their lack of current relevance leaves out the most basic reality in international politics. The requirements attendent upon national interest mean that for the United States—whatever the differences in rhetoric or style—American foreign policy for Nixon or Carter, Kennedy or Johnson, Eisenhower or Taft (had he been elected) is subject to many of the same constraints. A nation's resources and its national capacity set limits on its foreign policy, driving the nation back to build on its ideals, its example at home, the quality of its life and people. There may be differences of emphasis and degree. The law, someone has written, may evenutally be not only what the judge says it is but what suffragettes campaigning for women's rights wish it to become. Yet the limits of foreign policy, given the half-anarchic state of international politics, are more far-reaching than those affecting social change within an organized national community. To ignore this fact is to invite national setbacks and ultimately disillusionment for the people who have been misled and betrayed.

Single Moral Goals

Politics and foreign policy involve the balancing of competing goals. The nature of the moral decision is more than the determination of a single good. Choice is not simply arrived at; policy requires the weighing of many factors. Both intention and consequence come into play. We know the crucial role of choice in personal life. How surprising, then, that we overlook the significance of choice making in national and international life.

No one can question the existence or truth of certain general moral principles. We remember the words of Justinian's Institutes: "To live honorably, not injure another, to render each his due." The most profound and perplexing question facing national leaders is: "How are we to implement these general precepts?" To give the law more specific meaning and content, the American constitutional system sets up intricate and far-ranging machinery in its several branches. The citizen turns to contracts—"the greediest of legal categories." He has recourse to the law of torts for the "satisfaction of reasonable expectations." The law provides its proximate and ordering distinctions, which, as with innominate contracts, look toward the deliverance of a thing in expectation of a counterperformance. Law enjoins performance in expectation of counterperformance.

What are the equivalents of these sharply chiseled distinctions and rules when we turn to international morality and law? Jurists and moralists to be sure have laid down broad working principles, such as that of proportionality in war (the action not to exceed the evil it seeks to remedy). Equality, too, is defined in the language of equivalence or proportionality.

Yet justice, order, freedom, security, collective and national defense are competing and sometimes opposing goals. How are they to be arbitrated? Who decides between one and the other as the basis of a given policy? Foreign policy and politics at their core entail the balancing of purpose and goals. If freedom could guide foreign policy in every choice, the equation would be simpler than when freedom and justice compete. The United States as a world power must attend to the interests of old and new friends—Europe and Asia, the Arabs and the Jews, the Soviet Union and China, black Africa and the white settlers, leaders in the developing world and the poorest of the poor, North and South, East and West, free enterprise and Socialist states.

It is forever tempting to cut the Gordian knot, to choose as if there were no moral problem, to do business or give aid to one group of states and not another. Recently, some policy spokesmen have urged Americans to choose between China and the Soviet Union. Inescapably, nations must fix priorities, must choose among relative *goods*. Such choices, however, are almost never made once and for all. Interests and circumstances create new guidelines to fit new problems. Perception may grow keener with experience and maturity in the community of states. Old enemies (Japan and Germany) have become new friends, and new relationships with adversaries (China and the Soviet Union) must somehow be kept in balance with long-standing connections among preferred allies without provoking "diplomatic shock."

The moral problem persists, because foreign policy involves political choices obscured by faulty perception, controlled by national interests, and complicated by multiple purposes and goals. It will not disappear. It stands at the beginning, middle, and end of every undertaking in moral reasoning. No purpose is served by not attending to the complexities raised by what we have called the moral problem. It must be understood and confronted as an essential aspect of the normative approach to foreign policy. There is no escape from the weighing of moral and political alternatives. The moral decision is fraught with consequences, and we deceive ourselves in supposing that every choice does not involve gains and losses or benefits and sacrifices for those who are principally involved.

Moral Reasoning Reconsidered

From the founding of the American republic, two traditions have coexisted in America's approaches to moral and political problems—monism and pluralism. Each rests on certain underlying assumptions and is guided by certain premises. Each represents overall intellectual tendencies and political directions, not rigid doctrinal positions. Each provides broad philosophical perspectives and operative principles for thought and action in foreign policy. Not everyone who has espoused one or the other viewpoint has done so consistently or without being influenced by the opposing viewpoint. In setting forth these traditions, I do not intend to suggest that they are absolutes from which philosophers and policy makers have not departed in specific cases. As the basis for action, however, the two viewpoints deserve attention in any discussion of normative approaches.

Monism represents the search for a clear-cut and unequivocal moral position in foreign policy. It finds in a single moral end guidance in moral and political choices. Morally concerned men and nations can take unmistakable satisfaction from this viewpoint. For oneself and for relations with others, there are unquestioned benefits in taking an unambiguous moral stand. Leaders who are enjoined to stand for something in a troubled and anxious world can do so at least to their own satisfaction in proclaiming devotion to a single moral value. They are freed from the heavy burdens of expressing uncertainty and moral anguish on complex and perplexing moral and political choices. Moral certitude has often provided hard-pressed popular leaders with a formidable rhetorical weapon in the marketplace of political debate. The public can more readily understand policies that are justified as expressions of liberty or justice than those that reflect compromises between competing values and principles. Especially in countries in which moral philosophers or theoretical approaches have enjoyed at best passive acceptance or toleration by the wider public, the monistic perspective has tended to prevail.

In the formative period of the American republic, the emphasis on a single moral value expressed itself in the widespread sentiment for intervention on the side of the heirs of the French Revolution. "Liberty, equality, and fraternity" appeared to represent the selfsame moral purposes of the American republic. The grounds for joining the French in the War of the Fourth Coalition provided a strong rallying point for thousands of Americans who responded to the appeals of Citizen Genet. President George Washington resisted those appeals by a declaration of neutrality, not for want of faith in the principles of liberty and equality but because the national interest militated against engaging limited American forces in a struggle far from American shores. The possible gains would be out of all proportion to the costs and dangers involved.

In the twentieth century, President Woodrow Wilson crusaded in defense of national self-determination as a basis for world peace and security. When support for the crusade flagged in the Senate, Wilson appealed to the American people for support of his Fourteen Points and the creation of the League of Nations. At the Paris Peace Conference, after being greeted by throngs of Frenchmen who cheered him in the streets, he suffered defeat at the hands of European leaders who sought to preserve their nations' security through territorial settlements that protected their own national interests. The economies of the newly independent states in Eastern Europe were weakened by the disappearance of economic unities, provided earlier by the Austro-Hungarian and Ottoman empires. The final blow was struck by Hitler, who invoked the principle of national self-determination against those who sought to resist his drive to incorporate the Sudeten Germans in Czechoslovakia and Germans in other lands into the Third Reich. Wilson's championing of a single moral value helped in this sense to pave the way for German expansionism.

The Atlantic Charter was another single-minded approach to moral values. Winston Churchill, Joseph Stalin and Franklin D. Roosevelt endorsed the charter's principles with varying commitments and attitudes. Apparently, only Roosevelt believed in the moral and political absolute that peoples everywhere should have the right to establish their own forms of government free of outside interference. Churchill, who also saw the charter as a worthy declaration of moral intent, viewed it in more provisional and pragmatic terms. The reality of the European situation and the Soviet drive for expansion required compromises with the national self-determination imperative on both sides of the Iron Curtain. The balance of terror replaced national self-determination as the controlling principle of Western security.

Confronted with the clash between a single moral imperative and political realities, a second approach emerged—pluralism—calling attention to the multiplicity of moral and political values in world politics. Not only must each nation's policy makers recognize its own multiple interests, but they must also accept the contending interests of some 150 other nation-states. Although this approach lends itself less readily to bold national crusades such as those for national self-determination as a prescription for world peace, it has provided a more enduring basis for realistic moral and political thought in a pluralistic international society. Thus America has been required in the Cold War to merge its support for national self-determination with a clear recognition of the limits of its power and the need to resist Soviet expansionism while avoiding World War III. Freedom, stability, and peace have become the three points on a triangle in postwar American policy. None can be ignored at the peril of threatening the preservation of the others.

A treatise on morality and foreign policy must give attention not only to the historic policies of the United States but to the expressions of monism and pluralism in the prevailing approaches of American and European thinkers to morality and foreign policy. American scholars have tended to group themselves into those who looked to a single moral end as the broad highway to a peaceful world and those who recognized the need to order and relate competing moral goals. Most of the great debates have involved a clash of the two approaches and their relative influence upon policies and attitudes. Sometimes monists have espoused first one and then another moral or political objective, retaining the same intense commitment to their latest moral crusade. Habits of mind and thought are evidently more consistent than the objectives to which loyalties attach themselves.

Before World War I, Americans like Secretary of State William Jennings Bryan poured their energies into establishing numerous arbitration panels and arbitration treaties for mediating international disputes. As secretary, "the Great Commoner" showed little interest in other aspects of foreign relations. Bryan was persuaded that conflicts could be resolved when nations submitted themselves to cooling-off periods. American scholars joined in the crusade; leading international lawyers were enlisted as members of permanent arbitration panels, few if any of which were ever called upon to settle disputes. An astounding investment of trained professional manpower was devoted to the effort with little or no appreciable effect on international conflict.

In the 1920s, the aim was the outlawry of war, culminating in the Pact of Paris. Again the scholars joined the publicists in a concerted attack on aggression and warfare. What followed was not the elimination of war but Mussolini's invasion of Ethiopia, the Japanese attack on Manchuria, and Hitler's conquests, which spread tyranny and brutality. All the while, reformist scholars calmly continued to seek new—and irrelevant—instrumentalities for outlawing war.

During the World War II period, scholarly emphasis shifted to collective security on the premise that no nation could be secure if others were imperiled. Peace was seen as indivisible: "One for all and all for one." The Charter of the United Nations embodied this principle. Collective security was promulgated as the major peacemaking alternative to war-producing arrangements like alliances and the balance of power. The first task of scholars was not to describe traditional international politics but to provide measures for the collective enforcement of peace.

More recently, human rights have become the latest moral equivalent of war, the means of creating a new global moral consensus. Political leaders and their academic defenders have justified human rights with the same zeal and moral enthusiasm of earlier crusades. If stability in the developing countries and a new Strategic Arms Limitation Treaty stood in the way of a public campaign for human rights, so much the worse for these other foreign policy initiatives. Calls for caution and circumspection were overridden, much as warnings by critics of arbitration or the outlawry of war or collective security had been dismissed in earlier periods.

Pluralists have responded to these moralistic crusades, not by denying their moral validity, but by emphasizing the complexities and interrelationships with other moral and political realities. Thus, experienced practitioners and authoritative writers warned that arbitral procedures for international disputes operated within a different political and constitutional environment than arbitration within a sovereign state. The moral consensus achieved by labor and management within the nation was beyond reach for nations internationally. Constitutional arrangements are lacking on a worldwide basis to assure each side that peaceful change is attainable once arbitration replaces conflict. Means have to be found to safeguard national interests—another moral objective of states —at the same time that arbitration is being organized through a network of treaties and panels.

The outlawry of war, which was morally unexceptionable, was also in tension with international reality. Some nations at some times were persuaded that their goals were attainable only through war. For such nations, it was still a working premise that "war was a continuation of policy by other means." Until national leaders accepted that most, if not all, their cherished aspirations could be achieved peacefully, a thousand treaties outlawing war would have little effect. Therefore, attention had to be addressed to the causes of war and the conditions of peace. Pluralists pointed out that a fraction of the initiative and imagination directed to outlawing war could have been more usefully directed to ameliorating political and economic conditions in Germany and Italy. Such actions might have delayed or forestalled the rise of Hitler and Mussolini.

The cleavage between international relations scholars was if anything more pronounced over the issue of collective security. The pluralists were quick to point out in the 1940s and 1950s that even the most perfect blueprint for collective security conflicted with the imperative of national security. Nations who felt themselves endangered, as well as their responsible leaders, were unlikely to entrust national survival to others. The history of statecraft threw a long shadow over the hopes of moralists. Before collective security systems could become credible, nations would have to commit their forces to new collective security agencies. But the history of the League of Nations and the United Nations made abundantly clear that this was not the case. Before collective security could become a reality, other profound changes in the state system were required. More than bold statements of brave new purposes would be needed. The architects of peace would have to devote themselves to far-reaching transformations on many fronts.

The American human rights campaign found monists and pluralists once again divided on the pursuit of a worthy moral objective. Coming as it did in the wake of Watergate and the Nixon-Kissinger foreign policy of *realpolitik*, the Carter crusade attracted widespread popular enthusiasm, especially within the United States. Americans felt good that the country once again stood for something worthwhile in the world. The impact was at least as significant within the boundaries of the United States as in countries to whom the campaign was addressed. When pluralist critics warned that the effect could be destabilizing in certain strategic developing areas of the world and that human rights had to be measured against deep-seated cultural and economic realities in other countries, they were dismissed as being immoral. Questions about the effect on Soviet-American relations of pressing human rights charges within the Soviet Union were answered by saying that human rights and the SALT negotiations were unrelated. Because an all-out crusade is fundamentally at odds with a pluralist viewpoint, calling attention to competing moral objectives had little effect on policy and almost none on official rhetoric. The linkage of competing goals was denied, and policy makers talked glibly of a process of decoupling specific moral and political initiatives.

The contradictions and conflicts between the monist and pluralist views and recurrent problems for Americans in implementing a moral foreign policy point up the need to reconsider the historic traditions of moral reasoning. Nations approach the moral problem differently, and consequently they face different dilemmas. Britain's pragmatic approach earned it the name of "perfidious Albion." Germany in certain eras gained a reputation of "might makes right." America's devotion to high moral purposes—easier to preach than to practice—was reflected in its early emphasis on dignity and steady purpose. Indeed America's challenge is less to abandon its search for morality than to reconsider earlier traditions of moral reasoning in Western thought and its own political history.

Such traditions view moral reasoning as more than simply affirming a noble aim or objective. Theologically, some Americans have been attracted to the fundamentalist doctrine: "Believe in God and do as you please." Reinhold Niebuhr, who often polemicized against this theology, declared that even if all men were Christians this fact could not assure a solution of the atomic problem. Politically, the proclaiming of a goal such as universal human rights is not adequate in itself to the demands of political morality. Desirable goals and practical deeds must be joined. Moral reasoning, as defined by some ancient political philosophers, involved the balancing of good moral ends. The authors of the Federalist Papers applied this tradition to the founding of the republic. They found the doctrine of absolute states' rights as lacking in political wisdom as that calling for an all-powerful national government. While recognizing the need for what Alexander Hamilton called an energetic executive, they simultaneously called for strong legislative and judicial branches of government. The Federalists were closer than many present-day moralists to the ancients in rejecting the sufficiency of a single value, perhaps because their thinking was grounded in traditions of moral reasoning.

Pluralism—provided it remains rooted in an overall moral design and eschews cynicism—has more in common with the traditions of moral reasoning than a single-minded monist viewpoint. Pluralism runs the risk of relativism if it ignores ultimate moral goals such as liberty, justice, and equality—what the framers of the United States Constitution called the higher law. That law manifested itself, not in the fulfillment of ultimate principles in political practice, but in the formation of mediating principles that could be written into the Bill of Rights. The founders, however pretentious their claims, recognized one enduring truth when they proclaimed that love of liberty and equality was a heritage of the American republic, bound up with an inherited tradition and a particular cultural and political order. Not every people were yet endowed by their Creator with as favorable an environment as America for the flowering of liberty. From the beginning, America's purpose was the pursuit of multiple political values, expressed in the principles of liberty joined with equality.

The hope of a more viable approach to morality and foreign policy is dependent in the end on a return to moral reasoning rather than the headlong pursuit of any single moral value. This perspective transcends those simplistic views that describe what ethics and foreign policy are not and delineates practical concepts of what morality is and may become. It has room as well for moral maxims, which constitute approximations of morality in diplomatic and political practice. It recognizes, as statesmen have always been compelled to recognize, the interconnections between what is morally desirable and what is politically possible. It offers resources for confronting the moral problem as a perennial issue, a persisting impediment to morality and foreign policy. It calls on those who would be moralists to be political realists as well.

Moral reasoning provides the intellectual resources for approaching the great issues of theory and practice in morality in the history of American foreign policy. It offers a foundation for examining certain case studies in American foreign policy, including human rights and foreign assistance. It can help those who seek to understand the relative and the transcendent aspects of morality and foreign policy, the tragic element in international politics, and the relationship of science, morality, and transnationalism. Finally, it points to a reexamination of practical morality and prudence in politics. In summary, a reconsideration of moral reasoning as a practical alternative to abstract moralism or hopeless cynicism is the continuing challenge of anyone who would write realistically about morality and foreign policy in our time.

The Ethics of Major American Foreign Policies

The theologian Reinhold Niebuhr often warned that moralists who entered the foreign policy sphere were more likely to destroy a nation's ideals than were cynical realists. Evidently he feared that those who lacked a sense of the limits of foreign policy would proceed as if the values and goods that were attainable in the more intimate communities of the family, the locality, and the nation were attainable in the international community as well. Whatever Niebuhr's quarrels and debates with classical Greek thought, he was at one with Plato and Aristotle in believing that justice could be more effectively pursued by smaller communities like the city-states. He insisted on a recognition of the differences between such communities and the present-day world powers. From World War II until his death, he wrote about foreign policy, especially about American foreign policy and its moral basis.

One of the persistent difficulties in moral reasoning arises from one thinker imposing his intellectual framework on another's thought, which had been fashioned for a different era and influenced by a different set of circumstances. Karl Popper has been criticized for imposing his own modern scientific framework on the political philosophy of Plato, especially in his statement that Platonism is the antithesis of the open society. William M. McGovern in *From Luther to Hitler* oversimplified the relationship between Martin Luther's call to Christians to recognize the sovereignty of the ruler in the political realm and Luther's influence on the rise of Hitler.[1] Because Luther's doctrines led Christians to be politically passive, McGovern said, they prepared the way for the German dictator. Other writers who have criticized Thomas Aquinas, Augustine, or John Calvin have imposed a wholly modern scheme of thought on those religious thinkers from another era. A more recent example of this tendency is the attempt by such interpreters as Richard W. Fox, Ronald Stone, Tom F. Driver, Richard Shaull, and Harvey Cox to judge Niebuhr by the assumptions of their individual philosophies or theologies—revisionism in history, liberalism, liberation theology, or counterculture thought. None of these writers from Popper to Cox have first asked the questions: What was the intention of Plato or of Niebuhr? What were they trying to say and do? The question they appear to ask is rather: How did Plato or Niebuhr fail, measured against the most recent intellectual framework (with which the critics themselves are identified), whether of Cold War revisionism or countercultural thought? As the critics proceed, they appear to judge an earlier thinker or philosopher in the light of questions that he never anticipated or considered.

If any approach to moral reasoning is to receive its due, its interpreters and critics must consider and evaluate it on its own terms. To make Plato a Fascist is to ignore his basic purpose and the context in which he wrote. To attribute Hitler's National Socialism to Luther is to ignore the several historical and political movements and social forces that converged in Nazism and the economic factors that contributed to its emergence. To classify Niebuhr as a Marxist, a Cold Warrior or even, in oversimplified definitions, a liberal or a conservative is to overlook the historical development of his thought or the dialectic method of his approach. With almost any serious moral thinker, responsible criticism is more than applying to his thought a litmus test taken from a popular contemporary political ideology.

Of course, it is true that serious moral philosophers are not that numerous and that for less important writers critical analysis and evaluation may need to be less complex. For example, certain approaches to moral reasoning stem less from any organized system of political thought than from popular enthusiasm or public sentiment. Alexis de Tocqueville, one of the early observers of the American scene, pointed to feeling and sentiment as inescapable qualities of American society that determined the character of moral reasoning. Americans, he said, were not given to the kind of abstract thought evident in some European societies. Americans were a highly practical and pragmatic people. On political and religious issues, Everyman was his own philosopher. It was widely assumed that one man's thought on politics or virtue was as good as any other man's thought. This characteristic of American life resulted in large measure from the fact that the United States was not an aristocratic society. Instead, Americans had fled from aristocracy, and they resisted it whenever or wherever it manifested itself in whatever forms. In any case, ethical and political judgments were so subjective, so debatable on every point, and open to such an infinite range of interpretations that only the majority could decide what was right and wrong. Therefore, for most issues, including value judgments, the only arbiter was the majority vote of the people. If men differed—and it was inevitable they would, given the absolute equality of every man's views—the sole resolution of their differences had to be through the voice of the people. Majoritarianism was the only definite and certain, measurable and objective test of morality. Any other test was too subjective, too colored by bias and prejudice, too leftward or rightward leaning, or too dependent on the foreignness, localism, or parochialism of a given individual's thought. The only way out of an intellectual and moral impasse—the one sure path to the resolution of individual differences—was to have the people decide. Even if the majority ruled that incest or rape was morally justifiable, presumably the majority would be right.

It is not surprising, therefore, that in America the great public expressions of what was right and the prevailing modes and proclamations of moral judgment rested largely on political majoritarianism. A characteristic of majority thinking, as de Tocqueville pointed out, is to sift out and eliminate what is ambiguous, debatable, and confusing to the majority. Majoritarianism has little if any place for subtleties and nuances, for moral and political distinctions, and for discriminate moral judgments. It tends to settle on what is indisputably right or wrong as viewed by the mass of the people. It looks for good or evil, and it prefers absolute moral and immoral determinations rather than proximate ethical valuations. In searching out identifiable elements of morality, it depends on the least common denominators accessible to the understanding for all, not the quest for the highest and most exacting levels of moral reasoning. If this statement is seen as an exaggeration, consider some of the guiding precepts and doctrines of American thinking on foreign policy: specifically, four important doctrines that presumably rested on firm moral and political assessments of right and wrong made by the American people. Each doctrine was a response to particular historical circumstances, an attempt to solve particular problems. However, these responses have persisted long after the particular circumstances had passed. Often these ideas were forced into an entirely new framework, altering their purpose and intent. It could be argued that, in the same way Popper misconstrued Plato or Cox misinterpreted Niebuhr by judging them within a framework different from their original one, the neoisolationists of the 1920s and 1930s misconstrued the isolationist doctrines of certain of the founding fathers.

At first glance, the connection between debates in political philosophy may appear to have at best a tenuous relationship with debates over philosophies and doctrines of foreign policy. Whether historians and mere empiricists fully recognize it or not, the underlying basis of foreign policy involves philosophical inquiry and evaluation. It is as appropriate to ask the same questions about foreign policy as about individualism and collectivism as aspects of domestic politics. Thus Niebuhr's philosophy, to which we shall return in conclusion, can contribute to the great debates over American foreign policy, including debates over historic foreign policies. Without a viable intellectual and philosophic framework, foreign policy debates become little more than glorified current events.

No Entangling Alliances

The doctrine of no entangling alliances, or "splendid isolationism," was the foreign policy legacy of the first administration of the American republic. President George Washington offered as the first principle of United States foreign policy that the young fledgling state safeguard its national security and independence by limiting its political engagements with foreign powers. America ought not to become embroiled in the ancient struggles of Europe, conflicts it had little prospect of influencing or resolving, rivalries from which settlers in the new land had fled. The colonists and those who followed them to America had shaken the dust of Europe from their feet. Many had suffered persecution. Others had lost all they treasured most—their families and their possessions—in long, bloody, and recurrent strife. From all this they had freed themselves in a new and secure land. Few if any were anxious to return to the old scenes of oppression and to bitter national and religious warfare. They were making a fresh start on new soil not yet contaminated by nationalistic ambitions and historic rivalries leading almost inevitably, they thought, to deprivation, human suffering, and the most fateful forms of enslavement in struggles to the death.

President Washington's counsel of prudence, reserve, and abstention delivered to a relatively powerless nation fell on fertile soil. It was not that countervailing ideals and guidelines were not present and did not compete. Powerful commitments to liberty and equality drew some American support for direct intervention in foreign conflicts. Temporary political majorities strenuously pressed for active intervention, both military and political, on behalf of those countries and peoples whose political goals seemed to coincide with American national purposes and revolutionary aspirations. In its early stages, the French Revolution found much sympathy in the United States. Marquis de Lafayette sent President Washington the key to the Bastille. In the spring of 1793, Citizen Genet (Edmond C. Genet), the French minister to the United States, sought to win the support and, failing that, the benevolent neutrality of the United States for France's revolutionary war. However, local problems and factionalism divided the two nations. The French problem became acute for the American government with the execution of Louis XVI and the French declaration of war on February 1, 1793, against

Great Britain, Spain, and the Netherlands. The United States had completed an alliance with France in 1778. By 1793 the issue for America was whether it should help France, just as fifteen years before France had come to its aid. Or had its responsibilities under the treaty of 1778 ended on September 21, 1792, with the new French government? On April 22, 1793, President Washington announced a policy of neutrality. America would fulfill its responsibilities as a neutral and would expect in turn protection of the rights historically shown neutrals by belligerents in time of war. Citizen Genet, a Girondist who saw his nation under danger of counterrevolutionary attack in Europe, landed in Charleston, South Carolina, under instructions to seek a new alliance for France and to gain American assistance. He commissioned four privateers and launched them against any British ships off the American coast. He moved northward to Philadelphia rallying fellow republicans. When President Washington received him with cold formality and Secretary of State Thomas Jefferson presented him with a formal note warning that military commissions on American territory were an infringement of its sovereignty, Genet responded that he would appeal directly to the people. Washington was burned in effigy, and crowds of pro-French supporters denounced the neutrality proclamation. Washington was convinced, nonetheless, that the people would side with him as they weighed the consequences. He defied the people in the short run, since he believed that they would support his policy in the long run. In his farewell address, which was less an address than a presidential manifesto to secure the election of his chosen successor John Adams, he declared: "Europe has a set of primary interests, which to us have [but] a very remote relation. Hence she must be engaged in frequent controversies, the causes of which are essentially foreign to our concerns. Hence, therefore, it must be unwise in us to implicate ourselves by artificial ties in the ordinary vicissitudes of her politics, or the ordinary combinations and collisions of her friendships, or enmities."[2]

Nowhere did the phrase *entangling alliances* appear in Washington's address; the words were used for the first time by Jefferson in his inaugural address of 1801. Washington's prudence succeeded over the emotional response of thousands whom Genet aroused on behalf of the French cause. At one point, Washington had appeared to speak not for the majority but for a beleaguered and antiidealistic minority. History's judgment, however, favored his political realism and prudence, not the political evangelism of his foes and critics. It found him more moral than those who denounced his immorality—the hope of any democratic leader who resists the popular passions and emotions of the masses.

But history's judgment, as it became a part of the American tradition of foreign policy, went far beyond a judgment of the rightness of a given policy designed to meet an urgent problem in a particular time and place. The concept of no entangling alliances became a controlling doctrine of American foreign policy for decades to come because it corresponded with certain deeply held beliefs and prejudices concerning the American people and their mission in the world. It became a timeless moral and political principle from which a virtuous people could not allow themselves to retreat. Americans saw themselves as a chosen people, annointed to carry out God's will on the new continent. The idea of reserve, circumspection, and limits in avoiding foreign commitments that involved risk to the nation's security had a firm base in the political realities of the late eighteenth and early nineteenth centuries. It was a proximate moral and political principle founded on the national interest. Over time it became a rigid doctrine and an absolute moral creed because it satisfied the yearning of successive generations to retain the myth that they were a people apart. It was translated by Washington's successors from an operative foreign policy into a doctrine of political religion long after its usefulness as a guide to action had disappeared. And well into the twentieth century, it persisted in arguments over whether the conflicts in World Wars I and II were matters of any interest to the security and well-being of Americans.

Manifest Destiny

Contrary as it may seem, manifest destiny, or the "white man's burden," is consistent with a policy of isolationism. For the colonists, manifest destiny dictated the conquest of the wilderness, the march West, and America's continental expansion. Frederick Jackson Turner found his main clue to American national character in its response to the challenge of the frontier. Americans were driven by the inevitable logic that it was their destiny to rule the continent. The morality that justified such expansion was expressed by Senator Albert J. Beveridge: "God has made us adepts in government that we may administer government among savage and senile people."[3] Manifest destiny was also reflected in President William McKinley's report that he struggled with himself over whether or not to annex the Philippines. After praying all night, President McKinley not unexpectedly received divine guidance to yield to destiny.

Whereas the doctrine of isolation and no entangling alliances survived for almost a century and a half after its proclamation (implicitly on September 17, 1796, in Washington's farewell address and explicitly in Jefferson's 1801 inaugural address), the moralistic justification of manifest destiny was most strongly stated after the end of nineteenth-century expansionism. According to the foremost authority on the subject, Julius W. Pratt, "manifest destiny . . . became a justification for almost any addition of territory which the United States had the will and power to obtain."[4] It formed the basis for the Louisiana Purchase and the other annexations of territory by the United States in the nineteenth and early twentieth centuries.

The doctrine of manifest destiny had some of the characteristics of European imperialism, which Americans criticized. The nineteenth century was the great age of expansionism in Europe. The United States extended its authority and rule over North America in the early part of that century; European states successfully pursued their colonial conquests in the latter half. John L. O'Sullivan, the prominent New York editor who in 1845 coined the phrase *manifest destiny*, described it as the right of Americans to "overspread and possess the whole of the Continent which Providence has given us for the development of the great experiment in liberty and federated self-government entrusted to us." But the policy involved more than the territorial influence of Americans on one continent. Indeed its justification took on an undisguised religious character: "Its floor shall be a hemisphere—its roof the firmament of the star-studded heavens, and its congregation an Union of many Republics comprising hundreds of happy millions . . . governed by God's natural and moral law of equality."[5]

Manifest destiny as O'Sullivan described it, however, was not always the stated basis of American foreign policy in the mid–nineteenth century. By the end of that century, Darwinism, a more traditional brand of imperialism, and the successful settling of a continent lay behind what historians have called a "New Manifest Destiny." According to the Darwinian philosophy, America as a strong nation was bound to extend its authority over the weak. American imperialism was the external expression of the strenuous life President Theodore Roosevelt asked every American to undertake and—to all intents and purposes—a carbon copy of the late nineteenth century imperialism of Britain and Europe. As the European powers projected their rivalries into Africa and Asia, the United States brought several million alien peoples under its rule. Because continental expansionism had reached its limits and most of the land from the Atlantic to the Pacific was already under its control, the United States undertook to expand further southward and northward and across the Pacific Ocean to Japan. Because of Darwinism, traditional imperialism expressed in the settling of a continent, and the missionary spirit that had inspired the first manifest destiny doctrine, John Hay saw the new expansionism as a virtually irresistible force: "No man, no party, can fight with any chance of final success against a cosmic tendency; no cleverness, no popularity avails against the spirit of the age."[6]

The latest application of manifest destiny appeared following World War II. This chapter in American imperialism was the more remarkable because it was pursued in the name of anticolonialism. It is not necessary to accept the major assumptions of the revisionist Cold War historians that American foreign policy in this period was expansionist to serve the interests of dominant capitalist and commercial groups seeking markets in Europe and Asia. The evidence now is clear for the postwar era that the United States was repeatedly called on to shoulder responsibilities which Britain and the European states had carried before the war. On assuming these burdens, the United States seldom if ever saw itself as taking over the mantle of the European imperialists. Its task in education and science was to bring to the Africans and Asians the blessings that the colonial powers had denied them—self-determination and self-government, control of indigenous institutions, and national educational systems. Americans did not see themselves as replacing Europeans for narrow selfish or imperialist ends. Bringing the land-grant university or one-man-one-vote free elections to Africans was a latter-day expression of manifest destiny—making universal and worldwide the mission Americans had undertaken in the early nineteenth century within the territorial boundaries of the United States.

Wilsonianism and Collective Security

Ironically, doctrines of no entangling alliances and manifest destiny were predicated upon the continued existence of the old order in international politics even as they portrayed the American as "the new man." The Fourteen Points of President Woodrow Wilson combined a faith in American democracy—the idea of a war to make the world safe for democracy—and Wilson's profound conviction that "the day of conquest and aggrandizement is gone by." The old system of alliances, secret diplomacy, and the balance of power had passed; the new world of international cooperation, harmony of interests, and open diplomacy was dawning. It was considered immoral to question or doubt the emergence of this new order. Scholars were excluded from debates over its existence, not because they were judged to be bad historians or scholars but because they were considered immoral in their outlook. To latter-day Wilsonians, the fundamental issue in the troubled days of World War II was not the distribution of power between the Soviet Union and the United States, but the method of election of "members of the Security Council . . . as individuals, somewhat in the way that judges of the World Court were elected."[7]

The other dominant issue for Wilsonians was universal membership for all states in the United Nations. Clark Eichelberger, head of the United Nations Association after World War II and a tireless spokesman for the League of Nations Association in the interwar period, indicated: "If the principle of automatic membership had been adhered to [rather than giving the Security Council power over the admission of states], years of confusion as to who should be members of the United Nations would have been avoided."[8] But what effect would automatic membership have had on the struggle between the Soviet Union and the United States both within and outside the United Nations?

Nothing would be gained by replaying the debate between the supporters and the critics of Woodrow Wilson in this discussion. It is clear that Wilson's prepresidential views of international politics differed substantially from those he advanced in his public campaign for the League of Nations. As a member of the Inquiry involved in planning the peace after World War I, Walter Lippmann began as a staunch defender of Wilson but ended as his outspoken critic. Certain American secretaries of state, including John Foster Dulles and Dean Rusk, have defended Wilsonian principles with far more vigor when they were out of office than when they were responsible officials of government. What is worth observing in the present context is that Wilson's brave prophecy that old patterns of international politics were disappearing and that national interests were decreasing and being replaced by common world interests has, except in limited social and economic spheres, been refuted by history. Nor has formal membership in a universal international organization brought about an end to rivalries and strife. No matter how the prophets and followers of Wilson have tried to state his ideals as universal truths, they are still the result of particular attitudes, needs, and circumstances. Automatic membership in the United Nations after World War II would hardly have assured peace and harmony as long as the United States and the Soviet Union were engaged in an unremitting struggle for influence and power in Eastern Europe, Greece, and Iran. The system for choosing members of the Security Council could scarcely have been based on the election of respected individuals as long as United Nations membership was restricted to sovereign nation-states. It is tempting to draft blueprints for a new and better world, but responsible statesmen must act in the world *as it is*—a world of anxious, ambitious, and ideologically oriented states who put their own national security first. Yet not for a moment does this suggest that new international forums are not valuable and even essential as centers where statesmen can air their problems and negotiate both in public and in private within and outside the United Nations, especially when foreign ministers and heads of state gather in New York for the opening of each session of the General Assembly.

Wilsonianism and collective security are noble goals that call on nations to put the common good and the security of all nations ahead of their separate national interests. The realization of the brave new international order has not come about in our time. It is misleading, however commonplace, to assert that foreign policy can be shaped wholly in accordance with unrealized goals. To this day, Wilsonianism persists as an expression of American morality, whatever its limits and difficulties.

The Truman Doctrine: Making Containment Universal

The distance between Woodrow Wilson's ideas and the Truman Doctrine is too great to suggest, at first glance, an obvious and self-evident connection. President Harry S. Truman was of course Wilsonian in his early staunch commitment to collective security and to the United Nations, which he described as the cornerstone of American foreign policy. Yet he and in particular his secretary of state and adviser, Dean Acheson, soon turned to instrumentalities other than the United Nations to assure the maintenance of peace. NATO was one such instrument, and the Truman Doctrine was such a policy. What links Truman with Wilson and previous foreign policy doctrines was the tendency to turn specific foreign policy strategies into rigid and absolute political doctrines. We have the word of George F. Kennan, the author of the policy to contain Russian expansion "at points of our choosing," that he had never foreseen or intended containment being formulated on a global and universalistic basis. In the "Mr. X" article in *Foreign Affairs*, Kennan had urged that the United States resist Soviet imperialism through the application of unalterable counterforce wherever "they show signs of encroaching." He insists to this day, Walter Lippmann's criticism notwithstanding, that resistance should have been discriminating, selective, and determined by American national interests. But whatever the intent of Kennan's recommended policy of containment, the Truman Doctrine as proclaimed by the president came to be viewed as an American commitment to the defense of freedom everywhere in the world.

The global extension of the doctrine of containment was possible because it was coupled in the minds of a generation of American leaders with the resolve not to repeat the 1930s, whatever the price. Truman's advisers in the decision to intervene in Korea to halt the aggression against South Korea by North Korea did so under the long shadow of memories of the appeasement of Hitler at Munich. As they met with President Truman at Blair House late in the evening of June 25, 1950, each of them remembered the fearful price mankind had paid for failure to stop German aggression. Each man based his thinking on certain negative and positive moral principles: the resolve not to appease an aggressor and the use of counterforce to meet Communist expansionism. Having made that choice and having preserved thereby (or so they hoped) South Korea's independence, future policy makers saw no reason not to apply the Korean analogy to containment elsewhere in the world. From this line of thought, the road led almost inescapably to South Vietnam and one of the most fateful decisions in the history of American foreign policy.

It is argued that the Truman Doctrine was universalized to offset congressional inhibitions against a strong American policy of resistance to Soviet imperialism, but it is pointless to debate whether a more discriminating policy would also have gained congressional support. Responsible authorities can be cited on both sides of the argument. What is indisputable is that the Truman Doctrine is one more example of a policy designed to respond to specific needs but cast in a universalistic mold that made flexibility difficult for subsequent crises. At the time of Vietnam, the Truman Doctrine had outlived its usefulness, and the majoritarianism that had assured moral justification in the case of Greece and Turkey impeded adaptation and modifications when the conflict shifted to Asia.

It may seem farfetched to some to argue the connection between Washington's farewell address, manifest destiny, Woodrow Wilson's approach, and the Truman Doctrine. What these landmark foreign policy approaches have in common may be less apparent than what separates them from one another. If we step back, however, and consider the moral aspects and assumptions of each approach to a particular foreign policy problem, the connection becomes more apparent. What unites the four approaches is their common tendency to offer a total, all-inclusive explanation and justification for a single fixed course of action. Absent from them all is that tentative, provisional, and experimental quality associated with finely tuned policies in politics and diplomacy and the capability for adjustment to an ever-changing set of problems and facts. Assumed is the conviction that a single abstract doctrine can fundamentally alter and transform the world's realities. Ignored is the grim warning of William Graham Sumner:

> The worst vice in political discussions is that dogmatism which takes its stand on great principles or assumptions instead of standing on an exact examination of things as they are and human nature as it is. . . . An ideal is formed of some higher or better state of things than now exists, and almost unconsciously the ideal is assumed as already existing. . . . [All this] is popular because it is easy; it is easier to imagine a new world than to learn to know this one. . . . It is easier to catch up a popular dogma than to analyze it to see whether it is true or not. All this leads to confusion, to the admission of phrases and platitudes, to much disputing but little gain in the prosperity of nations.[9]

It would be comforting to think that there was no longer any need for warnings like Sumner's. All the evidence, however, points to a continued, if not an increased, need for voicing such concerns. However, the search for good and moral foreign policies raises questions today as serious as those discussed by Sumner. Such questions lead us to a deeper examination of moral approaches and foreign policy. They call for a better understanding of moral reasoning and the connections between transcendent and relative moral principles and for a further review of the theory and practice of morality embodied in certain examples of concrete foreign and global policies and the fundamental issues raised in their formulation and application.

Fortunately for America, the universalistic strand of American foreign policy has been accompanied by a more realistic tradition that began with Alexander Hamilton and continued through Henry Kissinger. A full discussion of American foreign policy would require attention to both traditions. Policies from the Monroe Doctrine through the application, if not the politics, of detente offer examples of the second continuing tradition. Moralism and realism have interacted in the formulation of key American policies; their dialectic is apparent in Franklin D.

Roosevelt's approach prior to Yalta. Liberals with a conservative bent—Roosevelt has been described as a Hudson Valley renegade—and conservatives such as Dwight D. Eisenhower, who recognized instinctively the limits of American power in Indochina, have shown themselves adept at reconciling ideals and power. It would serve no purpose, however, to ignore the impact of universalism on important historic American policies. The tendency toward universalism has most recently been evident in the Carter administration's initial formulations of human rights and disarmament policies. Nor is the issue disposed of by pointing to the retreat from universalism in subsequent policies. The urgent need is to diagnose the forces that have led to the original universalism and the consequences for American foreign policy—an unmistakable tendency to formulate great doctrines of foreign policy in absolute and universalistic terms.

Reinhold Niebuhr warned of identifying democracy with an optimistic view of history that experience would refute: "Democracy does indeed require some confidence in man's natural capacity for justice." But it also "challenges every pretension of wisdom and balances every force with a countervailing force."[10] It questions secular optimism as the true foundation of democracy. Niebuhr sought to offset this danger with precepts of practical morality or proximate ethical norms. Both cynics and idealists, he believed, misconceived the relationship between moral principles and realist calculations, the former by ruling out morality and the latter by overlooking realist demands. Their errors could be remedied by searching for intermediate or proximate norms that reflected ideals but were responsive to interests and power.

Leaders in the conduct of American foreign policy are right to identify specific policies with principles that are broader than narrow self-interest, for in personal as in national life too much self-centeredness can be self-defeating. At the same time, they need to recognize that policies are provisional and subject to a continuous process of review. The most nations can legitimately aspire to is some approximation of higher moral or universalistic principles. Nations, like individuals, are never as moral as they claim to be. Moreover, in affirming their own principles, nations must recognize the principles of others. What saves the national interest from excessive parochialism is a recognition of the possible mutuality of one nation's interests and those of other states. Prudence requires, therefore, both the acceptance of the tentative nature of concrete policies and the need to seek points of convergence with others. For Niebuhr the Marshall Plan was the most striking example of success in this search. With all its virtues, democracy—which was for Niebuhr the best practical approximation of a political system grounded on moral precepts—was imperiled by two illusions. The first was democracy's tendency to sanctify every practical measure, and the second was the assumption that the voice of democracy and of the people was the voice of God.

Foreign policy, therefore, is a practical art linking justice and power, not an exercise in moral philosophy. Power without justice within a state leads to tyranny, but justice without power means impotence. In foreign policy, national self-righteousness blinds a people to the necessity for continuous adjustments to ever-changing realities. Dogmatism drives out prudence, which became for Niebuhr in the last fifteen years of his life the cardinal political virtue. Because he was a child of reformist religion, which had looked for final answers to social problems, Niebuhr learned from experience the importance of understanding the political process. He came to see that compromise has its own moral content, particularly in respecting the aspirations and interests of others. Political reformers and self-righteous nations are likely to go wrong when they claim to have discovered what is absolutely right and therefore beyond compromise—an error to which his own country was not immune. Isolationism and globalism suffer fundamentally from similar intellectual and political misconceptions, and the remedy for both is basically the same.

The difficulties with practical morality in a democracy, particularly in foreign policy, stem from the public's insistence on clear-cut doctrines and blueprints. The way out for democratic leaders is to nudge the people toward viable alternatives, responding where necessary to popular pressures but refusing to be controlled by passions or events. Franklin D. Roosevelt, whom Niebuhr came to admire, did this in drawing a reluctant public into a great world struggle. Abraham Lincoln held to enduring political principles. In differentiating between individual and collective morality and in emphasizing proximate moral answers, Niebuhr provided intellectuals and some policy makers with an alternative to universal moral principles as the practical moral basis for foreign policy.

American Foreign Policy: Values Renewed or Discovered

On the surface, there is little if any resemblance between early American traditions and values and those undergirding American foreign policy today. Who in the present era would say with de Tocqueville: "I am firmly convinced that the Democratic revolution which we are now beholding is an irresistible fact"? Major trends in the world appear more and more to be crowding out this prophecy. Or, following Watergate, who echoes Michel de Crèvecoeur in proclaiming: "We are the most perfect society now existing in the world"? Who thinks of America any longer as the "simple, open, innocent, and guileless society"? How quaint and distant, now that America has become a highly industrialized, urban society, are Jefferson's words: "Before the establishment of the American States, nothing was known to history but the man of the old world crowding within limits either small or overcharged, and steeped in vices which the situation generates."[11]

Too many crises have followed one another too rapidly and too painfully to preserve these simple faiths. The effect of the crises has been to depress but not destroy pride and vision. Consider the turbulent events and secular trends of the twentieth century—the early decades of a nation struggling to find itself, combating bigness, rallying to the Progressives and Populists in some of the states, joining a war to end wars but repudiating Woodrow Wilson's other crusade for a league to enforce the peace. Next came the twenties, a return to normalcy as the weary nation, reeling from the strenuous life, regrouped and sought to reconstitute itself. The pendulum's swing, however, brought two subsequent decades of severe challenge and testing as a grim depression spread over the globe. Then ensued the nightmare of fascism, the consequent worldwide warfare and destruction, and the holocaust with its savage mass murders in gas chambers and concentration camps. Instead of challenge alone, response in the 1930s and 1940s brought some of mankind's finest hours, restoring the economy, turning back fascism, and exchanging hope for despair. The 1950s, as had the 1920s, ushered in an era of tranquility, this time by healing the noxious effects of McCarthyism and of a house divided against itself. The steady and calming force of a respected military hero as president enabled a war-weary, strife-torn people to renew and restore themselves, to gain a second wind before moving on. Yet even the mystique of a Dwight David Eisenhower could not entirely calm the storm. War clouds thickened over Berlin, Southeast Asia, and the Middle East. Economic growth slowed down, and a new sense of restlessness began to spread. When an attractive young senator promised to get the nation moving again, Americans were ready to respond.

What then of the 1960s and, so far as we understand them, the 1970s? What kind of an era have Americans known in these two decades? To what extent has it expressed once more the recurrent historical pattern of reform following retrenchment, of stabilization followed by the radical leap forward? As best we can perceive a period so close to us, the 1960s began according to pattern—dramatically illustrated by the New Frontier and the Great Society. It seemed that history was repeating itself. But a cluster of unforeseen accidents intervened—the assassination of three strong, trusted, and humane leaders; the spread of domestic violence; and the grotesque horror of the Vietnam War. At the same time, chronic problems surfaced and worsened—social decay in the cities, pollution and overpopulation, the progress by one minority lighting the torch for other minorities and ethnic groups.

Before the decade ended, the people called for a pause once more, another breather from the burdens of too much change. A world of constant uncertainty and kaleidoscopic transformations was more than they could bear. They grew weary of sacrifice, skeptical of intellectuals, saturated by the media, and dubious of the truth of any ideology. At this point, the promised land came to be viewed as a wasteland—a landscape of endless problems, half-successful strategies piled on strategies, resentments and racism, recessions and inflation, and technologies advertised as panaceas that actually became part of the problem. For a century and a half, Americans had been a shining example to others. New nations slavishly and often naively fashioned their doctrines of self-determination after the Declaration of Independence and modeled their constitutions after America's. Woodrow Wilson's Fourteen Points became a beacon for the oppressed.

Toward the end of the 1960s, the spotlight of international judgment fell on the United States—not kindly and magnanimously searching out its strengths and weaknesses but critically, sharply, relentlessly reminding the world that others were determined not to repeat America's mistakes. Those who came to visit the United States left, not applauding its successes, but reciting a litany of unsolved problems: the cities, consumerism, minorities, Vietnam. People listened, reacted, showed resentment, and then withdrew—a response as common to troubled nations as to anxious individuals. There was a sense that truth underlay the criticism. An Indonesian colleague serving on an international commission said that the one thing his country needed least was American films and television. He feared the social consequences of more than one national television channel in Indonesia for, if it had more, the hours would be filled with the same programs that had corrupted and weakened American society. To preserve indigenous culture, he said, his countrymen should resist the spread of plastic culture. Robert Penn Warren voiced a similar complaint when he returned to his birthplace and found passivity and self-indulgence replacing participation in civic and schoolboard affairs as the people turned first to watch and then to act out the less ennobling behavior they had viewed on television.

Many Americans then began to question their inherited values. Could it be that through technology they had conquered new worlds while losing their souls? Is it true, as René Dubois and others warn, that *things* are in the saddle and ride mankind? Are Americans driven by autonomous forces that are making decisions for them—by technology, scientific advance, and armaments research? It is simpler to describe the problem than to outline reasonable answers. Indeed there is a growing number of informed observers who doubt that Americans will find the answers. They speak of every society's inevitable rise and fall. A leading newscaster predicts that more people alive today will die of thermonuclear fallout than of cancer and heart disease. Past secretaries of state have repeatedly warned that America is poised between self-destruction and the dawn of a new era whose characteristics are left unexplored. Some point to a way back to sanity and survival, others challenge America to look ahead to a new society, and a minority believe that religion holds a key to today's dilemma. The problems seem so vast that they provide a thousand pretexts for indifference and inaction. What are the routes to renewal or, if it must be, to inescapable decline? What are the controlling values that can help or hinder the achievement of true goals and purposes?

It is easier, as George F. Kennan has remarked, to define by exclusion or to box in a problem by eliminating false answers or untenable solutions. More specifically, we may be able to approach the definition of a principle or policy by delineating what it is not. More than a decade ago, the brilliant if controversial legal scholar Edmond Cahn sought to illuminate justice by outlining examples of injustice in his book *The Sense of Injustice* (1949). One way to identify operational values is by looking at what they are not.

The first negative value is a personalism that overrides the necessary constraints and responsibilities of wise foreign policy. Contemporary Americans are ambivalent about their heroes, and we are told that young Americans have none. Individuals doubt one another but seek a superior force in which they can place their trust. In aristocratic regimes, the higher qualities of certain leaders are recognized, as illustrated by de Tocqueville:

> When the ranks of society are unequal, and men unlike one another in condition, there are some individuals wielding the power of superior intelligence, learning, and enlightenment, while the multitude are sunk in ignorance and prejudice. Men living at these aristocratic periods are therefore naturally induced to shape their opinions by the standard of a superior person, or a superior class of persons, while they are averse to recognizing the infallibility of the mass of the people.

In democracies, the opposite is true. Individualism makes each man less prone to place faith in another man or class of men and paradoxically increases man's readiness to believe the multitude. Since men are all endowed with equal means of judgment, truth is seen to reside with the greater number. As de Tocqueville said: "When the inhabitant of a democratic country compares himself individually with all those about him, he feels with pride that he is the equal of any one of them; but when he comes to survey the totality of his fellows and to place himself in contrast with so huge a body, he is instantley overwhelmed by the sense of his own insignificance and weakness." The majority rules, therefore, and imposes its will with "a singular power, which aristocratic nations cannot conceive; for it does not persuade others to its beliefs but . . . makes them permeate the thinking of everyone by a sort of enormous pressure of the mind of all upon the individual intelligence." [12]

Faith in public opinion becomes a species of religion, the majority its ministering prophet, and the executive its chief spokesman, interpreter, and representative. The executive plays such a role because for every faith, however diffuse, there must be a focal point; an individual must become the symbol. Consider the adulation shown for America's most dynamic leaders: Wilson, Roosevelt, Kennedy. When, if ever, has a comparable respect been shown for a particular Congress or any other assemblage of men, with the possible exception of the Constitutional Convention? The moral burdens thus placed on the executive and the temptation to hubris are overwhelming. Whether or not one is a member of the elect or the best and the brightest, one comes readily to believe it. Personalism is an almost inevitable outgrowth of the set of forces de Tocqueville described, although he also described counterforces. A chain of events is set in motion that leads the executive or his principal representative to believe that only he speaks the will of God. President

Woodrow Wilson appealed to the people at home and abroad over the heads of Congress. The power of such wartime leaders as Franklin D. Roosevelt had roots in the belief that they spoke for history and destiny. Secretary of State Henry Kissinger, because of extraordinary natural ability and the accidents of history involving the weakened role of a fallen president and his successor's inexperience in foreign affairs, took on a personal image enjoyed by few if any secretaries. Kissinger, however well his personal standing may have served him in the capitols of Moscow and Peking, was threatened by the virus of personalism. He thought he could read the American mind more accurately than his critics when he said that the American people wanted their leader to be a "lone cowboy riding into town," but this notion was fraught with serious perils. If one man is the sole trusted leader, only he can negotiate. If only one man is the recipient of policy guidance, only he deserves to speak with the president. (Compare this with Secretary of State Rusk's insistence, during the internal debates over Vietnam, that Undersecretary George Ball should make his case directly to President Lyndon B. Johnson.) Shuttle diplomacy, like summit diplomacy earlier, is the product of the misconception that only one man has the knowledge and authority to negotiate for his country.

Criticisms of Secretary Kissinger, or earlier leaders to whom much is owed for significant accomplishments, ought not to be based on the petty or the trivial. If critics have something to say, they should address fundamentals and in so doing, two questions surface. Is America in danger as a nation when every rise or fall in prospects for world peace is measured by the personal success or failure of a chief executive or a secretary of state? What are the consequences for American policy around the world when the secretary is engaged for weeks at a time on a particular peace mission? Who is left tending the shop, coordinating and giving direction to the actions of others? Foreign policy experts on Mediterranean problems appear in general agreement that the 1970s crisis with Turkey and Greece and the failure of American policy in Cyprus were caused more by what was not done in the first week of that crisis than with other subsequent failures, including the failure of Congress to back administration policies. It is difficult to see how anyone totally engaged for weeks on end in the search for a settlement between Israel and Egypt could have redirected the effort and attention needed to deal with a major new problem. When one adds to this the enormous drain of physical and mental energy that shuttle diplomacy entails, the criticism falls not on an individual but on a faulty concept of the office of the secretary of state. Personalism is defective in principle because foreign policy requires full mobilization of the talents of all parties in America's constitutional system, not a monopoly by one of the officers of government.

The second and perhaps more controversial commentary on the ordering of values in foreign policy has to do with ideological crusades. Americans are naturally prone to make foreign policy a quasi-religious and messianic endeavor. Neither men nor societies can live without dogmatic beliefs. Man is driven to seek great causes to explain what is happening in the world. In part this results from conditions where "life is so practical, so confused, so excited, so active, that but little time remains . . . for thought." Through broad and sweeping formulations, men are spared the trouble of studying particulars. They gain a high return from a small measure of attention: "If . . . they think they discern a common relation between certain objects, inquiry is not pushed any further; and without examining in detail how far these several objects agree or differ, they are hastily arranged under one formula, in order to pass to another subject." Comparing various nations and political systems, de Tocqueville observed that "if aristocratic nations do not make sufficient use of general ideas, and frequently treat them with inconsiderate disdain . . . a democratic people is always ready to carry ideas of this kind to excess and to espouse them with injudicious warmth."[13]

This penchant for the most general formulation, which is magnified in the television era, is coupled with a mood of national self-righteousness to which de Tocqueville and other observers have called attention:

> The Americans, in their intercourse with strangers, appear impatient of the smallest censure and insatiable of praise. The most slender eulogy is acceptable to them, the most exalted seldom contents them; they unceasingly harass you to extort praise, and if you resist their entreaties they fall to praising themselves. It would seem as if, doubting their own merit, they wished to have it constantly exhibited before their eyes. Their vanity is not only greedy, but restless and jealous; it will grant nothing, while it demands everything, but is ready to beg and quarrel at the same time. . . . It is impossible to conceive a more troublesome or more garrulous patriotism; it wearies even those who are disposed to respect it.[14]

At first glance this description seems so remote and distant from present-day America as to deserve no further discussion. Americans, especially in 1980, may be guilty of "doubting their own merit" but hardly of a "troublesome [and] . . . garrulous patriotism." It is more probable that Americans *need* to raise the flag in international assemblies and speak out for their not inconsiderable achievements and contributions, especially when they are condemned on every side. They are faced with a new distribution of power and opinion in international bodies. In the same way that responsible civil rights leaders were vilified and condemned by extremists in the late 1960s, the majority of developing countries in the United Nations continuously denounces American imperialism and colonialism. In Daniel Patrick Moynihan's words: "The arithmetical majority and the ideological coherence of . . . [the] new nations brought them to dominance in the United Nations and, indeed, in any world forum characterized by universal membership."[15] This dominance has meant a minority role for the United States on many issues.

Is it any wonder that American leaders should cast about for new ground to stand on? It would be more surprising if responsible officials were not actively in search of policy positions. Three alternatives present themselves: (1) to speak up for American know-how and virtue, (2) to withdraw from an interdependent world, or (3) to find a new basis for establishing mutuality of interest with those who condemn America but who may yet have common goals and purposes. The first alternative was pursued by the administration during the short tenure of Ambassador Moynihan at the United Nations. Although the second alternative enjoys somewhat greater support now than when the United Nations was founded, it has generated little active support among major political leaders. (States may exhibit various degrees of engagement and withdrawal, and passivity or inaction may sometimes accomplish many of the aims of outright withdrawal.) The third alternative involves long and hard work to discover points of community and identity among nations in temporary disagreement. This means striving to learn as much about the achievements and virtues of others as one knows about one's own. In 1976 the so-called Stanton panel on the organization of the United States government for cultural and educational programs (chaired by the former president of CBS Frank Stanton) faced this choice about the fundamental goals of cultural programs. One group on the panel asserted that the sole aim should be to proclaim American values to the world; another—the majority view—urged that equal weight be given to understanding the values and cultures of others.

It is both appealing and logical that Americans should speak as boldly and freely as leaders of other nations. In Moynihan's words, "It is past time we ceased to apologize for an imperfect democracy." It is possible that those who criticize America for its failings would be embarrassed if an American were to point to *their* shortcomings as well: "It is time we grew out of our initial—not a little condescending—supersensitivity about the feelings of new nations."[16] All this argues for a strong, forthright voice in world assemblies.

The line between speaking up for America and embarking on an ideological crusade, however, is a fine one. Spokesmen beginning with one approach may imperceptibly shift to the other. The roots of national self-righteousness run deep in the nation's soil and the American psyche. For twenty-five years, America was engaged in a Cold War between East and West that gave ready legitimacy to every major program of defense and diplomacy. How tempting to embark on a new Cold War, this time between North and South. The conceptual basis is remarkably similar: a monolithic rival to whom America is opposed, an ideology that sees America as the enemy, and a messianic urge to convert others to America's form of inherited truth. However, it is difficult to believe, particularly for one who has worked in Africa and Asia, that the political and economic systems of some seventy or eighty countries are all cut from the same cloth, however similar their rhetoric or social organization. Moreover, a description of any one of them may be quickly outdated. (Moynihan, writing in March, 1975, stated: "The Third World has . . . its share of attractive regimes. . . . Half the people in the world who live under a regime of civil liberties live in India."[17] Madame Gandhi came to power before the ink had dried in Moynihan's statement.) Caution is needed both in praising or in condemning states for their virtues and their failings lest the pattern change before the echoes die away.

Third, it is a negative virtue, and a common illusion in democracy, to believe that moral and political choice involves choosing a single value, making it an absolute, and defending it despite all the consequences. Americans are tempted to focus on one value, such as recent interest in "speaking for and in the name of political and civil liberty." Liberty is superior to all other values because those who have pursued it have done better economically and socially and have tended to support other values. In Moynihan's words: "This is so, and being so, it is something to be shouted to the heavens in the years now upon us. *This is our case.* We are of the liberty party, and it might surprise us what energies might be released were we to unfurl those banners."[18] We remember the call for a worldwide defense of freedom made by a young president in his 1962 inaugural address, which was followed so closely by the Bay of Pigs fiasco in Cuba. In foreign policy, as in politics, there is more to wise choice than standing for a single, even if estimable, value. If Americans are to support those values of peace, security, and justice, they need to look again at their interrelationships and the ever-changing context in which policies are worked out.

The first positive principle that deserves stating is that values, in foreign policy as in life, are multiple, not singular. They compete and are sometimes in conflict. No one value can be a guide to the formulation of policy, whether it be peace, liberty, justice, or equality. Conflicts between values are not accidental or exceptional; conflicts are part of the nature of things. Americans believe in freedom of speech, but public safety requires that no one cry fire in a crowded theater. Technological progress is based on freedom of thought and scientific pursuit, but an individual cannot engage in secret scientific activity that would endanger the security of the whole society. The value conflict is more acute in foreign policy because moral choice and action differ on the individual and collective levels. Political groups and nations pursuing their varied aims need to mobilize and generate popular support. Statesmen can seldom speak in whispers; their language must inspire, excite, and arouse. Apparently, citizens need to feel that they can achieve through the actions of states what is denied them in their personal lives. Therefore, national goals and achievement are cast in exaggerated form and stated in hyperbole. It is not enough to reopen contacts with China or to meet at the summit with the Russians. The public must be given a television spectacular and strong language about the twentieth century's most far-reaching foreign policy triumph—most far-reaching, that is, until the next. The mass media is made for overkill; group passions settle for nothing less.

Individual values can be more personal and tentative, unpublicized and uncalculating. Nations and groups expect a *quid pro quo*, want something in return, and view good deeds in terms of trade-offs. When foreign assistance is given, they look for expressions of thankfulness and gratitude. Individual morality differs because it is closer to direct human interrelationships and because men often do good without being able to trace the consequences. Interpersonal ethics are less often a bargain between parties. The individual can sacrifice himself or his interests to serve some higher purpose ("I give my life to find it," or "Greater love hath no man than this, that a man lay down his life for his friend"). Representatives of the nation or group sacrifice themselves only at great risk, given their responsibility to their publics. Because they must claim so much, they have trouble with William Wordsworth's definition of morality: "That best portion of a good man's life, / His little, nameless, unremembered, acts / Of Kindness and of love" ("Lines Composed a Few Miles Above Tintern Abbey").

In foreign policy, as in life, judgments on values come down to on-balance discrimination. Not only do good and bad values compete, but good values are themselves in rivalry. Operating value principles are not absolutes but are related to other principles. The United States stands for liberty, but it also stands for equality and justice. De Tocqueville fervently held that equality was the source of American democracy, but he added: "Because I attribute so many different effects to the principle of equality, it might be inferred that I consider this principle as the only cause of everything that takes place in our day. This would be attributing to me a very narrow view of things."[19] In personal life, value choices come down to balancing the competing moral claims of self and family, personal security and professional interests, and short-term and long-term good. Above all, moral judgment involves living with ambiguity. We cannot know the consequences of our acts, however noble our intentions. The Protestant Reformation gave birth to the nation-state, the French Revolution to crusading nationalism, and the conquest of Hitler to the rise of the Soviet empire. Moral judgment, which is often closer to action than to thought, demands that we live with the consequences of our acts, some of which are irretrievable.

A second proposition directed toward value formulation is that the social environment has radically changed. Therefore, today's moralists must cope not so much with ambiguity as with a deep and all-pervasive sense of pessimism. The overall atmosphere is not dominated by the theory of progress any more but by a sense of powerlessness, impotence, and despair. Curiously enough, pessimism may have its origins in two contradictory sources—the corrupting influence of power or the enfeebling effects of powerlessness. The former results from a weakness in man, the latter from situations beyond his control. Lord Acton's famous dictum about power is worth recalling. He had written a highly critical review of Mandell Creighton's *Papacy in the Reformation Epoch* (1897), condemning the author's failure to hold the papacy accountable for the Inquisition, the torture chamber, and the stake. Subsequently, Acton wrote in a letter to Creighton:

> You say that people in authority are not to be snubbed or sneered at from our pinnacle of conscious rectitude. . . . I cannot accept your canon that we are to judge Pope and King, unlike other men, with a favoured presumption that they did no wrong. . . . If there is any presumption it is the other way, against holders of power, increasing as the power increases. . . . Power tends to corrupt and absolute power corrupts absolutely. Great men are almost always bad men, even when they exercise influence and not

authority; still more when you superadd the tendency or the certainty of corruption by authority.[20]

Today's pessimism, however, derives less from the corruption of power than from limitations in man's capacity and ability to deal with problems that outstrip human and material resources. A leading American publisher tells of a series of breakfast meetings with all of the declared 1976 presidential candidates. The one impression he carried away from every meeting was that the candidates were overwhelmed by the complexity of current issues. None had answers to the problems of the arms race, tax reform, inflation, pollution, or the growing proportion of Americans supported by taxes paid by a smaller and smaller proportion of the producers of wealth. No one had persuasive solutions to these urgent problems; no one was able to speak confidently from the conviction that he had discovered significant new answers. Because of a prevailing sense of powerlessness, the strongest candidates politically may be those who promise and offer least. To do nothing is to fail in nothing.

In the search for values in public and foreign policy, we must recognize, therefore, that we are not surfeited with new ideas or new possibilities. We are in a period in which leaders must grope and feel their way without much assurance that any new approach will work. We may have to settle for piecemeal approaches, delaying actions, the staving off of disaster. Fortunately, the United States throughout its history has produced men of action who made reasonable choices when the moral and intellectual basis for decisions was unclear. De Tocqueville wrote:

> The man of action is frequently obliged to content himself with the best he can get because he would never accomplish his purpose if he chose to carry every detail to perfection. He has . . . to rely on ideas that he has not . . . [explored] to the bottom; for he is much more frequently aided by the reasonableness of an idea than by its strict accuracy; and in the long run he risks less in making use of some false principles than in spending his time in establishing all his principles on the basis of truth.[21]

This highly tentative and problematic approach may be the most we can hope for when few if any solutions are in sight. It would be pleasant to have a general theory of disarmament, inflation, or the production and consumption of wealth. In its absence, we may have to place our faith in men of action of the type de Tocqueville so vividly described.

Paradoxically enough, the gravity and severity of our problems and crises generate new concern for values. The Spanish romantic and mystic Miguel de Unamuno wrote: "Let us so live our lives that, if there is no life after death, it will be an injustice." To paraphrase and adapt this, we should approach our insoluble problems as if there were answers. In this way, we may find partial ameliorations of stubborn and resistant issues. Most of the final solutions to problems are more destructive than the problem itself. So we need to reinstitute the ancient tradition of moral reasoning with its balance of competing moral and political claims. Value approaches having nothing to say about the tragic elements in life—poverty and suffering, hunger and disease, fears and frustrations, disappointment and despair, self-doubt and failure, disillusionment and divorce, setbacks and losses, death and defeat—have little to tell us about life. The first aim of a public philosophy should be to rediscover such resources, renew men's interest in enduring political thought, and strengthen determination to bring problems within such a framework. To understand all this may be better than to shout to the heavens.

American Democracy and the Third World: Convergence and Contradictions

Abraham Lincoln prophetically defined the issues that faced both the young American republic and today's fledgling nations in the question: "Must a government of necessity be too strong for the liberties of its people, or too weak to maintain its own existence?" The political history of mankind is a dramatic struggle between these two opposing tendencies and requirements. Lincoln's question gives us a basis for understanding contemporary national and international politics. His formulation identifies a problem common to North and South, East and West. However, we need to remind ourselves of the differing points in time and history from which nations struggle to reconcile order and liberty. Americans are proud of their nation's goals and political heritage, but the realization that they have benefited from two hundred years of trial and error plus a two-thousand year legacy should encourage humility as well. The new nations, by contrast, have enjoyed at most a few decades to wrestle with such issues.

In a word, the relationship between American democracy and the Third World is one of both convergence and contradiction in values, interests, and necessities. Neither community of interests and similarity of heritage nor conflict of aims and purposes can supply more than a partial and fragmentary view of these relationships. Out of the analysis of such similarities and differences on North-South international politics, a fuller picture may emerge.

Two classic statements in Western thought describe the connection between liberty and order. John Stuart Mill viewed liberty thus: "A people may prefer a free government but if from indolence, or carelessness, or cowardice, or want of public spirit, they are unequal to the exertions necessary for preserving it, if they will not fight for it when it is directly attacked . . . they are more or less unfit for liberty." In Lincoln's letter to Horace Greeley, he wrote: "If I could save the Union without freeing any slave I would do it; and if I could save it by freeing all the slaves, I would do it; and if I could save it by freeing some and leaving others alone, I would also do that. What I do about slavery, and the colored race, I do because I believe it helps to save the Union; and what I forbear, I forbear because I do not believe it would help to save the Union." [22] In the contemporary international system of nation-states, commitments to liberty and order go hand in hand.

The clash and the interplay between liberty and order is one example of the unending conflict in politics between goals and values. If one value, and one value only, could be the lodestone of human conduct, how simple life would be. But values cluster and compete. Freedom and order, liberty and justice, individual rights and national security clash and contend with one another. No one is served when men prate about values and ignore man's terrible predicament in having to choose —a choice not simply between good and evil, but often between competing goods and more often still between lesser evils. The eternal dilemma exists because we want to do good—but what is the good?

American leaders in the first quarter of the twentieth century proclaimed that democracy was on the march and that freedom was the last best hope of all mankind. By the third quarter of the century, the warriors for democracy were in disarray, and Third World leaders were announcing that Western parliamentary democracy was unsuited to urgent problems. How remote from present-day expectations are the words of Woodrow Wilson addressed to the United States Senate on January 22, 1917: "I am proposing government by the consent of the governed. . . . These are American principles, American policies. . . . They are also . . . [those] of forward looking men and women everywhere, of every modern nation, of every enlightened community. They are the principles of mankind and must prevail." [23] In 1980, rather than the tree of liberty being watered by the blood of tyrants, it is the tyrants seemingly who prevail—not tyrants obsessed necessarily with prestige and private gain—although this too is sometimes their aim—but tyrants who are technocrats, administrators, pragmatists, and realists. Some are benevolent, some social reformers, many better educated than their countrymen. Some take their inspiration from the West; others are the children of traditional oligarchies; still others are weaving together strands of Western and anti-Western thought in a curious many-colored world outlook. Some are lip-serving Marxists with little understanding of either the theory or the practice of Marxism. Most are Socialists, like the societies for which they presume to speak, but Socialists prepared to tolerate if not seek out private investment at home and abroad. A significant number have come to power as consolidators struggling to bring inherited postindependence programs into balance with their country's resources.

As military men, the new oligarchs bring to their tasks the strengths and limitations of their profession. Their limitations are all too ominous and visible. Long queues of hungry people seeking daily food allowances testify to basic unmet human needs, not only in poorer countries but in such Third World countries as Ghana, which once had surpluses of financial and commodity reserves. Even Third World economic societies that have freed themselves from their more blatant excesses and extravagances are not yet geared to root out the deeper causes of social unrest. Their leaders suffer from that brittleness of thought and action common to technocrats and militarists who have moved from military decisions involving all-out victory and defeat to less certain forms of decision making in the ambiguous realm of politics and diplomacy. Lincoln, John F. Kennedy said, was a sad man because he learned that in politics we cannot have everything we want. Social criticism in some new countries is offensive to comparatively strong and decent national leaders, who are convinced that they are doing what is best for their countries. The democratic principle of "the indispensable opposition" described by Walter Lippmann is for them premature. It is painful for military elites to acknowledge and call on the necessary expertise of other elites (intellectual, religious, or social), particularly on any continuing basis; but expertise of all types is needed on the broad front of social problems.

At the same time, such ruling groups are acting on certain facts and truths which others may have overlooked. Order precedes liberty and justice, Reinhold Niebuhr wrote, even in developed societies. James Madison pointed to the same principle in 1829: "The propensity of all communities is to divide when not pressed into a unity by external dangers. . . . There is no instance of a people inhabiting even a small island, if remote from foreign danger, and sometimes in spite of that pressure, who are not divided into alien, rival, hostile tribes. The happy Union of these States is a wonder."[24]

For new nations, the problem of order has its special urgency and, along with such urgency, certain unique characteristics. The old political order with its traditional unities and coherence is eroding, if not disappearing, and nothing of comparable strength has yet taken its place. Anticolonialism, the main rallying point as the new nations approached independence, is tailored to the politics of protest more than to the politics of governance. Modernization, which serves contemporary social scientists and some historians as an ordering concept, has always seemed more descriptive of technical rather than organic social change. The new military administrators in developing countries are aware of the vacuum that exists and are taking what steps they can to institute a new order. They may provide provisional forms of order through recognizing that authority rests on the prestige of continued legitimate rule—a factor in maintaining order in traditional governments since the rise of the first empires in Egypt and Babylon. But authority has also rested historically on the claim that political order is an extension and application of the cosmic order, leading to all the idolatrous claims made for the priest-kings and god-kings of Egypt and Babylon. Gulielmo Ferrero in his *Principles of Power* (1942) distinguished between legitimate and illegitimate governments by pointing to the authority of the former and its capacity to gain either implicit or explicit consent and the inability of the latter to rule except by force and fraud. Writing of this distinction, Niebuhr observed:

> The significance of this distinction is that it places both democratic and traditional governments in the category of "legitimate" governments. The former relies upon explicit consent for the authority of a particular government, but must also rely on implicit consent for the authority of the system of government by popular will. The latter is more legitimate than pure democrats are inclined to believe because it has enough implicit consent to dispense with fraud and to rely on only a minimum of force. In short, the source of power is the authority of a government to gain consent without force.

Before the rise of democracy, legitimate governments drew their authority from their ability to maintain order, if order was not gained at too great a price of justice. It was taken for granted, in part because of certain religious and ideological assumptions, that concentration of power in government was a necessary evil, bound to lead to some injustice. When injustice became intolerable, as in the later stages of absolute monarchy, the authority of government collapsed. In other words: "Justice is always a secondary, though not a primary, source of authority and prestige. The primary source is the capacity to maintain order because order is tantamount to existence in a community, and chaos means non-existence." [25]

It may seem far-fetched to apply these concepts of Western political thought to the developing countries, and yet without them it is difficult to comprehend the ongoing acceptance and authority of governments in Third World countries. Even a world-respected leader like President Julius Nyerere of Tanzania, whose roots are in the democratic tradition, justifies the authority of government and the role of a one-party system in these terms. In effect, he is saying that his country is poor and cannot afford the full panoply of democratic institutions. Governments in the Third World rule by implicit consent of the people who, having found the authority of colonial power too vexatious, have turned to local regimes as expressions of nationalist and social revolutions. The unanswered question in some Third World countries is whether military regimes will, as they seek to impose order, prove even more vexatious to the claims for justice of their people. It must be acknowledged that human rights and individual freedom are even more restricted in some Third World countries today than when they were a part of alien colonial regimes. For the present, however, a majority of such regimes justify their rule as the means to achieve order, even though they often employ dictatorial policies and structures. Communist nations, whose colonialism is more recent in Africa and Asia, find few contradictions in cooperating with and in granting technical assistance to such regimes. But, as Niebuhr prophesied fifteen years ago, "the disadvantages from which the West suffers are more desperate than we have ever admitted to ourselves. In fact, there is a danger that we will be driven into a new fit of hysteria once we recognize the true state of affairs." [26]

As we enter the last quarter of the twentieth century, the grave risk in North-South problems, as it was for the third quarter-century in East-West relations, is that the West, in particular the United States, *will* approach such problems in a fit of hysteria. It has become as rewarding politically to condemn Third World leaders and governments at the United Nations as it once was to denounce the Soviet Union and international communism. Our reactions will determine whether the world is divided in two once more, and it is not reassuring that such reactions involve Americans who are a proud and impatient people. De Tocqueville wrote: "The Americans, in their intercourse with strangers, appear impatient with the smallest censure and insatiable of praise. . . . It would seem as if, doubting their own merit, they wished to have it constantly exhibited before their eyes."[27]

No one would contest that Americans need to raise the flag in international assemblies and to point to positive goals and accomplishments that others may overlook, whether from design or ignorance. It is illusory to suppose that American power and influence will increase through the appeasement of critics. Former Ambassador Moynihan was on solid ground when he declared: "It is past time we ceased to apologize for an imperfect democracy." Yet strong words that may bring political dividends in one political setting may give offense to national pride and prestige in another arena. Words must be judged in the context of the different publics who are listening, of democracy and foreign policy, of worldwide domestic and international politics. For example, Ambassador Moynihan in an autumn, 1975, speech to the American Federation of Labor declared that the Organization of African Unity had in General Idi Amin the leader one would expect them to have. With this statement he offended, not so much the organization or General Amin (who surely deserved condemnation), but his fellow African leaders whose chairman he was solely by virtue of rotation of office within the organization. The sovereign and responsible governments of African member states, not Amin, were aroused. Given the makeup of their political constituencies and the strong and sensitive force of young nationalism, African leaders had no alternative but to strike back. Flamboyant and ill-considered Irish wit rent the delicate fabric of a coalition of African moderates. Overnight, the leadership of those African states—formerly exercising restraint within the Arab-African bloc in votes on Israel at conferences in Kampala and Lima—retaliated. American political rhetoric, fashioned in part for American domestic politics, left Africans no alternative. Ambassador Moynihan seemed to forget that the United States since World War II had been catapulted into a position of world political leadership it did not seek, that responsible leaders in the world arena speak not to one audience but to many, and that the first order of business for a world leader is building working political coalitions for common ends. "Politics," Woodrow Wilson once explained, "is the slow boring of hard wood." What goes on among diplomats and in the corridors more often serves this end than do political fireworks and spectaculars on the hustings. When values and interests converge or when potential if limited convergences can be perceived as the basis for building consensus, the task of the statesman is to nurture and strengthen—not destroy—the prospects of political cooperation.

Convergence

It is easier to point to the mistakes and contradictions of others than to formulate good foreign policy. What we must consider here are not the shortcomings of individual leaders but the points of convergence and contradiction between American democracy and the Third World. The picture is complex; it will not yield to oversimplifications. It is as false to maintain that all the germinal ideas for the governance of African societies originated in the London School of Economics as it is to argue that British socialism has not left its considerable mark in Africa and Asia. But the convergence of British socialism and some Third World regimes is not the only point of similarity. What makes the recent fit of hysteria in our approach to North-South problems so tragic is that the observer can identify six areas at least in which convergence is apparent: the human, historical, philosophical, institutional, traditional and cultural, and economic.

From the standpoint of human relations, many American and Third World leaders are old friends. An Indonesian appointed to one of the highest positions in UNESCO privately lamented the widening gulf between North and South: "We are graduates of your universities, trained by your most distinguished professors, and united in friendship to more Americans than any other people outside our own lands. Yet we cannot defend you in our councils when you condemn us en masse; we cannot speak well of you when you abdicate your role of world leader. Only the United States can lead the rest of the world, but you are not doing it." In nongovernmental fields—educational, scientific, agricultural, commercial, and even legal—the human ties between Americans and Third World people are based on mutual trust and long experience with common problems. I recently directed a review of higher education and development in Africa, Asia, and Latin America financed by twelve large donor agencies: the United States Agency for International Development, (USAID), the French Ministry of Foreign Affairs, the British Overseas Development Administration, the Canadian International Development Agency, the International Development Research Center of

Canada, the World Bank, the Inter-American Development Bank, UNESCO, the United Nations Development Program (UNDP), UNICEF, and the Ford and Rockefeller foundations.[28] When we decided to turn not to Western educators but to Third World leaders to conduct the case studies, a score of respected figures from the three regions were quickly identified as men whose educational and human qualities were well known to those of us in technical assistance. Their educational competence within their own countries and regions was as great as any comparable group of Europeans or Americans. Bonds of friendship and respect had developed between "us" and "them" over the past two decades. Incidentally, lest someone question their status and acceptance in their own countries, three became university rectors and presidents during and after the study, and three more received ministerial appointments. Referring to such people, my Indonesian friend commented: "It would be a tragedy of epic proportions if America were to squander its rich heritage of friendship and trust."

Historically, the past and present fate of many Third World countries has been hammered out in relationships with the Western democracies. Colonialism is a two-edged sword. Although providing an object and a target of resistance, it has also bequeathed a priceless heritage of institutions, beliefs, and values, not all of which are irrelevant to the lives and needs of indigenous peoples. For better or worse, the colonial powers have been present at the creation; without them, and in particular without the example of the British Empire freeing over a billion subject peoples, there might not have been a community of proud and independent new nations today. We and they, because of certain underlying values, have been partners in the unfolding of a momentous new historical era.

With all the vast differences separating rich and poor nations, well-placed leaders of some of the new nations share with us a common philosophical heritage. This is true from both a negative and a positive standpoint. Negatively, just as Marxism can be viewed as a Christian heresy, the programs for social justice and national development invoked in the Third World take their inspiration from regnant goals and ideas in the West—values professed but not fully realized. Much as upper-middle-class youth in the late 1960s invoked the values of their parents against them, the new nations in their social revolutions have invoked dream versus reality in the West and in the West's relationship with the Third World. From a positive standpoint, I cannot remember a discussion of education in the Third World in which certain democratic ideas were not prevalent. For example, in the case study of Tanzanian higher education, the authors described the process of changing an inherited educational system to reflect the goals of the country's social revolution but criticized the system for providing few if any opportunities for women. Another example stems from the debate over the relations of governments and universities in the Third World. The prevailing view in Asia and Africa is that the two are part of a single unified system. To speak of separation or conflict between them is to apply a Western idea not yet relevant in the developing world. Rector Puey Ungphakorn, Thailand's most respected intellectual, posed the historic Western view: "Past, present or future Asian students need independence of thought and independence of judgment. It is understandable that Asian governments should guide Asian universities and students. However, guidance can mean control. If there is too much control and suppression, students will go underground and their claims will become unthinking and unreasonable. No government can have an ironclad hold on its universities and students." Puey went on to say that the ideas he had expressed were not Western ideas but universal ones that all governments and all universities ignored at their own peril.

A more controversial area of convergence has to do with the affinity of democratic and Third World institutions—controversial because some of the institutions inherited by Third World countries are plainly not relevant to their needs. An astounding amount of adaptation and accommodation is going on, but I am impressed that much of it has left the inherited institutional structures intact. Surely this is true for the basic educational structures and the patterns of governance within universities. Indeed, Africans and Asians are using democratic procedures to reform the established systems of governance by university senates and councils. Younger and often more innovative faculty members are organizing their efforts through councils of deans or departmental leaders to break the hold of senior conservative faculty—in Brazil, the *catedratico*—within university senates. Most striking is that this struggle continues to take place within the established institutional framework and not outside it, as in revolutionary councils.

In the two other areas of convergence—traditional culture and economics—affinities have been noted between North and South. Some of the writings on the political process in the Third World suggest that tribal chieftains in the developing world, especially in Africa, have exercised political power with the implied consent of those they govern and serve. There were trade-offs and a bargaining process between chiefs and those who were subject to their power. Consequently, it would be inaccurate to describe the tribal system as totally authoritarian. Similarly, most of the discussions in the Committee of 77 at the United Nations and at the United Nations Conference for Technical Assistance and Development (UNCTAD) on a new international economic order assume the reform and not the destruction of the present international economic order. Let us negotiate about change, the Third World leaders appear to be saying, seeking broader representation and more equitable international commodity agreements to which all parties will give their consent.

Of course, it would be utopian to suggest that these points of convergence will persist or determine policy. However, it would be shortsighted to ignore their existence and to depict all Third World countries as having fallen permanently into the antidemocratic, authoritarian camp. Furthermore, to condemn all developing countries en bloc is to fashion a new dogma, to offer a self-fullfilling prophecy that carries within itself the seeds for the growth and development of the very forces democratic states ought to resist. America would better show itself to be the great and self-confident power it is if, as George F. Kennan has so often counseled, it viewed its role as gardener, not mechanic, sensitive to the natural forces struggling with one another in the world, most of which have little chance of being influenced or affected by America. If the United States adopted this more modest concept, it would be less likely to do harm and more likely to strengthen forces congenial to the deeper values it seeks to follow and uphold.

Contradictions

When we consider the democratic process as it affects the shaping of foreign policy, the contradictions between American and Third World experiences become apparent. Surely there is scant evidence anywhere in the Third World that foreign policy is being determined by the outcome of free public debate. Indeed, the usual formulation of democracy and foreign policy by definition excludes those normally democratic societies in which one ruler or a ruling political party presumes to express the will of the people without allowing them to express it for themselves. If the Third World countries approach democracy in foreign policy at all, it is as representative, not direct, democracy. But even here there remains a wide gulf between most Third World military governments and the ideas expressed by political philosophers such as Edmund Burke.

This leads to the crux of the matter—the quality of political leadership. Here we come face-to-face with a deeply troubling paradox in Third World leadership. For the United States, the founding fathers charted the course to independence and continued to guide the nation's destiny. The founding leadership for the new Africa and Asia comprised early nationalist leaders and popular demagogues whose claims for their nation and culture, although extravagant if not preposterous, were probably necessary for national identity and independence. To the extent that present-day Indonesians scattered over three thousand islands call themselves Indonesians, Sukarno's flamboyant nationalist rhetoric may have been more of a unifying force than Suharto's steadier and more rational administration. On the streets of Accra, more Ghanaians are familiar with the name of Kwame Nkrumah than the present-day military rulers with their much lower political profiles. The George Washingtons of countries such as Nigeria and Togo—men like General Gowon and Sylvio Olympus—have been victims of coups d'état or political assassination, not leaders honored and revered as was Washington in the years following the Citizen Genet affair. Some of the new nations lack the underlying political consensus, stability, and unity that America's founding fathers described as "a more perfect union," and consequently they are in a state approaching continuing civil war. The implications of this for commitments in foreign policy are obvious, although some measure of continuity is assured by the existence of cadres of permanent civil servants.

Then too there is another form of instability that leads to tension and contradictions between us. Although America needs to be more responsible and to recognize points of convergence, Third World leaders also have important responsibilities that have not yet been met. Leaders in Africa and Asia must do more to understand the predicament of their American friends. Loud and unqualified criticism of all that the United States tries to do in the Third World can be counterproductive. If Americans seek to help, they are called imperialists; if they withdraw when this criticism mounts, they are condemned as isolationists. To mention a particularly fashionable litany, many Third World leaders believe that the United States is unwilling to assist Socialist states on ideological grounds. Although there have been sharp differences of viewpoint and intense debates in the Congress, the last five administrations have all recommended and carried out cooperative programs, not only in Socialist countries but in Communist ones such as Yugoslavia. Rumania and other East European countries have been encouraged to initiate contacts and trade with the United States, and America now cooperates with the Soviet Union and China. Yet ill-founded charges and broadsides continue to be directed against the United States by Third World countries who ought to recognize that their unfair and unreasonable criticisms toward the West, especially the United States, may be as damaging as any criticism of them by the West. This applies also to the double standard toward democratic and Communist states. Third World countries often condemn the United States and other Western-oriented countries on the matter of human rights and remain silent toward or actually justify even worse policies by Communist states.

Americans pay a high price for democratic foreign policy. The government may adopt a permanent foreign policy and then find that, in a moment of public passion, an excited popular opinion will not support that policy. By contrast, in some Third World countries, the country's foreign policy is essentially that of its ruler. De Tocqueville's "natural defects" of democracy in the conduct of foreign policy pertain less to military governments in the Third World. Writing of Gaullist France, Raymond Aron explained that the advantage in dealing with a strong and determined leader is that he is able to keep his promises. General Charles de Gaulle was elected through democratic processes, and the new French constitution was approved by the French parliament, a process not followed in many Third World countries. Yet to equate those countries with France from the standpoint of an underlying political consensus is questionable, particularly in regard to the long-term forces at work on the African and Asian continents. These forces include the character of Third World nationalism, residual anticolonialism and an almost pathological concern with neo-imperialism, the antipathy of colored peoples to the West, and the precarious nature of political authority, especially in countries that have not experienced social revolution. Taken together, these volatile conditions within the new states shattered the Moynihan strategy at the United Nations and constitute important factors that even the strongest Third World leader cannot ignore. However divisive such forces may appear, Americans would be shortsighted to ignore the extent to which similar forces played a part in their own early history. Seen in broader historical perspective, American foreign policy has expressed its own form of antiimperialism toward European intervention in the Western Hemisphere—the Monroe Doctrine, the struggle for national indentity, the need for the myth of a chosen people guided to a promised land, the conquest of the frontier and the wilderness, and the flight from the wickedness and frustrations of the Old World. Ambassador Moynihan and Secretary Kissinger proceeded on the basis of different assumptions about common values and experiences, or lack thereof, between Third World countries and the United States. Kissinger's perspective has been used by the Carter administration, especially by Ambassador Andrew Young. My own experience with the international programs of a private foundation in the developing world leads me to believe that Kissinger and Young are closer to the truth. The real issue, however, is whether one or the other approach best defines and facilitates the task of the statesman in sizing up events and shaping them to his purpose. For the statesman knows that every decision he makes is connected with other decisions and that each has its consequences. He must live with the world as it is, including his mistakes in comprehending it. He cannot retreat to yesterday's world, start over again, and reconstruct his decision—a luxury enjoyed only by scholars writing after the event—nor is he able to suspend judgment until all the facts are in. De Tocqueville summarized the many difficulties of foreign policy in a democracy, particularly the American democracy, but he identified one advantage of an essentially pragmatic people: "The world is not led by long or learned demonstrations . . . [but] a rapid glance at particular incidents, the daily study of the fleeting passions of the multitude, the accidents of the moment, and the art of turning them to account decide all its affairs."[29]

The question remains, and it is the fundamental one: What are we to say about prospects for democracy and foreign policy in nations whose political systems are the antithesis of the democratic process? At both ends of the spectrum occupied by democracy and military rule, what is needed, of course, is wise leadership. At one extreme, no political system—particularly if it originated in democratic thought—can escape the need to attend to some expression of the will of the people, as recent African and Soviet experiences suggest. At the opposite pole, Americans ought not to forget their own experience with government from George Washington to Franklin D. Roosevelt. Urgent problems in the Third World—famine and overpopulation to mention just two—appear to require some measure of authoritarian rule. The great issue is how authoritarian rule can ultimately be brought under public scrutiny —the extent to which channels for the expression of the public will are kept open and free men are able to assert themselves. There are differences between totalitarian regimes in which such channels remain closed and one-party political systems in which the public will may ultimately find expression. Tanzania represents a one-party state; yet political debate and differences are aired in party councils if for no other reason than because its leader's political philosophy is basically democratic. But Julius Nyerere has argued that solutions to the poverty and misery of his people require strong guidance and leadership. America's severe crisis in the 1930s gives us at least a glimpse of the present gravity of the problems in Africa. The test may well be, as Niebuhr and Ferrero have argued, whether such governments are legitimate, whether there is at least tacit consent to their rule, whether they can be maintained without too much overt force. In any event, there is little that America can do to reshape these systems except to wish them well and to help them move toward some greater measure of freedom through moderation and restraint in American policies. But this need not lead to American withdrawal and retreat. With maturity, American leaders may learn to live in a world, and particularly with the Third World, where values sometimes converge but are also often in conflict.

Reconciliation Without Political Power

Two traditions of political thought confront one another whenever students of politics or men of affairs have sought to reconcile conflicting viewpoints. Writers and political leaders have weighed opposing approaches to the relationship between American democracy and the Third World—the one emphasizing the convergence of their values and interests and the other their contradiction. The first tradition looks forward to the early resolution of differences by maintaining that either the American democracy and the new nations have basically common interests drawing them together or, contrari-wise, that their present policies and social systems are in contradiction and cannot under present circumstances be reconciled. The most effective spokesman of the latter view was President Gerald Ford's ambassador to the United Nations, Daniel Patrick Moynihan. The most determined and outspoken representative of the former view was President Jimmy Carter's envoy to the United Nations, Andrew Young. Moynihan stressed contradictions between North and South to the exclusion of common interests; Young in his tenure assumed that the values of African states and the United States need only be identified to be harmonized. It would be premature at this time to attempt any serious evaluation of Ambassador Young's conciliatory approach. Despite the fireworks he has set off along the diplomatic trail, Young's approach to relations with African leaders has significantly benefited from his conviction that Africans and Americans could cooperate if they understood what each valued most. Front-line

African diplomats and statesmen have responded to his more affirmative approach and to his demonstration that black Americans share a common heritage with the leaders of black Africa.

Yet historians, paradoxically enough, may find that Young and Moynihan have more in common than may at first appear. Both have focused on only half of a profound human problem and have tended to consider a part of reality as if it were the whole. One has recognized the points of convergence and the other the contradictions between industrial and developing countries. In doing so, each assumes that he has described everything that is fundamental in African-American relations for any foreseeable future. In effect, both Young and Moynihan have treated as all-inclusive only one dimension in such relations. Each is less a pluralist than a monist in his political and ethical thinking. If one had to choose between Young's more positive and Moynihan's more negative views, there would be every reason to opt for the approach of President Carter's ambassador. The risk with Young's approach, however, is that failure to recognize the growing conflicts and tensions between North and South may lead to disillusionment, just as a too-simple American idealism in the early stages of the Cold War brought on harshly dogmatic and unyielding attitudes when contradictions between East and West became only too apparent.

Fortunately, there is another political tradition more tested and revered than the one inspiring Moynihan and Young. It is a tradition associated with Abraham Lincoln. At its core is the belief that statesmen must live with antinomies or conflicting values and social forces, as well as with goals that converge for men and nations. Had Lincoln in his day been faced by the all too self-evident reality of conflicting and converging interests of the new and the older states, he would have called attention to both sides of that reality. He would have grasped both horns of the dilemma, even as he continued to uphold the necessity of understanding the prerequisites for liberty and order. It is always tempting, most of all for politicians, to prophesy an easy reconciliation of stubborn opposing realities. The tradition that calls for political reason and moral judgment in dealing with seemingly incompatible factors teaches that men must accept both sides of reality as two parts of the whole and, in the case of North-South relations, the inevitable underlying convergence and contradiction.

The Problem of Human Rights

Not since the days of Woodrow Wilson and Franklin D. Roosevelt with their Fourteen Points and Four Freedoms have ethical principles received greater prominence than in the political campaigning and presidential statements of Jimmy Carter. Looking back, President Carter's crusade for human rights has a certain air of inevitability about it, given his personal background, political acumen, and the previous administration's legacy of the Watergate and Vietnam issues. Washington observers have noted that the human rights issue fits Carter like a glove. The determinants were his religious beliefs, his fundamentalist origins, the moralist streak in his nature, and the successes of the civil rights movement in the South. Less often mentioned was the influence of the men around Carter, liberal foreign policy advisers in search of a credible alternative to Secretary of State Henry Kissinger's *realpolitik* and such remote spiritual mentors as the Reverend Theodore Hesburgh, president of the University of Notre Dame. Political realities linked Carter's moral instincts with the need for: restoration of confidence in the integrity of government at home and abroad, restatement of the higher law principles on which American democracy was based; the building of a new coalition reminiscent of past Democratic groupings of otherwise diverse forces made possible by the fortuitous coincidence of attitudes on the left and the right (liberal Democrats saw the lack of a moral base for foreign policy as supporting right-wing repressive regimes, while foreign policy conservatives in labor and business blamed concessions to the Soviet Union on the amorality of American negotiators), the appeal of the human rights issue to minorities (notably, Jews, the right, the South, Baptists, liberals, and labor), and exploitation of the foreign policy differences between Ronald Reagan and Gerald Ford to the embarrassment of the incumbent president. The issues of Watergate, Vietnam, the CIA scandal, and the Chilean coup d'état were political targets. Although candidate Carter was himself cautious about leveling blame on President Ford, an electorate listening to his roadside campaigning could scarcely miss the point. Along with the customary negative methods of attacking those in office, Carter strategists early saw the need for a new and more positive message.

If motivation for a human rights stance is now obvious, candidate Carter was at first slow to invoke the principles of human rights. He raised them in a Democratic issues forum in Louisville, Kentucky, in late 1975 and in a speech on foreign policy in Chicago, Illinois, the following March. He returned to the subject in a speech on human rights in October, not surprisingly delivered at Notre Dame. Not until the second debate between Ford and Carter did the Democratic candidate assert his views with determination, centering the attack on President Ford and Secretary Kissinger for not protesting Soviet violations of Basket Three of the Helsinki agreement. (The first basket dealt with security and postwar European boundaries; the second with trade and scientific and technological exchanges; and the third with freedom of travel, marriage between citizens of different states, and reunification of families.) In this one decisive political thrust (an issue that Patrick Caddell, Carter's pollster, called very strong across the board), Carter appealed to the followers of Senator Henry Jackson and others concerned about Soviet treatment of the Jews (Carter in his Notre Dame speech had also spoken of Soviet pressures on the five million Russian Baptists) and to liberals concerned with Korea and Chile. It mattered little that his stand reversed an earlier decision to shy away from foreign policy issues, given Ford's and Kissinger's greater experience, or that some witnesses reported that Carter heard about Basket Three for the first time in San Francisco just before the second debate. Carter had previously been potentially vulnerable to criticism for being leftist on foreign policy and too passive on the threat of Eurocommunism, but during the second debate, on this single issue, he showed Ford as slow to answer the evils of communism. A human rights campaign, one Carter strategist observed, was an outgrowth of America's basic assumptions. Another adviser noted that the people who first urged Carter to make human rights an issue may not have anticipated how receptive he would be for personal reasons. There followed the letter to President Carter from Andrei Sakharov, the Soviet nuclear physicist and dissident leader, on January 28, 1977; President Carter's reply made public by Sakharov on February 17; the State Department's charge against Czechoslovakia for arresting and harassing signers of Charter 77 (a petition to the Czech government for protection of rights outlined in the Helsinki agreement); and President Carter's messages in February to Leonid Brezhnev and Ambassador Anatoly Dobrynin, as well as several public statements making his intention clear to speak out when human rights were threatened. In March Carter declared in a speech at the United Nations: "No member of the United Nations can claim that mistreatment of its citizens is solely its own business."

The outstandingly able Washington journalist Elizabeth Drew has written: "Having arrived, through a variety of circumstances, at a policy idea, the Administration's next problems were to define it, to find methods of implementing it, and to reconcile it with various conflicting goals." Most of the activity went on inside government. One foreign policy official explained: "I know there was no specific planning for a particular human rights campaign or program, such as it is. . . . Fate intervened—happenchance things, letters—that blew the issue up unexpectedly. . . . [Response] drew such enormous attention and acclaim—especially from the right . . . [and] gave the President maneuvering room." To make a policy idea operational, it was necessary to sharpen the issues; deal with Congress, which in the Kissinger years had enacted legislation to introduce human rights considerations into foreign policy; moderate the style (Secretary of State Cyrus Vance spoke of avoiding stridency); establish methods and machinery (Patt Derian, a civil rights leader, was elevated to the post of assistant secretary of human rights); apply human rights to specific issues, such as military assistance to certain Latin American, African, and Asian countries; and develop a conceptual framework. The problem was, as one official put it: "How do you express this value [human rights] in tangible terms?"[1]

Secretary Vance undertook this in a speech at the University of Georgia Law School on April 30, 1977, distinguishing between governmental violations of the integrity of person (torture, arbitrary arrest, denial of a fair public trial); fulfillment of vital human needs, such as food, shelter, health care, and education; and the right to civil and political liberties, such as freedom of speech, press, religion, assembly, movement, and participation in government. Developmental loan assistance by multinational assistance organizations, the World Bank for example, through which the United States channels about one-third of its aid to developing countries, presented a special problem. So did the linkage of human rights with the Soviet-American SALT talks. Human rights was made a part of the PRM (Presidential Review Memorandum) process of American foreign policy under the chairmanship of Undersecretary of State Warren Christopher, but outside groups were also enlisted. From June 14–16, 1977, a group of international lawyers, diplomatists, theologians, Third World authorities, and diplomatic historians met with high-ranking State Department officials in Charlottesville, Virginia, under the auspices of the University of Virginia to explore the fundamental issues and to search for a rational framework for human rights. Participants pondered the present need for a human rights policy in the context of the late Reinhold Niebuhr's wise counsel: The more Americans indulge in an uncritical reverence for the American way of life, the more odious they become in the eyes of the world, and the more they destroy their moral authority, without which both economic and military power become impotent. "The irony of our situation lies in the fact that we could not be virtuous (in the sense of practicing the virtues which are implicit in meeting our vast world responsibilities) if we were really as innocent as we pretend to be."[2]

The Ubiquity of Moral Choice

A nation, particularly a democratic nation and most particularly the United States, tends to view its actions as taking place within a moral framework. On one hand, it sees itself as subject to certain moral limitations and judgments; on the other, it looks to national goals and historic traditions as the explanation and moral justification for its course of action. Seldom if ever is foreign policy defended by arguing solely for national survival or national power. Americans and most other people speak rather of standing for moral purposes beyond the state: democracy or communism, freedom or equality, order or justice, and historical inevitability. Whatever cynics may say, foreign policy tends to be articulated in moral terms, even in some authoritarian regimes, whether those terms be social justice, economic equality, the overthrow of colonialism, national liberation, or the end of an unjust status quo.

To know that men and nations espouse goals that transcend national defense or survival is a first step or approach—but not a solution—to the moral problem. In fact, it is more a claim than an approach; it may bespeak what George F. Kennan and Hans J. Morgenthau, two participants in the deliberations, called moralism as distinguished from morality. Moralism is the tendency to make one moral value supreme and to apply it indiscriminately without regard to time and place; morality, by comparison, is the endless quest for what is right amidst the complexity of competing and sometimes conflicting, sometimes compatible, moral ends. Paul Freund of the Harvard Law School based his 1976 Thomas Jefferson Memorial Lecture of the National Endowment for the Humanities on Lord Acton's aphorism: "When you perceive a truth, look for a balancing truth." According to Freund, Western civilization suffers from the decline of the ancient art of moral reasoning, the essence of which is weighing and balancing not only good and evil but competing goods.

Freedom and order, liberty and justice, economic growth and social equality, national interest and the well-being of mankind are each in themselves worthy moral ends. How much simpler moral choice would be if the leader could select one value as his guiding principle and look upon all the rest as secondary or instrumental. In every human community, however, the choice between right and wrong is endlessly fraught with complexity and grounded in deep moral pathos. There is an inescapably tragic character to moral choice. Within the family, men all too often may be driven to choose between family interests and professional responsibilities, between devotion to one and neglect of the other. Loyalty to spouse and children may conflict with caring for the needs of aging parents. With the nation, freedom of speech and assembly may clash with the requirements of security and order. States' rights may collide with loyalty to the federal union; and when the conflict remains unresolved, a tragic civil war may ensue. The right to a fair trial may clash with the right to know and the freedom of the press. Even within the most developed democracy, every political and constitutional principle coexists and is related to every other principle. Each is at most a partial expression of morality; democracy's survival depends on recognizing the fragmentary character of all values, as Reinhold Niebuhr wrote, "Our best hope . . . rests upon our ability to observe the limits of human freedom even while we responsibly exploit its creative possibilities."[3]

Within the family and the democratic nation, however, forces are at work to protect fragmentary values and interests—to hold moral absolutism in check and to prevent men from erecting a single principle into an all-controlling moral dogma. The rights of individuals are weighed against the rights of the group. Society has long-established procedures and institutions through which claims and counterclaims are weighed and adjudicated. Political and constitutional rights and social legislation are invoked to prevent abuses that threaten the weakest elements of society, including minorities and the powerless, children, the infirm, and the aged. The law of love that lies beyond the reach of large collectivities (political parties, corporations, and organized churches do not love one another) is at least theoretically a practical possibility within the family. Within the family, however, some form of distributive justice may prove to be man's highest moral attainment, as even the most loving husband and wife or parents and children can attest. Justice within the family involves giving each party his or her due; often this is as much a matter of calculating needs and interests as of unselfish love.

Within the nation, the Bill of Rights and the constitutional system mediate justice for individuals and groups, minorities and majorities, the weak and the strong. Just as love is mediated through justice in the family, the higher law principles on which the Constitution is based support the unending quest for rights within American society. The health of democracy rests finally on the possibility of minorities becoming majorities, on some approximation of justice, and on a common-sense recognition that no single value or principle is a final guide to moral rectitude. To paraphrase Niebuhr: The triumph of common sense prevents anyone's strategy from being carried through to its logical conclusion. There is an element of truth in each position which becomes falsehood precisely when it is carried through too consistently. Democracy is a "saving faith." It is "an attitude, not a program."[4] It preserves community despite the upsurge of successive political movements.

Diplomatic and Legal Perspectives on World Politics and the Emerging Community of Nations

The moral problem, as exemplified within the family and within democratic nations, is more readily comprehended and understood than it is within the fragile and embryonic community of nations. Some 150 nations make up international society, each with its own political and economic system, institutions and practices, needs and traditions. Each has its own requirements of governance, its necessities of state, and its own rights and restraints inherent in its political order. For manifold reasons, the moral problem for politics among nation-states is more complex than among families and democracies. The first duty of a national statesman is to preserve the union—a requirement that both limits his actions and directs some of them along lines that may be offensive to ideas of personal morality. President Lincoln pointed out in his letter to Horace Greeley that his primary purpose was to save the Union, whether this meant freeing all, none, or some of the slaves. His choice based on national morality was not necessarily the choice he would have made from the standpoint of personal morality. Nor could he assure national unity without paying homage to domestic political realities. Louis Halle has written: Lincoln, in his Emancipation Proclamation, "excepted from its provisions the slaves in certain border states that were represented by members of Congress whose political support he needed. The self-proclaimed representatives of morality won applause . . . by denouncing him as one of the wicked, but the wisdom that comes only with the passage of historical time has at last preferred him to them, even on moral grounds."[5]

The demands of statecraft have sometimes been even more severe than those dictating Lincoln's choice. The Italian nationalist Count di Cavour has said: "If we had done for ourselves what we did for the state what scoundrels we would be." The classical definition which some consider a popular misconception of the diplomat is an honest man sent abroad to lie and deceive in the interest of the state. From Callières to Stephen Kertesz, writers have contested this view. Harold Nicolson amended it: "Yes, but he must also return to negotiate another day."

The crux of the matter, as viewed by most students of diplomacy, is that foreign policy is conducted by governments as a function of their duly constituted responsibility. It must serve the purposes of government, and it must be determined by the national interest and the dictates of national security. On this point, members of a well-known group of American authorities on diplomacy differ in emphasis but agree in their conclusions.

Hans Morgenthau, an uncompromising champion of political realism, argues that the conduct of foreign policy is not devoid of moral significance. Political actors come under moral judgment; they express the values of their societies. However, the contemporary environment of international politics paradoxically shows signs of both moral improvement and moral decline. Advances in respect for human life have certainly occurred since the fifteenth and sixteenth centuries when, for example, the Republic of Venice carried on its rolls an official poisoner whose employment depended on his success in disposing of the leaders of adversary states. Compare this with the sweeping moral indignation of Winston S. Churchill when Joseph Stalin at Teheran proposed—half mockingly but not wholly in jest—that fifty thousand German leaders be summarily shot to put an end to the threat of German aggression. Or contrast it with the force of public reaction in the United States to disclosures concerning possible plans for political assassinations by the CIA. At the same time, the decline of international morality in other areas indicates that moral restraints are weakening if not disappearing; for example, in distinctions in wartime between combatants and noncombatants. According to the Hague Conventions of 1899 and 1907, only soldiers ready to fight were considered combatants and objects of war, but by World War II this distinction had effectively been obliterated in the saturation bombings conducted by both sides. The international environment, therefore, is marked by a decline in international morality brought about in part by the technology of warfare and in part by a diminution of standards concerning the sanctity of human life.

Therefore, in war and peace the world has seen moral improvement and decline. Universal moral principles are filtered through circumstances of time and place and through national concepts that determine their application. In peace, there remains an enormous gap between American deference for human life, Stalin's massacre of the Kulaks, or Hitler's mass extermination of the Jews, for example. Short of taking human lives, some societies engage in the worst forms of torture. (In Saudi Arabia thieves are punished by cutting off their hands.) The overarching characteristic of today's international environment is that particular moral imperatives are obeyed by particular nations at particular times and not by others.

George Kennan goes further than Morgenthau when he writes: "The governing of human beings is not a moral exercise. It is a practical function made necessary, regrettably, by the need for order in social relationships and for a collective discipline to control the behavior of that large majority of mankind who are too weak and selfish to control their own behavior usefully on the basis of individual judgment and conscience." Ambassador Kennan declares further that government, particularly democratic government, is an agent and not a principal. No more than any other agent (for example, the corporation or the church, especially since the Protestant Reformation) can it substitute itself for the conscience of the principal. In a strongly worded statement concerning the American government as agent of the American people, Kennan asserts:

> The government could undertake to express and to implement the moral impulses of so great a mass of people only if there were a high degree of consensus among them on such questions as: what is good and what is bad? And to what extent is it the duty of American society to make moral judgments on behalf of others and to improve them from the standpoint of those judgments? Such consensus would be difficult to achieve even if we were dealing with a highly homogeneous population, with firm and unanimously-accepted concepts of an ethical nature as well as of the duties and powers of the state. In the case of a polyglot assemblage of people such as our own, it would be quite impossible. If our government should set out to pursue moral purposes in foreign policy, on what would it base itself? Whose outlooks, philosophy, religious concepts would it choose to express? Imbedded in our population are hundreds of different traditions, beliefs, assumptions and reactions in this field. Are we to assume that it, the government, knows what is right and wrong, has imparted this

knowledge to the people at large, and obtained their mandate to proceed to bring about the triumph of what is right, on a world-wide scale?[6]

Opposed to the views of diplomatic writers is a large and respected body of writings from international law. Philip C. Jessup, the former American judge on the International Court of Justice, has singled out five criteria as essential to "an ethical and therefore a successful foreign policy: sincerity, loyalty, legality, humanitarianism," and what he has called "proper objectives." By sincerity he means the same as honesty or an absence of deceit, vital especially in peacetime. A government suffers bankruptcy from such labels as "perfidious Albion," which can mean that it is not to be trusted in the future. Jessup acknowledges that there may be imperatives which lead to deceit of a government's own citizenry, but these must find justification, if at all, under "proper objectives." Louis Halle, who belongs to the first group of diplomatic writers, offers another perspective:

> From 1955 to 1960 . . . the United States regularly sent its U-2 spy planes over the Soviet Union at high altitudes to locate military installations and report on military activities. Presumably, such planes would have been able to detect any preparations for a surprise attack on the United States in time to give warning. . . . A Soviet system of espionage operating inside the United States was alert to detect any preparations for a surprise attack on the Soviet Union. This mutual espionage contributed to the preservation of the peace, because the observations of the spies on either side, showing that the other was not preparing a surprise attack, enabled each to remain calm and restrained. If such observations had not been available, each side might have been the victim of panic-making rumors that would have impelled it to feel that its survival depended on striking before the other was able to realize some rumored intention of doing so itself. . . .
>
> However, in 1960 when an American U-2, illegally violating another country's air space, was shot down in the middle of the Soviet Union, many moralists in the West were shocked to learn that such espionage by the United States had been going on, for they regarded it as both immoral and incompatible with the advancement of the cause of peace.
>
> Peace is more secure today, and the prospects of arms control are better, to the extent that the Soviet Union and the United States,

through their espionage (in which satellites have replaced spy planes), can each be sure of what armaments the other possesses.[7]

There are significant differences between diplomatic analysts and international lawyers, therefore, on truth telling. The former are more inclined to say that, although there is a universal moral code for truth telling, there are differing social contexts in which it is applied. In personal and national affairs, men operate within a society where lying is seldom necessary. Mayor Richard J. Daley's creed for Chicago politics affirmed that a politician's last resource is his word and that lying does not constitute good politics: "If you must lie, it is better not to say anything." International affairs differ from personal and national affairs just as the conditions of civilization and the conditions of nature differ. Because of the half-anarchic character of international society, "one man is to another as a wolf." However, for the international lawyers, truth telling is an aspect of sincerity plus loyalty plus legality. Law's basic norm—*pacta sunt servanda*—is found in America's moral creed, the Koran, and other religious teachings. Pragmatism and morality came together in the Hague and Geneva conventions on the treatment of civilians and prisoners, evolving as they did from the pragmatic test of reciprocity. Judge Jessup states: "The principle or rule that a treaty secured by the application of force or threats to the person of the negotiator is void is an illustration of a moral base for a legal rule. The bombing of Cambodia by the Nixon administration is an example of illegal, immoral and bad policy. The Mayaguez affair is another similar example as it was also deceitful in its alleged justification."[8]

Judge Hardy Dillard, another representative of the legal perspective at Charlottesville and formerly the American judge on the International Court of Justice, goes further. International law, for him, is not a legal straitjacket or an abstract and inflexible set of rules. It can be made to serve the security interests of the United States. Its putative advantages in specific policy choices can be measured against its costs. For him, the U-2 flight was a mistaken act because its alleged advantages were outweighed by its costs. Law has a constitutive function by ordering the bully to do what is right. It is designed not to settle but absorb disputes. Today the world is governed by a network of international treaties. Some 760 volumes of United Nations treaties, designed to regulate international life, have been registered since World War II. Although nations are free to invoke or not invoke this body of law, it remains a guide to policy decisions.

It is fallacious to say that law is obligatory and policy voluntary. *Pacta sunt servanda* for Judge Dillard does not mean that all treaties have to be observed at all times. The ultimate value of Article 2, Paragraph 4, of the United Nations Charter on the use or threat of force against the territorial integrity of sovereign states or of international treaties regarding human rights is that certain moral and political positions are stated, policies have been forged into solemn agreements, and important matters are no longer solely a matter of domestic jurisdiction. To paraphrase Justice Oliver Wendell Holmes, taking law into account is not a duty but only a necessity; the end products or results of diplomacy cannot be ignored. Moralistic finger shaking may prove more an irritant than a solution; but in every policy decision, the good of invoking the law must be weighed against its disadvantages. All history is a tension between heritage and heresy. Law and policy must mediate conflicting demands for stability and change. *Taking* a moral stand is different from moralizing about it.

Workability Versus Abstract Principle in the International System

Two fundamental issues separate the diplomatic analysts and the international lawyers on matters of morality and foreign policy: workability versus abstract principle and continuity versus change in the international system. Diplomatists put the stress on workability: the objective of foreign policy should be closely related to the reduction of as much human suffering and injury as possible, not the unqualified triumph of abstract principle. Moral appeals to mankind in general or the masses too often constitute not morality but Pharisaism. Whatever the short-term advantages of this approach, it has floundered in the long run because a self-proclaimed moral individual or nation requires others to follow its own assumed perfection. Manicheanism, which sees the world as divided between the good and the bad has infected American thinking on foreign policy. Since World War I, Americans have divided the world into peace-loving and aggressor, freedom-loving and Communist states. Used as the basis for foreign policy, this attitude ignores the test of workability. The almost inevitable result of Manicheanism is a moral crusade, war or the threat of war, and genocide. (It is worth remembering that certain Allied leaders, who fought against Hitler's extermination of millions of Jews, saw the "solution" to the German problem in the extermination, in turn, of thousands of Germans.)

Workability is also the test applied by certain diplomatic historians, notably the Cold War historian Norman Graebner, another participant at Charlottesville. History suggests that whenever the United States has introduced towering humanitarian objectives as the guide to policy it has added to, rather than diminished, human suffering and has subsequently been forced to abandon unworkable policies. In our time, Secretary Dulles' liberation foreign policy offered by the Republicans in 1956 as a more dynamic alternative to the postwar policy of containment inspired Hungarian freedom fighters to revolt, only to discover that American national interest and the facts of geography and power required a more cautious policy and precluded American intervention.

For the first thirty years of America's history, the new nation was a moral and political example for the rest of the world. Benjamin Franklin wrote: "Establishing the liberties of America will not only make the people happy, but will have some effect in diminishing the misery of those, who in other parts of the world groan under despotism." Thereafter, every major European revolution against monarchy and aristocracy evoked popular demands that the United States underwrite its cause and thereby that of humanity. Graebner observes, however, that "never were the repeated references to the American mission in the nineteenth century the actual determinants of policy." These demands collided with an even stronger American tradition that the nation concern itself with those finite goals which served the national interest. Alexander Hamilton warned in his "Pacificus" and "Americanus" letters that the only sure guide was the national interest. George Washington resisted the popular mass movement aroused by Citizen Genet for intervention in the French Revolution on grounds that "no nation is to be trusted further than it is bound by its interest; and no prudent statesman or politician will venture to depart from it." Even American idealists such as Thomas Jefferson, James Madison, Henry Clay, and Abraham Lincoln, especially when responsible for decision making, were less concerned with American involvement in revolutions abroad than with building a good society and preserving national security. When President James K. Polk in 1845 sought to universalize the American interest in the Western hemisphere under the Monroe Doctrine, John C. Calhoun argued in the Senate that the ends of policy had to be calculated by the means available. It was, he maintained:

> the part of wisdom to select wise ends in a wise manner. No wise man, with a full understanding of the subject, could pledge himself, by declaration, to do that which was beyond the power of execution, and without mature reflection as to the consequences.

There would be no dignity in it. True dignity consists in making no declaration which we are not prepared to maintain. If we make the declaration, we ought to be prepared to carry it into effect against all opposition.[9]

Graebner argues that a shift in the American approach to foreign policy occurred with President Woodrow Wilson, foreshadowed by President William McKinley's defense of the Spanish-American War and the acquisition of the Philippines based on sentiment rather than clearly defined national interests. Previously, Graebner indicates, "none of the nineteenth century revolutions in Europe or Asia succeeded or failed because of what the United States did or did not do. They reflected the worldwide trend toward self-determination and democratic forms of government, supported by the American model, nothing more." With Wilson, idealism and sometimes moralism replaced political realism as the cornerstone of a new world order. Maintenance of the status quo was identified with universal democracy and the Versailles peace structure; Americans linked that status quo with the abstract moral and legal principles of the League of Nations rather than with a body of clearly defined interests to be defended through diplomacy and war. The goals of a universal moral order were in tension with the policies of nations who could not see their interests as served by strict observance of the requirements of the new world. The Japanese and the Germans turned to war in part because their leaders were able to rally their publics against the real and imagined injustice of the status quo and in part because the principles of peaceful change did not satisfy the interests of all nations equally. (The British, French, Belgian, Dutch, and even American empires were left untouched by the peace settlement.) Graebner writes: "In its relations with Japan the United States sought peace. But its proposals [fueled by the moral indignation of leaders such as Cordell Hull], based on the assumption that the right belonged totally to the status quo, sought not compromise but capitulation. The capitulation never came." History repeated itself in some respects following World War II. American efforts to apply the doctrine of self-determination failed to undo specific repressions that existed behind the Iron and Bamboo curtains. Graebner concludes: "The Wilsonian appeal . . . could not prevent the destruction of the Versailles order; the postwar appeal to the Atlantic Charter could not restore it. . . . What the American experience, in many ways unique, has demonstrated is the fact that policy goals unsupported by generally recognizable interests will not receive much credence elsewhere."[10] There is no dignity in goals that a nation is not prepared to pursue after consideration of all possible consequences.

International law's response to the diplomatic historians is to question whether words and solemn commitments do not have an effect of their own. Important ideas enshrined in the American Declaration of Independence have been written into solemn international treaties; for example, the Declaration and the Covenants of Human Rights. (The diplomatists asked whether failure to ratify the Covenants gave America a strong platform from which to speak.) Words and ideas document that there is something universal about human rights; even the vocabulary of the Communist and totalitarian states attest the existence of fundamental freedoms. (To paraphrase Niebuhr: hypocrisy is often the tribute that vice pays to virtue.) A nation acts by speaking out for its values; silence can be costly. (In international law, Dillard went on to explain, protest indicates nonacquiescence, but failure to protest does *not* indicate acquiescence.)

Policy makers see the importance of arousing public support for foreign policy. It could be argued that in recent years the rest of the world has come to believe again in the American vision, testimony to the power of words and ideas. In the days of the founding fathers, the United States was powerless to work its will; now that it has become the most powerful nation in the world its words are more surely attended to. Some saw in this fact new responsibilities; others warned against the corruption of power. Perhaps Niebuhr's counsel helps reconcile these differences: "Nations, as individuals, may be assailed by contradictory temptations. They may be tempted to flee the responsibilities of their power or refuse to develop their potentialities. But they may also refuse to recognize the limits of their possibilities and seek greater power than is given to mortals." [11]

For the international lawyer, the national interest is too narrow a concept. Enforcement of laws is misconceived if keyed exclusively to physical enforcement. ("The Supreme Court has spoken, now let it enforce its decision" is one perspective. This must be weighed against the success of the courts, for example, in requiring former President Richard Nixon to give up the tapes despite the president's powers as commander in chief.) Until Iran in late 1979 rebuffed the World Court, only one nation refused to abide by a judgment—Albania in the Corfu Channel case. Judge Hersh Lauterpacht wrote that the French Declaration of Human Rights was more powerful than all the battalions of Napoleon. Dillard agreed on the futility of nations proposing things that cannot be done effectively and raising false expectations (for example, rolling back the Iron Curtain). He quoted Lord Balfour on the need for restraint in making grievances public. However, to say that nations should not propose what they cannot enforce is too narrow an approach, Dillard insisted; there are other pressures. Law may not command, but it can affect what nations do in justifying their actions. If moral statements and standards are irrelevant, why do nations bother to justify themselves by those standards? There are signs that even the Russians respond and are sensitive to moral appeals.

Continuity Versus Change in the International System

The second issue between diplomatic analysts and international lawyers is the nature of international society—its propensity for continuity or change. The diplomatic school sees the world of American foreign policy as subject to many of the same rules and constraints known at the founding of the republic. To the question posed by the historian Carl Becker at the end of World War II, *How New Will the Better World Be?* they answer that it is neither wholly new nor necessarily better. Why? Because of the nature of man and international politics and the persistence of the nation-state system.

In an unpublished paper prepared for the Charlottesville conference, Hans J. Morgenthau stated that the purpose of American foreign policy "is not to bring enlightenment or happiness to the rest of the world but to take care of the life, liberty and happiness of the American people."[12] At the same time, he acknowledged that national interest in contemporary American foreign policy must be defined in terms that transcend nineteenth-century concepts of national interest. In a certain sense, all nation-states, large and small, are obsolete; they no longer adequately meet human needs within national boundaries. Man's protection of the environment and the preservation and distribution of natural resources require the cooperative efforts of communities of sovereign states. Yet, however obsolete the present international system may be, national leaders are still held responsible for the wise conduct of their nation's foreign policy, thus maintaining the requirements of historic international politics until the day when a new international system may come into being.

International lawyers are more inclined to argue the existence of a new and better world, the birth of an embryonic world community. The Charter of the United Nations and the Declaration and some nineteen Covenants of Human Rights are said to embody core principles of human rights and fundamental freedoms foreshadowed in the American Declaration of Independence. To defend human rights abroad, therefore, is not to act in contravention of Article 2, Paragraph 7—the domestic jurisdiction clause of the United Nations Charter. Judge Philip C. Jessup quotes Secretary of State Elihu Root, writing in 1906 to the American ambassador in St. Petersburg regarding a protest concerning the persecution of Jews in Russia:

> I think it may do some good, although I do not feel sure of it. I do not know how it will be received. It may merely give offense. I am sure that to go further would do harm. I am sure also that to publish here the fact that such a dispatch has been sent would do harm, and serious harm to the unfortunate people whom we desire to help. Any possible good effect must be looked for in absolutely confidential communication to the Russian government. The publication that any communication has been made would inevitably tend to prevent the Russian government from acting, to increase the anti-Jewish feelings and to make further massacres more probable.

But then Judge Jessup adds that the situation today may differ "since human rights have become the subject of international agreements." He concludes: "I favor the position of President Carter."[13]

Guidelines for Human Rights from the Diplomatic and Legal Perspectives

No one who favors a human rights emphasis in American foreign policy would suppose that diplomacy and law could provide all-sufficient and comprehensive principles and guidelines. As we have seen, the human rights approach of the Carter administration can be understood only in the context of American presidential politics. Political scientists and political observers are needed to help explain its dynamics. To theologians, a policy initiative such as human rights illustrates creative activity at the "moral margins." Idealism and realism are forever in tension, but policy makers have the opportunity of acting at the margins of idealism. Every religious and moral system has its models of the good leader and of exemplary human conduct. Perhaps each society or civilization should be judged on its own models. If Americans judge human rights practices solely by American standards, they are guilty not only of ethnocentrism but of innocence abroad. A nation aspiring for world leadership cannot long survive unless it seeks righteousness at the heart of its national life and in the world. The great challenge for America is to maintain a proper tension between its clear approximation of righteousness and the limits and relativity of its moral base. President Carter has to a considerable extent restored a self-doubting and uncertain country to a sense of integrity and awareness of its national purposes. He is trying to institutionalize this mission and forge administrative mechanisms for achieving it. The test of so noble an effort viewed from the Third World will be whether an America that has discovered anew its historic moral beliefs can relate them to a rapidly changing world. Ways must be found to view human rights as one aspect of the search for a new morality by the majority of the world's people. Viewed against the background of the goals and strivings of others, a more moral American foreign policy can lose much of its rigidity and compulsiveness without losing its moral content. A persistent American weakness throughout history has been impatience. Americans are more inclined to speak to the world about their own purposes than to listen, to seek self-understanding first and only belatedly mutual understanding. A true moral international order requires America to join with other nations and peoples in an effort to resolve their ethical dilemmas as well as its own.

If there is one point on which diplomatists, lawyers, theologians, and Third World spokesmen can agree, it is the mistake of depending wholly on governments to legislate and articulate human rights. The foreign policies of nations are set by what their publics tacitly or openly support. An unsolved problem is how to connect a realistic vision of a future world order with the people's sense of participation. Freedom for people to participate has not been a hallmark of the United Nations; but recent world conferences on the environment, food supplies, population increase, women's rights, and human settlements have provided a forum for people as well as for governments. Government-to-government relations are essential in the present stage of international relations but so are relations among people and among political parties. There are grave risks, as Communist states have learned, in leaving all public declarations on issues such as human rights to beleaguered chief executives; when they speak, the nation's court of last resort is exhausted prematurely. Political leaders of great powers are in danger of talking big and doing nothing. (President Theodore Roosevelt sensed this when he spoke of talking softly and carrying a big stick.) A friendly Third World observer, Soedjatmoko of Indonesia, asks why parliaments, political parties, and civic and religious organizations in Western countries cannot carry some responsibility for speaking out on human rights. The diplomatic historians and international lawyers echo this view, and all conclude that any American president will have to reserve some of the rhetoric and hectoring for the participants in nongovernmental relations, much as the United States Information Agency (USIA) learned somewhat painfully that it had to leave cultural relations to the broad international scholarly and cultural community.

There is a deeper philosophical problem, however. No one has discussed this more profoundly than has Soedjatmoko. The acceptance of a pluralist and democratic international order, urged by the diplomatic school of thought, is more than the intellectual acceptance of otherness; it requires trust in those who are members of different cultures and political systems. The root question is whether we are capable of trusting the essential humanness of other people even when their leaders appear to be gangsters. Once we are capable of doing this, we will find those who share our ideals. Within all systems there are bound to be people who embrace common values, but there exists in some Western countries an almost desperate compulsion to force other political systems to accept a common code. A more realistic and promising approach would be to help people within different systems who yearn for another way of life. Westerners ask: Who are such peoples? One answer is to point to the dissidents; but they may be no more than the tip of the iceberg. American leaders experiencing political pressures from the right and the left may all too readily point to them in order to prove the results of their policies. (One PRM–State Department in-house study spoke rather euphorically of an eighteen-month time frame for human rights; another cautioned that "it is realistic to believe that within four years our efforts will render many if not most governments" conscious of the need to take human rights into account.) Given American domestic politics, pressures exist to make the search for dissidents the beginning and the end. Seen from outside the United States, America's style and attitudes toward human rights too often appear confined to the problems of dissidents. When the United States speaks through private or public instrumentalities, it should ask whether its statements about human rights are designed to make Americans feel good or to be helpful to peoples and forces in other nations who support human rights. Some critics abroad see the present human rights campaign as a jag of moral self-indulgence. They ask about moral consistency. Americans glamorize the dissidents, but when they emigrate to the United States, they cannot find work. Immigration laws, supported by some of the very people who preach human rights, weaken the force of America's moral example. Dissidents are not only intellectuals but working people, technicians, and artists. Is it not fair to ask what the United States is doing to help them or how far it has gone to join with others in confronting the mounting international refugee problem?

International lawyers and Third World leaders alike recognize the need for new instrumentalities for advancing human rights. Recent administrations from Kennedy's to Carter's have not pursued a particularly consistent course. Critics within their ranks have variously characterized the United Nations as "a theater of the absurd" (Daniel Patrick Moynihan) or "a shambles on human rights" (Patt Derian). Nevertheless, it seems clear that the United States cannot act alone on human rights. It must take the lead internationally and confront with others a whole panoply of problems on the issue, compounded by the incapability of some of the weaker states to do anything about them. There is a profound inner contradiction between shouting about international treaties and international law and shying away from the United Nations —like praising national legislation but refusing to accept congressional action because of its seamy side. The pulpit from which America speaks to the world would be a stronger one if its actions matched its words; for example, in the ratification of at least one of the nineteen Covenants on Human Rights, perhaps the one on genocide. The case for ratifying the Covenants rests not primarily with their legality but their consciousness-raising potential. Everything points to the importance of raising the human rights effort to the level of international cooperation. Once the United States has ratified at least some of the Covenants, its leadership position within and outside the United Nations will be stronger. America should also look for new ways of reducing nationalistic reactions against intervention and new international rules for pushing back the barriers of domestic jurisdiction without counterproductive effects. The special problem of traditional international law is that it carries a "made in the West" label. The new nations see legal arrangements as instruments designed to preserve the status quo in a colonial era. The taint of Western dominance can be removed, if at all, only through new legal instruments and treaties arrived at by the participants in more representative international bodies.

Greater cultural sensitivity and empathy are also needed for the peculiar social and political problems of the nations of Africa and Asia. Indeed the proposal has been made by a Third World spokesman that a National Endowment for Human Rights be created with the primary objective of helping Americans understand the reasons for inhumanity in certain cultures. Why do certain systems moving through stages of political and economic development transform themselves while others do not? An agency created by government or by a group of foundations might finance studies of the social, moral, and economic preconditions that allow certain societies to deal with their problems in a more humane fashion. Significantly, some officials in the Carter administration began their pronouncements on human rights in January and February, 1977, immediately upon taking office. This would scarcely suggest that such officials possessed a very keen awareness of the complexities of the issue.

Diplomatists and diplomatic historians fashion guidelines for human rights on the assumption that mankind will continue to live in a culturally pluralistic world. The diplomatic perspective, more than the legal one, leads inescapably to an attitude of caution and reserve affecting human rights. George F. Kennan speaks for the diplomatists when he writes:

> To my mind liberty is definable only in terms of the restraints which it implies and accepts. And human rights, too, operate only within a system of discipline and restraint. But if you talk about discipline and restraint you are talking about something that enters into the responsibility of government. Do we, then, in undertaking to decide what "rights" should exist in other countries, propose to tell the peoples and governments of those countries what restraints should also exist? And can one, then, try to tell another country what rights ought to be observed in its society without telling it what sort of government it ought to have?[14]

The diplomatists insist that some of the demands for human rights reform, naively or not, have amounted to calls for a change of government, for example, in the Soviet Union. The vast Soviet empire has held together a collection of disparate Soviet Socialist Republics by limiting the rights of ethnic minorities. Once the rights of a few minorities are recognized and their freedom of movement established, the whole structure of the Soviet empire could crumble. The issue of human rights in the Soviet Union, therefore, is not peripheral but strikes at its very *raison d'être*.

Respect for domestic jurisdiction causes diplomatists to question a crusading approach to human rights. Routine interference in the essential conduct of the affairs of one government (that is, in its definition of its rights and duties) by another is a recipe for disaster in political relationships. Furthermore, history offers little support for the assumption that moral intervention changes institutions and practices elsewhere; sometimes such intervention can even make the situation worse. Given the realities of national sovereignty, methods such as quiet diplomacy, the private offering of incentives and rewards, and sustained individual contacts are more likely to yield results. Workability is a companion principle to respect for domestic jurisdiction. Together they provide the diplomatists' main guidelines for action in human rights as in other spheres of foreign policy.

Despite caution and reserve, diplomatic analysts and students of international politics are not willing to see the people and government of the United States do nothing about human rights. They would, without any question, have private groups and intellectual and moral leaders speak out; they would have Americans concentrate and work harder on being a moral and political example to the world (but not a preacher from a somewhat tarnished pulpit); they would urge any administration to articulate its traditions and beliefs in broad and fundamental terms (one diplomatist commented wryly that he would favor a Gettysburg Address by the president as often as it promised to produce positive effects); they would select as targets of criticism especially blatant and egregious violations of human rights; they would strive for more effective ways of orchestrating views on human rights with other essential American goals that at a given moment were even more vital to human survival (for example, an arms agreement with the Soviet Union); they would strongly urge that any human rights approach be viewed as a sustained and long-term effort toward building moral consensus, respect, and trust. For enduring advancement in these areas, moral steadiness and political wisdom are more important than a crash program inspired by moral revulsion to the Kissinger conception of foreign policy or than the imperatives of short-run advantage as they present themselves in American domestic politics.

The question that can be raised (and international lawyers often raise it) is whether the acceptance of international politics in its traditional forms leads to moral cynicism. Are there not risks of sanctifying what exists and ignoring what might be? Acknowledging such risks, political realists warn of an opposite danger, as recounted by President Lincoln.[15] During the Civil War, Lincoln was visited by a group of Presbyterian ministers with a petition calling for the emancipation of all the slaves. Lincoln replied to his religious petitioners that in every great contest each party claims to act on the will of God. Though God cannot be for *and* against the same cause, each believes it is following the divine will. Lincoln went on to say that if God had revealed *His* will to others, one would suppose He would have revealed it to *him* because of his duties and responsibilities. He was anxious to learn the will of God and to follow it, but this was not the day of miracles. He explained that he could not do otherwise in making moral and political choices than "to study the plain physical facts, ascertain what is possible and learn what is wise and right." Lincoln's position, as historians see it, was one joining cosmic humility and political realism. The best guide for the attainment of human rights may still be Lincoln's threefold approach: studying the facts, determining possibilities, and seeking (not proclaiming) what is right and just. The moral code is subject to historical and cultural forces; understanding them is fraught with the gravest consequences, for the stakes of moral and political judgment have never been greater than in a nuclear age.

Human Rights and Morality: A Framework for Thought and Action

For many Americans the issues of human rights have become synonymous with morality; some assume that morality enters foreign policy only when human rights are added to the equation. Ignored are the various moral purposes that must guide policy makers. It would be difficult to chart advances in moral purpose if a nuclear war left only a pitiful handful of survivors who would scarcely have human rights in any country. Moreover, preachments on human rights ignore a more difficult matter—that of establishing and maintaining governments which protect both freedom and security. Lincoln grasped the need to balance the two when he asked: "Must a government, of necessity, be too strong for the liberties of its own people, or too weak to maintain its own existence?" Having fought and won long and fateful battles to preserve the union and to extend liberties to all the people, Americans preach to the world from a favored and privileged pulpit.

Looking at foreign peoples, it is easy to forget the essential disjunction between power and morality, a disjunction never wholly resolved in any country and leading to the religious concept of the tragic dimension of life. The success in the United States of a largely pragmatic politics and the beneficence of vast natural resources prompt Americans to forget the tragic element in life and the inescapable limitations of even a great power. Lincoln understood that the essential irreconcilability of power and morality forces any leader to bow in humility and to throw himself on the mercy of Providence. The limits of a nation's power affect its capacity for moral influence. Power and morality in politics ought never to be isolated from one another, yet what is essential in theory is almost impossibly difficult in practice.

Consider a field far removed from human rights—the conduct of war. In warfare, every military action is designed to serve a tactical purpose, and tactics are related to strategy as strategy is related to the objective of the war. The nation-state comprising the highest embodiment of the values and interests of the community determines the policies on which objectives are based. War not directed by policy would be a senseless thing without an object; the military system must be subordinate to the political. Unfortunately, the former has its own requirements; it has to work according to its needs. Military affairs has its own grammar, as Karl von Clausewitz put it, even when military strategy rests on political logic. Military bases are needed and may be situated in countries with repressive regimes; raw materials necessary for the conduct of war may also be located there. Public opinion in Britain favored mandatory sanctions against Italy in 1935 even at the risk of war. Collective security might have proven itself, and the ideals of joining together to halt an aggressor represented a clear ethical imperative. But ethics, in Clausewitz's words, can never be "a despotic lawgiver."[16] The experts in military grammar, the British Chiefs of Staff, pointed to the growing power of Nazi Germany and the increasingly overt aggression of Japan as the real threat. To risk even a successful war against Italy and expend military resources which might be needed against Germany ran counter to military necessity. Americans need scarcely be reminded that military strategy and necessity, as the military saw it, required that America defeat Germany in World War II as expeditiously as possible. That concept of military necessity, however sound, helped create a new threat to the security of Europe.

Michael Howard, the renowned British military historian, has argued that to say that strategic considerations should be subordinated to state policy does not say very much: "The world of power remains stubbornly autonomous; the suzerainty of ethics may be of quite Merovingian ineffectiveness." To make of either power or morality a wholly autonomous reality is to condemn it to the crudest forms of coercion or irrelevance or both. Instead, Howard has proposed another framework for considering ethics and power—as dimensions of politics. He writes:

> Political activity takes place in a two-dimensional field—a field which can be defined by the two co-ordinates of ethics and power. The ethical co-ordinate (which we may appropriately conceive as vertical) indicates the purposes which should govern political

action: the achievement of a harmonious society of mankind in which conflicts can be peacefully resolved and a community of cultures peacefully co-existing within which every individual can find fulfillment. The horizontal coordinate measures the capacity of each actor to impose his will on his environment, whether by economic, military or psychological pressure.

Successful political action must recognize both dimensions. To concern oneself with ethical values to the total exclusion of any practical activity in the dimension of power is to abdicate responsibility for shaping the course of affairs. However, to accumulate coercive power without concern for its ethical ends is "the course of the gangster, of St. Augustine's robber bands." Each one-dimensional course by itself is self-defeating, and the coordinates if indefinitely prolonged become circular. Therefore, "obsession with ethical values with no concern for their implementation is ultimately unethical. . . . Thus political action . . . needs to be diagonal. . . . The more ambitious and wide-ranging the ethical goals, the greater the power mechanisms required to achieve them."[17] Power and morality must be harnessed, and purposes must be balanced by capacity.

Michael Howard's framework for relating morality and power has its application to human rights, not in offering policies for concrete and individual sectors of rights but in suggesting directions and a course to follow. The statesman, in pursuing his diagonal course guided by the two coordinates, must be like a pilot reading a compass bearing from which he cannot diverge too far in either direction. Too fanatical a concern with moral absolutes may destroy capacity for effective action; too little concern for ethical values may produce short-term military or political advantages but destroy a nation's moral standing and prestige. Again, Reinhold Niebuhr's phrase best articulates the principle underlying this approach: "Politics will, to the end of history, be an area where conscience and power meet, where the ethical and coercive factors of human life will interpenetrate and work out their tentative and uneasy compromises."[18] We can only hope that President Carter will find this phrase a helpful guide as he continues to proclaim and act on human rights.

Foreign Assistance and the Moral Imperative

If there exists any sector of foreign policy based on the moral imperative, it would appear to be foreign assistance. The elements of such an imperative can be traced back to earlier moral and religious thought. For a great power such as the United States, the ancient injunction "from him to whom much is given, from him shall much be expected" has meaning and relevance. Edmund Burke's words were prophetic of twentieth-century America's role when he wrote that his nation was set on a conspicuous stage and that the whole world marked its conduct. When all is said and done and every rational argument adduced, the core justification of foreign aid is the moral imperative that the rich ought to help the poor.

Universalism is another part of the moral imperative. St. Augustine wrote that the brotherhood of man goes back to a common ancestry all of us share in God's creation of the first man. However much modern civilization has diverged from this original world view, the force James Reston has called "residual religious faith" has continued to exert its influence well into the twentieth century. Frederick T. Gates, the Baptist minister who became John D. Rockefeller's principal adviser, asked in 1911: "Is there not something within us, an instinct, which is the harbinger perhaps of better things, an instinct of humanity, which cannot be fenced in by the boundaries of merely national patriotism, a sympathy which transcends national boundaries and finds complete expression only when it identifies us with all humanity?" This vision found its way into the charter of the Rockefeller Foundation, which proclaimed the new organization's purpose as one of serving "the well-being" not of Americans or southerners or minorities alone but of "mankind throughout the world." The foundation's mandate was inseparably linked with a religious heritage. The trustees' formal resolution to extend around the globe the hookworm research and public health program of the old Rockefeller Sanitary Commission—work that had been originally limited to the South—called to mind for one trustee "a response to the same entreaty which had greeted St. Paul: 'Come over into Macedonia and help us.'" [19]

For others more humanist and rationalist than religious in their belief that knowledge was the patrimony not of nations but of all humanity, the war against disease and suffering required a common front drawing on the resources of all countries. The peoples of the world had to face the enemies of mankind, not as isolated groups behind national boundaries but as members of the human race in frightening propinquity to disaster. Raymond Fosdick, the brother of the famous American preacher Harry Emerson Fosdick, was preeminently a humanist. A lawyer and close adviser to Woodrow Wilson, he almost certainly would have played a central role in the League of Nations, perhaps as its first secretary general, if the Senate had not opposed American membership. In his president's review of the Rockefeller Foundation in 1941, Fosdick chose as his organizing theme the importance of the common fund of knowledge and the scientists who never thought of flags or boundaries or served a lesser loyalty than the welfare of mankind. Men everywhere from birth to death, in war or in peace, were the beneficiaries of such knowledge, and no nation had a monopoly on discovery or excellence. Fosdick found that internationalism had a wholly practical basis. In war:

> An American soldier wounded on a battlefield in the Far East owes his life to the Japanese scientist, Kitasato, who isolated the bacillus of tetanus. A Russian soldier saved by a blood transfusion is indebted to Landsteiner, an Austrian. A German soldier is shielded from typhoid fever with the help of a Russian, Metchnikoff. A Dutch marine in the East Indies is protected from malaria because of the experiments of an Italian, Grassi; while a British aviator in North Africa escapes death from surgical infection because a Frenchman, Pasteur, and a German, Koch, elaborated a new technique.

And in peace:

> Our children are guarded from diptheria by what a Japanese and a German did; they are protected from smallpox by an Englishman's work; they are saved from rabies because of a Frenchman; they are cured of pellagra through the researches of an Austrian.[20]

The doctrine of universality for organizations serving mankind, such as the Rockefeller Foundation, drew on twin sources of inspiration—theology and reason, or the New Testament and the Greco-Roman tradition. Like the roots of American democracy, these have reinforced and counterbalanced one another. Despite their tension, they have also corrected certain tendencies inherent in each. Religion, as it enters the sphere of public policy, runs the risk of sanctifying and making absolute more proximate and immediate social and political solutions. Greco-Roman thought, with its greater clarity on the polity and things political, is likely to underestimate nonrational qualities, such as compassion and concern for the weak and downtrodden. As long as religion and political reason work together, they provide a reasonable basis for helping others; to the extent that they are pulled apart and weakened, the underlying basis for "going over into Macedonia" or mobilizing known skills and human resources in the service of mankind loses part of its strength.

This idealized picture of the grounds for foreign assistance appears somewhat removed from most present-day debates on foreign aid. Modern civilization, embarrassed by the pretentiousness of moralistic rhetoric, has thrown off not only the excesses of moralism but many of the abiding truths of morality. This in part accounts for morality's rather precipitous decline in some places. The inescapable fact of life in every human community, whether the family or the world, is that we need one another. Not fully understanding yet fearing one another, we hurt one another. Interdependency and dependency are more closely linked than either moralists or rationalists recognize. There is a profound moral center to every serious endeavor at international cooperation in that men seek to become what by their nature they are capable of becoming but are denied by all those forces that pull them apart.

In any discussion of morality and foreign policy, it is vital to consider the setting in which the problem must be approached. Too little has been written by the defenders of foreign aid about the context of this issue. In the annual round of debates accompanying the work of congressional committees reviewing aid legislation, the tacit assumption of defenders is that all foreign aid is beneficial, while the opponents contend that it often harms American interests, wins no friends, and leads to dangerous involvements and war. In thinking about aid, America must make an unusually stubborn effort to think clearly about the soundness of its objectives and measure its achievements against such objectives. The validity of concepts underlying actions must be tested. Successes and failures must be analyzed and the contributory reasons traced.

The need for such a review is magnified by the more responsible criticisms of foreign assistance. Americans, we are told, have a deeply ingrained tendency for reducing stubborn political and military problems to economic ones, which are more readily managed and controlled. This American preference for economic solutions to political and military problems is powerfully reinforced by the wishes of the recipients of economic support, who prefer the profitable transfer of economic assistance to the more uncertain process of diplomatic and political bargaining. It is appealing to the electorate to be told, as they were by candidate Carter in the 1976 campaign, that "it is likely in the near future that issues of war and peace will be more a function of economic and social problems than of the military security problems which have dominated international relations in the world since World War II."[21]

Writing on foreign assistance, Hans J. Morgenthau in his criticism asserts:

> This outlook assumes that the highly developed and rich nations of the world are responsible both in terms of cause and effect and in moral terms for the plight of the Third World. The developed, rich nations . . . owe their development and wealth primarily to the colonial exploitation of the nations of the Third World, hence, they are morally obligated to compensate the nations of the Third World. . . . That moral obligation . . . is reinforced by the general moral principle of equality which frowns upon the extreme inequality among nations and imposes upon the advantaged ones the moral obligation to share their advantages with the disadvantaged ones.[22]

In refuting this viewpoint, Morgenthau first calls attention to the great variety of Third World nations. Saudi Arabia is rich, and Chad and Niger are almost hopelessly poor; some nations are committed to policies of nonalignment, whereas others, such as Cuba, receive several million dollars a day from the Soviet Union. It is inconceivable that a single American policy can do justice to their different circumstances and needs. It would be closer to the truth to say that there must be nearly as many policies as there are such nations and that policies must be based on the interests and power of the United States.

In elaborating this viewpoint, Morgenthau enumerates five different categories of Third World countries, each posing its particular issues with different implications for American foreign policy: (1) nations that presently, or at some predictable future time, possess a nuclear capability (America must consider assistance to such nations in terms of their threat to the regional or world balance of power); (2) oil-rich nations that have the negative power of denying an essential raw material not only to the industrial nations but to other disadvantaged states; (3) countries that by moving into the Communist orbit build up a psychological momentum on behalf of communism which can presage further inevitable Communist advances, thus affecting the worldwide balance of power; (4) countries that reflect the polycentric character of world communism and whose policies are determined by considerations of national interest rather than dogmatic consistency in support of the Soviet Union or other rivals of the United States (Morgenthau writes: "Anticommunist military dictatorships support Soviet foreign policies, and governments who proclaim their 'socialism' . . . are at least not necessarily hostile to the interests of the United States"[23]); (5) nations whose foreign policies are of little interest for the foreign policy of the United States however much they may touch humanitarian or theoretical concerns of some Americans (such as the theory of economic development). Because of the disparity of interests and power among the five categories of Third World nations, it is unrealistic to speak of them simply as representing a North-South problem. In any event, this lacks the stark character of an East-West confrontation in which the prospect of mutual annihilation is present.

The main burden of Morgenthau's criticism is directed toward the social reformist view that the nations which enjoy an abundant standard of living have a moral responsibility and are at least partly to blame for the suffering and misery of the less fortunate Third World countries. Morgenthau notes that the West has been made conscious of such differences because of the revolutions in transportation and communications; the inferior status of the poorer nations did not come about overnight. Awareness of their plight coincided with the rising ascendancy of the moral principle of equality and equity. Americans are morally embarrassed by their riches and guilt-ridden by the gap between rich and poor. In pursuing its own interests the West does so with a bad conscience. The Western democracies in particular find themselves in a position analogous to that of 1938 when the German claim to a part of Czechoslovakia was advanced in the name of the moral principle of national self-determination. The ill-fated resolution of that conflict in the Munich Settlement was explained by the London *Times*: "Self-determination, the professed principle of the Treaty of Versailles, has been invoked by Herr Hitler against its written text, and his appeal has been allowed."[24]

Morgenthau distinguishes the moral argument in favor of the equalization of the standard of living throughout the world from humanitarian or disaster aid to nations in distress: "Humanitarian aid is justified by a sudden national catastrophe, the consequence of which the affected country finds it hard to remedy from its own resources. Worldwide differences in the standard of living are the result of a complex conjunction of natural, cultural, economic, and political factors, which outside intervention may be able to modify in specific instances but cannot expect to eliminate on a worldwide scale."[25] He finds in the impossibility of achieving this objective—even with the best of intentions and the most extensive commitment of resources—a negation of moral obligation. He quotes a principle of Roman law to support his argument: *ultra vires nemo obligatur* (beyond his ability nobody is obligated). In other words, the rich nations cannot be expected to bring about the transformation of the poorer countries if it lies beyond their capacity and power to do so.

The remedy of inequalities in food scarcity, for example, depends less on agricultural technology and collective generosity than on political interest and will. The perpetuation of poverty and of food scarcity is more a question of political and economic choices within the deprived countries (influenced by official and private corruption, bureaucratic mismanagement, and inefficient distribution) and of deficiencies of soil and climate than of the selfishness of the rich: "If one wants to rid the world of hunger, one has to rid these societies of the arrangements that have caused it. More likely than not, that means radical reform, if not revolution."[26] The United States has been caught on the horns of a dilemma: it has followed a policy of establishing stability in a world largely in a prerevolutionary or revolutionary condition. It has followed an antireformist and antirevolutionary strategy in dealing with these nations and in formulating policies that are essential to eliminate economic inequality. It has supported equity in words and stability in deeds but, according to Morgenthau, has failed in both. Extensive foreign aid programs will continue to fail unless America resolves this dilemma through far more drastic actions than have heretofore been taken.

Cultural and Educational Assistance

The critics of foreign assistance, however negative their conclusions, appear to be calling for greater specificity in discussions of mankind's well-being. Three widely separated efforts to study education and culture illuminate the relationship of education to the context of a society. The moral principle underlying these efforts is mutual understanding, respect and empathy for the most urgent needs of a particular people. The first is a broad-based inquiry into America's cultural relations with Africa, India, Japan, the Middle East, and Southeast Asia, initiated in the early 1970s by the Hazen Foundation and culminating in a publication in late 1972 with the rather immodest title *Reconstituting the Human Community*. The second inquiry with more immediate political ends was the report in 1975 of the Stanton Committee (Frank Stanton was formerly president of CBS) on the reorganization of the government for cultural, educational, and informational programs. A third and spiritually associated effort was a study of higher education for development sponsored by twelve large donor agencies (United States Agency for International Development, Britain's Overseas Development Administration, French Ministry of Foreign Affairs, two Canadian assistance agencies, UNICEF, UNESCO, United Nations Development Program, the Ford and Rockefeller foundations, the World Bank, and the Inter-American Development Bank). All three inquiries saw culture as a unifying theme; all three put social change and innovation in the forefront of social objectives and traced their interconnections with culture.[27]

Higher Education and Social Change

There may be merit in beginning with the third of the three inquiries since it is the most far-reaching and the most ambitious undertaking. The mandate of the study may be reduced to four words: "Take time to listen." The twelve large donor agencies sought not to tell others what to do about higher education but to learn from developing-country experience. The operating principle was cooperation. The consortia established by the donors for agriculture and health served as precedents. The Rockefeller Conference Center in Bellagio, Italy, had been the home of a series of working conferences on development assistance programs. Following these earlier discussions, a core group of fifteen agencies was formed for further deliberations. Representatives met on three occasions to exchange and share information. In contrast to the founding meetings of the agricultural and population groups, representatives from the less developed countries were present from the outset.

As chairman of the higher education consortium, I can testify that we underestimated the complexity of our mission. Education is as many-sided as the culture it represents. Its aims and goals are multiple, not singular. The agricultural consortium, by comparision, which evolved into the agricultural consultative group, had one primary mission: increasing agricultural production. The means it pursued were defined in a singularly straightforward way—by support and expansion of the network of international agricultural institutes created by the Rockefeller and Ford foundations in the Philippines (rice), Mexico (corn and wheat), Colombia and Nigeria (tropical agriculture), India (arid land agriculture), and Kenya (animal health). The mission of this cooperative venture was to assure the continuation of the international institutes and their worldwide attack on hunger. The mission of the educational consortium was diffuse, complex, and in many of its aspects debatable

—to train educational and government leaders, produce faculties, improve the overall educational system, solve problems, and further cultural relations. Education, most educators were agreed, had to pursue a threefold task of training, research, and service. But what were the priorities? Were the needs and manifestations of this threefold task everywhere the same? Were educational instrumentalities recognizable and definable in every culture, or were there sharp differences in form and character? How were educational goals identified and pursued, and what was the moral and intellectual framework of educational thinking? In short, increasing food production was a relatively simple, unambiguous, and measurable goal; vitalizing and improving education was not.

In mid-1974 the educational consortium decided to initiate a twenty-five-year review of the results of assistance to higher education in Africa, Asia, and Latin America. Since the decision coincided with mine to leave the Rockefeller Foundation, I was asked to direct the study. I accepted but set one condition. To fulfill the mandate of listening, I felt it was vital that field studies be conducted by national educators from within the three regions. To those of us who had been involved in higher education in the developing countries, these educators were well known and respected. Although they were not necessarily skilled educational researchers, they had the "knack of sizing up"—a quality often found in individuals of broad practical experience. They also had access to the centers of policy and decision making and were privy to the inner workings of their own educational systems. Not one was an authority on the newest and most fashionable research techniques, but the weight and relevance of some of their findings suggest that cost-benefit analysis is not the only route to truth. P. C. C. Evans signaled the novelty of this approach: "The resulting study represents not only a major contribution to the literature on higher education in the Third World, but also *a radical departure from customary practice, in that local educational experts in the countries concerned were asked to undertake the study rather than the expatriate personnel* [italics added]." [28]

What were the reasons for this "radical departure," and why were the strengths of the Third World educators of such importance in the mid-1970s? Primarily, it had become clear that the environment of international educational cooperation had changed in the late 1950s, when higher education programs like the University Development Program of the Rockefeller Foundation had been launched. At that time Americans abroad could still be visible and recognized leaders, such as James S. Coleman, the political scientist, and Philip W. Bell, Paul Clark, and

Michael Todaro, the economists, in East Africa. It was possible for Americans to speak of a shared common experience and to claim that their own development was not too dissimilar from the new nations. Americans reminded themselves and friends in the new nations that at the turn of the century life expectancy in the United States was forty-seven; that one out of every four or five children died at birth; that of the population of 76,000,000, 65 percent lived in rural areas; that they had no income tax, no social security, and no laws governing poisonous drugs or spoiled meat. However pure America's motives and good its intentions in reaching out to others by reciting its own quite recent underdeveloped state, we know, looking back, that Americans were morally pretentious to claim that the factors which had transformed the American scene would work magic in other cultures.

This was true particularly of higher education. As W. Arthur Lewis has argued, universities may be either transmitters of culture, as in the developed world, or destroyers of culture. The British saw their public schools and universities in the nineteenth century as institutionalizing the heritage of Periclean Athens. An educated man had to know something about every aspect of human knowledge and participate actively in public discussion. American educators, at least in part, have adopted this legacy and expressed it with equal force. By contrast, as Lewis observes:

> The situation in less-developed countries is complicated. . . . The university, far from transmitting the culture, is rather part of the forces that are eroding traditional society. Much that the traditionalists weep over, and think so special to their geography, is really no more than the universal culture of poverty, which could not possibly survive development. But the university is one of the destructive agents so, despite the small ratio of the cohort which it gets, it has inescapably to define its creative cultural role.

The problem goes even deeper. Long-established traditional social systems are breaking down in the less developed countries. Extended kinship is losing out to the nuclear family. Religion has less hold; tribal and ancient loyalties are disappearing. Because of such changes, young people seek a new code of social ethics to define rights and obligations and patterns of behavior. In Lewis' words:

> The students who pass through our hands are particularly bereft of signals because they are joining a new class, which has not previously existed in less-developed countries, and for which no traditional code exists within their own cultures. They are

creating a new middle class of professionals, managers, scientists, artists, and so on. When this class emerged in Western Europe, slowly from the fifteenth century onwards, it inherited the code of the medieval guilds. . . . Latin America and Africa also have their handicraftsmen but, except in Sudanese West Africa, these are a small part of the labor force. The new middle class has therefore to grow into an ethical code which is not part of its tradition.[29]

The building of values, then, is one of the tasks of universities in less developed countries. To Lewis' mind, they "have done this part of their job poorly," failing to recognize its urgency and not setting up programs to deal with it. He explains: "Our graduates, however much admired for their technical proficiency, tend to be scorned in their own countries for their lack of social conscience, their desire to get rich quick, and their lack of responsibility." The prevailing approach in some developing countries is to require some form of national service either before university entrance—an emphasis on manual or farm work in China and Tanzania—or after graduation in the practice of one's profession. This approach contrasts with the teaching of the humanities and the social sciences in the Western world. Uncertain that national service can give the graduate a stronger social conscience, Lewis asks: "Is it really possible to teach to 20-year-olds in college basic ethics which they should have learned in secondary school at 15 or at home at 12?"[30] Lewis asks whether the university as the trainer of skills, advancer of the frontiers of knowledge, or service agency represents common guidelines for education around the world or whether education is not the same everywhere. In turn we may ask: Are there suggestions and recommendations that derive from the study of higher education, or must we resign ourselves to the uniqueness of the educational enterprise wherever we find it? In one sense, this was the underlying question of the twelve-donor agency study, although it was not the primary question that prompted the study.

The primary operating assumptions of the study were threefold. First, mutual interdependency has replaced or is replacing one-way dependency and one-way flow in cultural relations. Within the Third World, local and regional leadership has unmistakably come to the fore. Time has run out for expatriate leaders who might wish to call the tune. Outsiders must be on tap, not on top. This need not mean that educational partnerships are out. There remains the need for international service by Americans, educational linkages and programs foreseen by Title XII of the Foreign Assistance Act. Since World War II, however, new world forces influence education. These include the quest in the developing nations for national identity, human dignity, and a place in the world.

Second, what Americans and the British call institution building is still relevant to educational development in the developing world. This approach in the 1950s and 1960s was a step forward from the assistance of solitary individuals who, whether or not they returned from study abroad, were lost to their own societies. It is tempting to suppose that what we learn one day must be forgotten the next. It would be wiser to say with the philosopher that we have to live by what truth we can get today and be ready tomorrow to call it falsehood. We need to combine insights from the past and the present and remember again the words of William James: "It is not thinking with its primitive ingenuity of childhood that is most difficult but to think with tradition, with all its acquired force." There are certain rock-bottom principles essential to institution building. For those who would give assistance, these include continuity of help, concentration on a few centers of growth, and provision for a cadre of visiting career professors. For those who seek assistance, it means a plan for faculty development, positions to which trained manpower can return, and the wise use of a critical mass of teachers and researchers. It means local as well as overseas fellowships and such programs as the special lectureship plan instituted by the University of East Africa for stockpiling talent until establishment posts become available.

Third, educational institutions should not be seen as ends in themselves. Especially in the Third World, they must serve urgent community needs. In any country, a network of institutions will likely grow up. In the United States, this includes institutions to serve local and community needs (community colleges), others to meet regional needs (land-grant universities), and a few national universities (such as Harvard or the University of Chicago, which Howard Mumford Jones describes as "in but not of the city"). Universities may also be comprehensive or specialized, general or professional, arts-and-sciences oriented or technical. Not every higher educational institution is designed to do the same thing. The great criticism often leveled against developing-country universities has been that they were ivory towers reproducing privileged elites divorced from the most urgent needs of their peoples. Cast in the mold of Oxbridge, they offered courses more germane to the parent country than to their own; for example, an architecture course at the University of Ibadan in Nigeria emphasizing systems of central heating.

The process of the higher education study may be more important than its assumptions or its findings. The first step was to name three regional chairmen: the former rector of the Universidad del Valle of Cali, Colombia; Thailand's leading intellectual, who was to become rector of Thammasat University; and the former president of the National University of Ethiopia. Each selected the members of his own regional team and determined the institutions to be studied. Three staff members in New York prepared a fifty-page study plan and a series of study guides and working papers. As director, I participated in the founding and concluding meetings of each regional group and visited some of the case-study institutions. The regional directors brought their teams together to review all the case studies with the project director in attendance; each director wrote his own regional report. Two staff members in New York drafted a final report based on the case studies and regional reports; the three regional directors participated in the review and publication of the final report.

Midway through the project, the regional directors and I presented an interim report to representatives of the twelve agencies. The process reached its nadir at this point; for the Third World educators and me, this was the least satisfactory stage in an otherwise exhilarating experience. In less than a year, agency priorities had shifted; primary and secondary education and basic education so-called (which the agencies have yet to define) had supplanted higher education as a prime interest. Agency receptivity to higher education had visibly cooled, and the enthusiasm of regional educators received a dose of icy cold water at a review conference in February, 1975, in Geneva.

The study may still prove useful even if higher education has lost its glamour for some of the donor agencies. For one thing, the Third World educators, however serious their attrition, are beginning to find their way into high positions in government and international organizations. The study's importance, moreover, is not confined to education alone. As the London *Times* review suggests: "This is certainly a most valuable publication which is a must for all those interested in Third World Development."[31] Despite such melancholy trends as the abandonment of support for higher education by the Rockefeller Foundation, there are signs of revived interest by others. The United States Agency for International Development is beginning to respond to the political promptings of the land-grant university movement and to legislative pressure reflected in Title XII of the Foreign Assistance Act. The World Bank announced that 21 percent of its education budget for 1977–1979 is being devoted to higher education. The Ford Foundation is placing new stress on education and cultural development. Looking back on the recent flurry of passionately self-conscious declarations that donor agencies are choosing new paths, as one foundation president put it, "to make us famous," we recall the axiom: "It is better to understand a little than to misunderstand a lot."

The lasting importance of the higher education study may in the long run rest more with the questions it asked than in the definitive answers it produced. Having pledged themselves to explore what higher education was doing for development and social change, the participants in the study soon recognized the need to break down the problem into its component parts. They asked of the institutions they studied and of national leaders they contacted: Who is doing something about the most urgent community problems? Who is doing something about health, sanitation, nutrition, infant mortality, the major health problems, food production, and population control? Or about improving the rest of the educational system and furthering cultural development? Or about leadership training, jobs, employment, and the quality of life? In pursuing such questions, there is a need for appropriate concepts, methodologies, research strategies, and tools of analysis. Questions of approach cluster together: How are a people's most urgent problems identified? What are the means of grappling with such problems? Is the best attack through the development of education (institution building) or in fashioning new and unconventional approaches to education for development? Is the sound approach the traditional one of training leaders or skilled manpower, or is it in turning educational centers into little Tennessee Valley Authorities and striking directly at the problems? Where does one look for indicators of progress, statistics, and reliable data? What about the factors behind the statistics, whether the gross factors or the broad trends and tendencies? Beyond universities, who is innovating, and what is the degree of acceptance of their efforts? Who has taken the initiative—educators or government or business leaders, nationals or outsiders? At what educational level are the community's most urgent problems being faced—literacy programs, primary or secondary education, nonformal or higher education? What is required before a society asks that its own educational system address such problems—necessity or doctrine? How influential are notions about intellectual versus manual, blue-collar versus white-collar work? How, if at all, can one or more of these factors be changed? What are a nation's underlying educational premises as they relate to elitism versus mass education, rural versus urban education, participation and service? How is education handling the problem of quality versus quantity or openness versus denial of international ideas, especially in scientific fields? What price is a society willing to pay for development, and what are the boundaries it draws? What is included and what is emphasized concerning urban or rural needs; what is neglected and ruled out? Where does a people draw the line between too much national integration and too little, too much or too little order? What is the relation of education to government in terms of educational autonomy versus total integration or subordination? What provisions are made for the whole population, women and minorities, and the flow of competence and talent to the top?

I would not claim that our study dealt with all these problems or that clearcut, unambiguous answers to such questions are ever possible. Instead, the answers all too often become part of a wider political debate grounded in strong national and political ideologies; we each bring a vast collection of political allegiances and prejudices to such debates. Differences are often hard to penetrate because participants within any political and ideological system arrange the facts to fit deep-seated assumptions. What is lacking—what may be impossible to determine— is the precise and measurable effect of the overall system on educational innovation or of innovation on the system. Tanzania and Cuba, of course, come to mind, but the problem also exists in more familiar systems. Lacking a framework for pursuing these questions, the debate over success or failure becomes endlessly tiresome and virtually irresolvable. Debates between Moslem fanatics and western-educated Iranians and Turks are a dialogue of the deaf. In the absence of a single framework, the most we can do is look for central issues and leading questions.

It is also possible to go beyond the question to at least some of the answers, conclusions, and recommendations of such studies. The twelve-donor agency study provides six broad conclusions that can be compared with other inquiries for at least tentative future guidelines. First, the study challenged the view that the world's educational systems are either effective or ineffective and cursed by elitism and privilege. Of the former, the Reverend Theodore Hesburgh wrote: "Recent studies have shown that between 50 and 60 percent of the gains made in the developed countries during the past half-century are the result of better educated people, more basic research, and a much more systematic use of the nation's brainpower and talent."[32] The assumption that education in the less developed countries is bereft of any of these strengths and resources is clearly not borne out by our study.

Second, of twenty-six case studies (seven dealing with poor rural and urban areas, three with health delivery systems, six with reforming the educational system as a whole, six with jobs and employment, and four with more general development problems), at least twenty and possibly twenty-three higher educational institutions were adjudged as making significant contributions to urgent needs. What makes these achievements noteworthy is that many of these institutions are still in their infancy compared with European or American institutions that have a 200- to 800-year history. The findings for these institutions, however representative they may be, tend to refute the charge that universities in less developed countries are nothing more than ivory towers.

Third, the study indicated that an impressive amount of innovation and educational experimentation is going on, although more is possible. In the Cameroons, medical doctors and technicians pursue much of their training together and continue as practicing health specialists when they go into the field. In Kumasi, Ghana, and Monterrey, Mexico, economic consultancy centers have been established at the universities that bring businessmen on campus and students out into the business world and generate income in the process. In Colombia and Brazil, in Cali and Salvador, new health delivery systems have been instituted for poor rural and urban areas. In the developing world, work-study programs are beginning, and universities in most countries are experimenting with extension programs and year-round educational efforts.

Fourth, higher education in the less developed countries is and presumably ought to be more than university education. It includes subprofessional training (the Ngee Ann Institute in Singapore), development training (the Development Academy of the Philippines and the Asian Institute of Management), and applied business economics (several centers in Asia). To limit higher education to universities is to define education too narrowly; the future may lie with innovations such as community colleges or their equivalent.

Fifth, these positive developments ought not to obscure the problems, obstacles, and uncertainties. Systems of governance in universities are often an impediment to progress, such as the conservatism of the *catedrático* professor in Brazil. Students are suspect as being too radical in many developing countries. Risk capital is lacking but indispensable; innovation costs money and will engender resistance if new programs require that resources be transferred from old ones. All this makes the flight of certain American foundations from some less developed countries deplorable. Some countries lack a tradition of universities contributing to development; others lack the minimum in trained manpower. Almost everywhere, nations suffer from unsolved problems of governmental-university relations. The umbrella university is an educational innovation in Africa with its own peculiar strengths and limitations. In many developing countries, there is an overall educational explosion. Demands for primary and secondary schoolteachers expand exponentially. It is utopian to suppose that such difficulties are easily resolved.

Sixth, the most important conclusion may be the words to the donor agencies: Don't lose heart. Education in some Third World countries is responsive to some urgent problems. These efforts need legitimizing on their own merits, not as the success stories of parent universities in London or Paris but for Cali or Kumasi. Once higher education enters contested areas and begins to confront urgent problems, it is bound to suffer its own backlash. To have the weight of the world's scientific community and the twelve donor agencies behind important but risky endeavors in less developed countries will reinforce and legitimize local efforts. In international cooperation, it is commonplace for partners to blame one another. Through currently available methods of food production, the earth could be made to yield three times the amount of basic food crops, yet one-half the world's people are hungry or malnourished. In the United States, it has become fashionable to say that since World War II America has spent $90 billion in foreign aid (less than three-fourths the current annual military budget) and has one million Americans living abroad. On a cost-benefit basis, what has America gained from its foreign aid investment? The current study proclaims to the large donor agencies that the gain is substantial, not measured by the donor's fame but by what appears to be going on within the countries for the people most directly involved.

America's Cultural, Educational, and Informational Programs

The Stanton report on international information, education, and cultural relations is similar in substance and identified problems with the higher education study. The Stanton panel chose a twenty-five-year time frame for its appraisal of programs in the broad cultural and informational areas. Under the chairmanship of Frank Stanton, it began its labors in April, 1974, and published its recommendations in 1975 through the Georgetown Center for Strategic and International Studies. The proposals for reorganizing the government for cultural programs may be the most important part of the report but need not concern us here. Suffice it to say, they call for a separation organizationally of long-term cultural and educational programs, general news and information programs modeled after the BBC, and policy information programs by the State Department. More important for this discussion, the Stanton Committee early in its deliberations made a moral and intellectual choice that had far-reaching consequences for its recommendations. One group on the panel, spearheaded by particular United States Information Agency (USIA) leaders, insisted that the primary goal of American cultural and informational programs should be, bluntly stated, to sell the American way of life. Another group argued that cultural and educational relations have to be grounded in mutual understanding. Even in the communication of national goals, traditions, and values, effectiveness depends on understanding the goals, traditions, and values of others. For United States programs in cultural relations, no less than the assistance programs of the twelve donor agencies, it was "time to listen."

Reconstituting the Human Community

A third inquiry, no less important, was instituted in the early 1970s by President Paul Braisted of the Hazen Foundation—its goal to look at cultural relations through the prisms of six or more regional teams. I served as chairman of the American group and chairman of the international commission made up of the respective regional chairmen. At the first meeting of the international commission, I rather naively presented the draft report of the American group, citing the more conspicuous success stories in America's cultural relations. My American colleagues and I were quite unprepared for the response. Colleagues from the Middle East, Africa, Southeast Asia, southern Asia, and Japan let us know, firmly and emphatically, that our highly touted American success stories had far more debatable and ambiguous images within their regions. Even the Green Revolution, a source of American pride as a model of technical assistance and international cooperation, had both strengths and weaknesses, contributions and limitations, when viewed by Asia or Africa.

These reactions caused us to reexamine the vaunted achievements of American cultural relations. We had assumed that international cultural relations were seen most clearly through American eyes, partly because the audience we had in mind was largely American; our aim had been the reinvigoration of the American will to serve the world. International service, we learned, meant listening to Asia and Africa and rediscovering their goals and values, fears and perspectives. The final report, *Reconstituting the Human Community*, took as its first premise the necessity of examining cultural relations through Asian and African eyes and reaching out for mutuality of interests and understanding. Few reports of a private and citizen body have caught the imagination of people around the world as this one did.

Culture and Innovation

Six questions emerge from these three inquiries. First, can anyone pinpoint the sources of change or the major change agents in higher education for development? The answers point in not one but several directions. Professional schools within a university (the medical faculty in Cali, Colombia) may be a source of change, but so may the university rector (Salvador, Brazil) or government leaders (La Molina, Peru) or business leaders (Monterrey, Mexico) or a political party and its leadership (Tanzania). Outside private agencies with flexible funds may be the catalyst (the Rockefeller Foundation in Cali or the Ford Foundation at Ahmadu Bello University in northern Nigeria), but public bodies may also be catalysts (WHO and UNICEF at the Federal University of the Cameroon or the World Bank and the government of Singapore at the Ngee Ann Institute). Impulse money for educational experimentation may come from outside the country (UNESCO in Mali and the examples cited above) but also from inside (the Development Academy of the Philippines and Monterrey). The one generalization that can confidently be made is that almost always one or more uniquely qualified leaders make the difference (Dr. Monekosso in the Cameroons, O. D. Corpuz at the Development Academy of the Philippines, Julius Nyerere and Cranford Pratt in Tanzania). But the discipline from which the leader comes, his intellectual formation, or his experience cannot be set down in advance as a guarantee of innovation. Most have had a breadth of experience (for example, university plus government or its equivalent) and some contact with other educational systems. There is a mystery, though, about leadership that cannot be computerized: "The wind bloweth where it listeth, and thou hearest the sound thereof, that canst not tell whence it cometh, and whither it goeth."

Second, the most important human quality leading to innovation is the spirit of divine discontent, often beginning with criticism of the imperialists, expatriates, and outsiders. Successful national innovators then go on to criticize their own conservatives and traditionalists. Once a critical process has begun, it can be internalized. For example, Tanzanians, having linked higher education to the nation's social revolution, go on to criticize the system's failure to provide educational opportunities for women. Moreover, second-generation innovators are waiting to further the work of the first generation.

Third, the innovative spirit tends to be contagious and to spread. The presence of a few innovators in one or two disciplines encourages the faint-hearted elsewhere in the educational system. Innovative programs in medicine at Cali spread to the social sciences and humanities and in the Institute of Land Use and Economic Planning in Tanzania to changes in education and history.

Fourth, there are also countervailing and conservative forces at work that may be rekindled by progress and advances. Universities are part of their societies, not beyond pressures of the status quo. An innovator's reign may be short-lived. The governments with which innovators cooperate may be toppled, the enemies who were overcome may regroup, and advances in less sensitive fields (health or agriculture) may be blocked in economics and political science. Innovators seldom escape the constraints of their society; leaders may have to choose between effecting major but controversial accomplishments or building a broad consensus for more limited advances. All this constitutes no easy choice. A country may have to stockpile its innovators, keeping them alive during periods of consolidation and retrenchment, calling on them when the country decides to progress again.

Fifth, innovators and operators are not interchangeable. Planners and managers have a different makeup, but there is place for both. The great periods of advance in American industrial development have occurred when leadership was able to combine the strength of the two groups. Each tends to be impatient with the aims and objectives, style and approach of the other. Innovators need a mutual protection society in most bureaucratic structures lest individual initiative be wiped out.

Sixth, no one has cornered the market in educational and scientific innovation. Raymond Fosdick pointed to the infinite threads that bind men together and the essential unity of scientific advances: "In peace as in war we are all of us the beneficiaries of contributions to knowledge made by every nation in the world."[33] This unity is seen in all fields of knowledge. Therefore, it is vital that cultural interchange continue. No nation can manage alone. The seeds of innovation may come from near or far. The common factor for almost every innovator is an ability to draw on more than one cultural and educational heritage.

The world is passing through a period of great stress on cultural pluralism, ethnic difference, and political separateness—all based on substantial fact and reality. Yet mankind is not bereft of experiences and discoveries—educational, social, and political inventions if you will—that can be shared with others. No child patterns his or her life wholly on a parent's, but neither does a sensible parent abandon life's lessons simply to achieve reconciliation or gain favor with children. (There is an Indonesian saying, "It is a terrible thing to have a reasonable father.") In normal periods, each has something to gain from the other. We need one another; yet in the present period of social turbulence, we fear one another. If we could recognize the full extent of our mutuality of interests and the dimensions of our interdependence, we might yet help one another. In the most fundamental sense, that is the penultimate conclusion of all three inquiries.

International Agricultural Assistance

Foreign assistance programs in agriculture have enjoyed rather conspicuous success and are now a central focus of most national and international assistance programs. International agricultural efforts involve the cooperative endeavors not primarily of political leaders but of scientific and technical professionals, whose concerns are less regional or local than they are worldwide. Feeding mankind and averting famine is a global need. The evidence is clear that outsiders can help to increase a nation's food production through building on skills and traditions developed elsewhere in the world. For example, knowledge of rice-growing methods and techniques and rice varieties originally developed in Louisiana, Taiwan, and Japan provided a central core of experience for further experimentation at the International Rice Research Institute in the Philippines. Improved varieties and production techniques for the growth of corn and wheat developed in the Midwest have been used experimentally at the International Corn and Wheat Center in Mexico with significant adaptation and modification to fit local needs. One country's know-how, skills, and modes of production have been adapted to another's urgent problems.

The Moral Imperative of Service

In part the success of American agriculture can be attributed to the land-grant college system, which may be the most significant nineteenth-century educational innovation in the United States. The educational philosophy behind these institutions was not without its critics, including a group of English academics who described the land-grant colleges as "places where men are taught to throw manure about and act as wet nurses to steam engines." Whereas the distinguished universities of the East had dominated the American educational scene and had provided an example of institutions capable of producing broadly educated men, the land-grant institutions placed major stress on the practical and the applied sciences and arts. They also put the accent on service to the community with closer links between study and work. From the beginning, they pioneered in programs involving extension work and outreach, whether through training of county agents or short courses and summer programs in agriculture. They took education to the people through outlying branches of the central university or special curricula that have since been organized under the heading of lifelong learning. Much of land-grant education began with an urgent problem and community need. The system was structured to be responsive to this need. Land-grant institutions became important clearinghouses for information and know-how in agriculture and applied science.

All such programs had one underlying and dominant theme—an emphasis on service. In one sense, the idea of service was an educational one; the choice of service above teaching and research was the distinguishing characteristic of land-grant institutions (not to the neglect, however, of the other two components in the threefold makeup of higher education). Service involved developing techniques and programs for assisting the farmer, private corporations, and agencies of government. But the idea of service was also a moral principle; today this principle is in part responsible for the willingness of such institutions to make available their best scholars and scientists to the developing countries. It has become almost commonplace for land-grant universities to accord extended academic leaves to their strongest faculty members for three or four years of service abroad, much as famous research universities grant long research leaves to their most outstanding scientists. Some land-grant universities have in effect two faculties in certain fields—one for teaching and research at home and the other for comparable work abroad. Provision is made in university budgets for a small cadre of professors for international service. Moreover, a number of land-grant colleges have taken the lead in initiating sister-university relations with institutions in the Third World. It would be impossible to explain their willingness to undertake such missions without reference to their commitment to service.

The main sources of the service ideal can be traced to the influence of at least four factors: individualism, communalism, parochialism, and universalism. The American farmer was a symbol of sturdy individualism and of stubborn determination in the face of ever-changing conditions of wind and weather. Early settlers demonstrated unmatched resourcefulness in conquering the wilderness and in meeting suffering and adversity; because of their courage and inventiveness, the specter of hunger and famine, which threatened other societies, was not as menacing to the new Americans. Such triumphs against great odds produced a new breed of fearless and outspoken leaders whose thinking and assumptions were rooted in local soil. Social and political movements such as populism, the Farm Labor party, and the Progressive party drew on the drive, ambition, and discontent of such men. They spoke out against early injustices and exploitation by the railroads, the utility companies, and a government that was remote and indifferent to their needs and problems. The nation's agriculturalists were blunt and plainspoken men and wary of domination by the favored few of an Eastern elite.

Individualism by itself is not an adequate description of rural motivation. When disaster struck, the community helped raise homes or barns that had been destroyed—and then celebrated in song and dance what cooperation had accomplished. Individualism and communalism coexisted in practice, however much they conflicted in theory and logic. Because men had learned to help themselves, they were better able to help others. Service had its birth in these early community beginnings, so it should come as no surprise that the children of rural forefathers were responsive in the mid-twentieth century to calls for help from abroad.

At the same time, paradoxical as it may seem, no group in American life has been, from a certain standpoint, more parochial. The American farmer has protested the acts of faraway governments, resisted cries for help by the cities, and questioned internationalism whatever its creedal or political formulations. Rural areas have cradled isolationism, welcomed opposition groups such as America First, nurtured xenophobia, and doubted the wisdom of any foreign involvements. Whatever the prime motivating factor—whether fear and resentment of the rich and the powerful or the Jeffersonian belief that it was impossible to discover human virtue outside of small cities and rural areas—agricultural America has affirmed loyalty to what was staunch, manageable, and immediate and has questioned cosmopolitanism and internationalism as leading to an effete way of life.

Yet rural peoples have also clung to an opposing dream—a belief that the good life was rooted in religion, hard work, and the family. Men who lived close to the soil were assumed to have an extra measure of integrity and moral stamina, whether they happened to be in Iowa or Nigeria. Their religious heritage had bound them together in the Christian missionary movement, and it was not too far-fetched for American agronomists or plant pathologists to perceive continuity between their missionary forefathers and themselves as they worked in a secular and scientific world. Religious precepts taught that all men were brothers. Mankind everywhere had both spiritual and material needs, which the privileged few were duty bound to help alleviate. Not surprisingly, therefore, despite its strain of parochialism, rural America rose to the challenge of feeding the world. Its universalism was linked to the simple and rudimentary aspects of life even as farm people continued to look with barely concealed distaste and suspicion on clever international diplomacy or high-flown language concerning world power and national interests.

The Internationalizing of Agriculture

The poorer nations have called on American agriculture for help because of their desperate struggles to feed their people. American efforts to help others have their origins in private and public emergency and rescue operations. When disaster struck, whether in catastrophes of nature or unremitting famine, Americans were among the first to respond. The Food for Peace Program of the government is only the most recent large-scale attempt to help the starving and the homeless. That needy people turn to America for help testifies to its recognized humanitarianism and to its successful agricultural system. Negatively, it shows a dissatisfaction with the efforts of other nations—notably those of the Soviet Union—to feed large populations.

Thus the American approach to feeding the world has been a response to appeals from Third World leaders. By the 1960s, African leaders in particular showed restiveness with existing assistance programs. Sir Eric Ashby chaired a commission which recommended that Africans consider using the organizational and educational approach of the American land-grant university. Asian and African universities, whose agricultural faculties had experienced at best limited success under British, French, and German tutelage, requested American technical assistance. Several went so far as appointing American agricultural educators with land-grant college backgrounds as deans of their agricultural faculties. In India seven agricultural universities were created, modeled after the land-grant universities. Indonesia turned to the Ford and Rockefeller foundations to strengthen its agricultural institutes and universities. Kasetsart University in Thailand drew heavily on the agricultural staff of the Rockefeller Foundation and at least three land-grant universities. The University of the Philippines reorganized its system of agricultural education with help from Cornell University and the International Rice Research Institute (IRRI). Zaire, Tanzania, Ethiopia, and Kenya have sought help and guidance from American agriculturalists. It is difficult to think of a major country in Africa or Asia that has not been touched by American agriculture.

American Agriculture's Influence in the World

It is natural to ask for reasons to explain the influence of American agriculture abroad. How can we account for its warm reception, particularly in the developing world? What have been its working principles, and how generally have they been applied? American agriculture places first priority on increased food production; such an emphasis is obviously in tune with urgent needs in most Third World countries. Fifteen thousand people die each day of starvation somewhere in the world. The passionate concern of American agronomists or plant pathologists to conquer hunger never goes unnoticed when they serve in developing countries. Their insistent demands that every agricultural university have at least one experiment station symbolizes their conviction that every agricultural student must learn to grow a crop.

Agricultural research at Third World universities ought never be research for research's sake. Universities must have links with agricultural ministries; academic agriculturalists should not be isolated from the principal actors on the agricultural scene. Some governmental research stations in agricultural ministries have been joined with agricultural research faculties, for example, in new universities such as Ahmadu Bello in northern Nigeria. Americans who have served in agricultural universities or research institutes have insisted that trainees put on overalls and go out into the field. Book learning has not been considered sufficient. Training and research have been integrated. When the Rockefeller Foundation agricultural team went to Mexico, it organized its efforts in a new Office of Special Studies within the Ministry of Agriculture; not long thereafter it created a first-class graduate school of agriculture at Chapingo. Here and elsewhere in developing countries, highly qualified professionals worked with local agriculturalists. No one doubted their professional competence, their commitment to mastering the language and learning about the culture, and their intention to stay. They made long-range commitments as members of a career service established by the Rockefeller Foundation and the land-grant universities. The concept of a career service culminated in 1975 with the establishment of an International Agricultural Development Service (IADS) composed of agricultural specialists who had served in one or more developing countries and were available for service elsewhere.

From Bilateralism to Multilateralism in Agriculture

The efforts of the land-grant universities were strengthened and reinforced by what were called country programs, established by agencies such as the Rockefeller Foundation. In 1943 that organization, after careful study and research, launched its first country program in Mexico in agricultural research and training, followed by successive programs in Colombia (1950), Chile (1953), the Philippines (1959), India (1960), and Nigeria (1962). Not only did these programs recruit skilled professionals, but they helped foreign scientists and technicians develop an identity and an esprit de corps. These agriculturalists constituted small, close-knit bodies who never for a moment doubted that they could increase agricultural production. They boasted that they could help a country move from a crop deficit to a crop surplus. In Mexico, Pakistan and India, and parts of Central America, they succeeded, at least for the basic food crops. Because of such undertakings, Mexico, for example, was able to terminate at least temporarily the importation of corn and wheat, thereby protecting scarce foreign exchange reserves.

The notable achievements of such country programs led to more strenuous regional efforts and to the creation of international agricultural institutes manned by experienced leaders from the earlier programs. The International Health Division of the Rockefeller Foundation had paved the way by showing what could be done throughout the world in medicine and public health. The aim was to build on country programs, to keep their human capital intact, and to make the resulting work available on a wider geographical basis. In the 1960s a coalition of some twenty-five or thirty private and public agencies joined to form an agricultural consultative group. The consultative group saw itself as both a policy-making and a fund-raising body, and it set out to strengthen the financial base for the international agricultural institutes. Its efforts assured that funds from $50 million in the 1970s to $200 million in the 1980s would be available to provide for the expansion of cooperative activities in agricultural research and training in the developing countries.

Such efforts and other related ones were the prelude to a far more determined resolution in the 1970s to meet the problem of world hunger. In 1972 the World Food Conference brought together representatives from both the developed and the less developed countries. The conference was a response to the desire for a North-South dialogue. It represented the same type of producers' and consumers' conference that had been held in the energy field. Such a meeting was a further sign of the equality of nations as exemplified in the composition of the United Nations, but it indicated that the existing United Nations specialized agency in agriculture—the Food and Agriculture Organization (FAO)—had left something to be desired. Culminating a bilateral attempt by a small private group in Mexico, the World Food Conference represented an expansion worldwide of the important work begun in the 1940s to feed mankind.

Overcoming World Poverty

One persistent criticism of foreign assistance programs in agriculture and education has been that they did not reach the people. Beginning in the 1960s, the United States under the leadership of President John F. Kennedy sought to reorient American foreign assistance efforts. Most dramatically, the Alliance for Progress for Latin America was a reformist foreign assistance measure designed to meet the threat of Castroism within Latin American states. A veteran observer of the Latin American scene, Herbert L. Matthews, wrote:

> In the whole of Latin America, the rich are getting richer and the poor poorer. . . . The Alliance for Progress was created primarily to tackle this essentially social problem, but social imbalances . . .

are devilishly hard to correct. . . . There are revolutions and revolutions. The fascist military type in Latin America comes from the right; the socialistic-communistic from the left; and in between is the sort of peaceful, voluntary, gradual but genuine type of revolution which the Alliance for Progress is trying to promote. Latin America is such a dynamic area of the world that it is bound to have revolutions. The only unknown factor is: what kind?[34]

At least two obstacles confronted the Alliance for Progress. First, it called on the rich and privileged to make concessions. Historically, few oligarchies have had the vision to sacrifice power in advance of revolution. Second, Latin American oligarchies have believed that in the end the United States might embrace reform in words but that its deeds would be guided by the need to protect private corporate investments and its fear of any revolution which, justly or unfairly, was labeled Communist. The leaders of such governments did not have long to wait for their estimate to be substantiated. In 1961 the Dominican dictatorship of Rafael Trujillo was overthrown. Not long thereafter, Juan Bosch, whom many considered a true democrat, was elected president. Seven months later Bosch was overthrown by a military coup d'état, dedicated to reinstating a rightist state. In April, 1965, forces led by Bosch revolted against the military dictatorship. As viewed from Washington, their movement was soon threatened by Communist control. Fearing a second Cuba in the Western Hemisphere, President Lyndon B. Johnson ordered American intervention on behalf of the military junta before it was clear that "Castro Communists," as the Johnson administration described them, had taken over the pro-Bosch movement. American intervention in the Dominican Republic confirmed the suspicions of Latin American oligarchs that where anticommunism and the Alliance for Progress conflicted, the former would take precedence.

By the late 1960s, the fear of communism had somewhat abated, producing a mood of complacency and resignation. Nonalignment became more acceptable, and observers noted the beginnings of a thaw in the Cold War. Certain situations—for example, Peru's expropriation of Standard Oil property and Salvador Allende's election in Chile—were not forcibly resisted. Foreign assistance dropped to its lowest point—less than one-half of 1 percent of the gross national product. Technical assistance replaced capital development projects, and at one stage in 1971, the Senate refused to pass any aid bill. The Alliance for Progress was abandoned, and the Nixon administration urged that more assistance be channeled through international lending agencies including the

World Bank. Disillusionment with foreign aid spread not only in the United States but in the Soviet Union as well. Foreign assistance was one policy that had no significant constituency, and rapprochement between the great powers made help to the poorer nations less likely.

The basic problems of poor countries remain, however. In the 1970s far-ranging nationalist and social revolutions engaged the populations, directly or indirectly, of two-thirds of the world's people. As the rich became richer and the poor poorer (the individual in many poor countries barely exists on an income of less than twenty-five cents a day), the future of many new and weak nations was in doubt, to say nothing of the survival of their people. The challenge to the American conscience was clear; mankind could not exist in two worlds, one rich and one poor. The problem of poverty was indivisible. In the words of the Pearson Commission (which conducted an international review of foreign assistance programs under the chairmanship of Lester Pearson, former prime minister of Canada):"If the rich countries . . . concentrate on the elimination of poverty and backwardness at home and ignore them abroad, what would happen to the principles by which they live? Could the moral and social foundations of their own societies remain firm and steady if they washed their hands of the plight of others?"[35]

The United States Congress made clear that it would not appropriate funds for foreign assistance unless aid was designed to help "the majority poor." The Agency for International Development responded in kind and went further to concentrate its resources on efforts intended to meet "basic human needs." Where recipient countries were unable to demonstrate that external assistance was being channeled to the poor, aid commitments were teminated. Programs for an elitist few (higher education) were replaced by others giving aid and training to the thousands (basic education and elementary-secondary education). Having found that earlier assistance efforts stressing higher education and capital development for the developing countries had not led to rapid modernization and immediate economic growth, Americans turned to a new design for eradicating world poverty with a characteristic single-mindedness.

Paradoxically, the first wave of criticism came from the developing countries themselves. Seen from the Third World, everytime the United States becomes outspokenly moral, its foreign assistance allocations drop. (The termination of significant assistance programs in the name of the majority poor or of human rights did not go unnoticed.) It is difficult to explain to people in developing countries thus cut off that stress on helping only the poor or those who respect human rights is not simply a means of putting a good face on the unwillingness of the American people to provide substantial foreign aid. Furthermore, however laudatory the attack on poverty everywhere, Americans need to remember that projects directed to the attack on poverty require far more national than foreign financing and basic changes in the structure of national as well as international society. The Indonesian Soedjatmoko asks: "Is it right for another country, the United States, to insist that a developing country spend a certain percent of its GNP or its national budget on poverty or social development thus foregoing economic development?" The poverty emphasis in foreign assistance has meant lowering the level of more general capital-forming foreign aid. It can make a developing country incapable of continuing other long-term projects that have no immediate bearing on poverty but that may at some future date determine its capacity for both growth and social justice. Americans, in a characteristically headlong rush to solve a pressing world problem, have not adequately recognized this key ethical and political dilemma.

Beyond this, Third World leaders warn of another paradox in American policies. They ask what has happened to countries that have addressed themselves single-mindedly to the problem of poverty. They warn of the taint of hypocrisy involving American words and deeds. China, Cuba, India, Allende's Chile, Jamaica, and Tanzania have sought to eliminate or substantially reduce poverty; but the United States has either shown little interest in their efforts or actually tried to destabilize the regimes of such countries. Certain Third World leaders argue that they are unable to devote the proportion of their resources to poverty programs required by the United States. Even if they were able through extraordinary efforts to do so, what guarantees would they have that the United States would not shift its policies tomorrow? All this may seem far-fetched to well-intentioned Americans, but other peoples who have read American history suggest that official rhetoric and proclamations have often been poor guides to future foreign policies.

Furthermore, it is a mistake to isolate poverty from the total needs of the country. The American experience with blacks should have indicated that a direct attack on the poverty of black areas is only one (and sometimes the least successful) method for assisting the disadvantaged. The American approach to equal opportunity within its boundaries has sought to widen social and educational opportunities, open up business and the professions to qualified blacks, and enable them to move to other neighborhoods. What is needed on the world scene is a broad-gauged approach comparable to equal opportunity efforts within the United States.

Fundamental to all the rest, however, is an urgent need to build new constructs of theory and practice for the achievement of development with freedom. As Soedjatmoko has observed, almost every development theory leads away from freedom; this includes, we may add, some of the policies aimed at the elimination of poverty. Japan and Germany developed on an alarming scale by limiting freedom and became totalitarian monsters; only military defeat made it possible for liberal forces to emerge. Outsiders who would help must face up to the fateful clash between freedom and growth in the developing world. The United States, while advocating freedom, has trained thousands of foreign economists, scientists, and military leaders who return to their countries with a narrow and elitist technocratic view of development. There are in the Third World countless people who yearn for development but remain respectful of freedom. When they look to most of the universities in the West, however, they find among both liberal and socialist thinkers an acceptance of the notion that development requires the subordination of freedom. Soedjatmoko asks: Who is doing anything to help with the search for alternative development models? Those who train the world's economists are not civil rights leaders or theologians. Western intellectuals do little; hard-pressed nationalist leaders are too embattled to think straight. Latin American "*dependencia* theories" help explain certain weaknesses and help vent nationalist anger. They do little to provide guidelines for development and freedom. Traditionally, Latin American nations have been shaped by literary, legal, and historical thinkers; but today's realities have become too complex for them.

One approach to the development and poverty problems of Third World nations would be for educators and foreign assistance officials to step into the void between yesterday's classical training and today's studies in the social sciences. When developing-country social scientists return from training abroad, they become either narrow governmental technocrats who are morally crippled or opposition leaders no less crippled but also politically polarized and full of nationalistic hatred or members of prestigious national research institutes doing useful but limited research not directed to broad social problems. The problem becomes more complex because much of American foreign policy in the developing countries is shaped not by the State Department or the United States Information Agency (USIA) but by military-to-military relations. The military in many Third World countries, and to some extent in the United States, is narrowly anti-Communist, largely defense-minded, and therefore unable to accept the need for social and economic change. There is no intervening civilian mechanism or perspective. As long as this condition persists, all well-meaning attempts at eliminating poverty or promoting human rights from outside the developing countries seem unlikely to succeed.

Conclusion

No one can doubt that morality and concern for the downtrodden and less privileged constitutes an important basis for the necessity of continuing foreign assistance. Political leaders in the United States who have fought for foreign aid programs, men such as the late Senator Hubert H. Humphrey, have needed a high degree of political courage, for foreign aid seldom has a substantial political constituency. It depends instead on moral and political convictions that the strong have a responsibility to help the weak, that human suffering around the world ought to be everyone's concern, and that mankind, despite national boundaries, is indivisible in its needs and aspirations.

Yet foreign assistance as policy, distinguished from noble intent, faces all the complex problems of foreign policy in general. It cannot ignore the imperatives of national interest or the unique cultural and social circumstances in particular developing countries. Foreign aid has its critics. Their fundamental questions and criticism cannot be overlooked. Maybe the most effective foreign assistance policies are those addressed to specific areas of human need (education and food production) rather than to universal problems that are affected by the form of government and political culture of the recipient countries. The theoretical basis for foreign aid is rudimentary at best. More attention must be directed to conflicting American policies, such as military assistance efforts, which tend to build or reinforce status quo regimes that oppose social change and the alleviation of poverty. For the United States, foreign assistance confronts policy makers with a clustering of painful choices. At the same time that we seek to enhance political stability in the world, we are undertaking to bring about social change. Once again, the problem is one of choosing between conflicting goals and values, a dilemma we have failed to resolve in the past three decades.

On an intermediate level, the task of foreign assistance is to seek out viable programs to improve coping with urgent community problems. Americans bring unique human skills to some but not all areas of human need; education and agriculture have evolved in the United States in ways that promise some success in helping others. The foreign assistance programs of every country should proceed from strength. Since we cannot do everything to help mankind, we do most when we undertake what we do best at home and abroad. The present stage of the evolution of international society and the requirements of both peace and justice demand that we do nothing less. Foreign assistance rests on a moral imperative but also on American national interest. As such, foreign assistance must follow the same tenets of practical morality on which all foreign policy should be based.

The Transcendent and the Relative
in Morality and Foreign Policy

Every discussion of ethics and politics or ethics and foreign policy comes down in the end to a debate over a transcendent versus a relativist ethic. These questions are raised repeatedly: Does an ethical system provide principles that can serve as guides to action? What are the standards it seeks to establish? How viable and relevant to the social order are its principles? What ordering of priorities among ethical and political principles takes place within the ethical system? How does such ordering relate to mankind's most urgent problems? What are the inner consistencies of a given ethical theory and its essential coherence as a body of thought? And if we accept the proposition of the Harvard philosopher John Rawls that a theory however elegant or economical must be rejected or revised if it is untrue, what can we say about the truth of a given ethical theory?

Before turning to the issues that arise from these broader and more far-ranging questions, a qualifying statement about international relations theory is in order. It is self-evident that international relations theory is not philosophy in the broadest sense. For example, it is not an attempt to define the nature of truth or to locate man's place in the universe. It does not ask with theology, "What is ultimate truth?" nor with philosophy, "What is man's highest end in life?" This has led philosophers such as the late Leo Strauss of the University of Chicago to question the validity of a philosophy of international relations. Strauss asked whether a philosophy for world politics was not as problematical as, for example, a philosophy for New York's sanitation workers. At one level in his questioning, Strauss was correct in stating that theorizing about international politics takes place at a more immediate or less universal level of discourse than general philosophy and suffers from the fact that common moral principles are hard to find. International theory is unlikely to ask: What is the best possible state? What is man's highest end? Its focus is more often upon power and morality or the preconditions of peace.

At the same time, it would be the height of intellectual arrogance (a condition from which philosophers and their disciples are not immune) for one school of thought to claim a monopoly over philosophy or to imagine that a single intellectual tradition had preempted all truth. Edmond Cahn, one of the twentieth century's most original jurisprudential scholars, asks: Where is the legal theorist to find the concepts and principles necessary for the illumination of the broad dimensions of his field? Writing in the late 1940s, Cahn answered: "The choice would be rather difficult if we did not have the benefit of indications visibly and repeatedly inscribed in the history of philosophy. The life of any reflective undertaking has been shown to consist in the clash and conflict of hostile principles. . . . That is why the ideal is habitually set off against the positive, identity against time, the free against the determined, reason against passion."[1] Cahn's approach to philosophy is more or less congruent with the preeminent concerns of contemporary international theory as here formulated. The central themes he explores, not surprisingly, are justice and power, freedom and order, and security and change. They are themes that ought to be found in almost any serious international relations text. Their prominence in both the legal and the international relations philosophical traditions suggests that certain recurrent issues are more fundamental to the various realms of inquiry than Strauss's criticism would appear to suggest. We may carry the discussion further, however, by exploring some of the basic questions set forth at the outset of this chapter.

Guides to Action

In both law and political philosophy, the natural law tradition has been praised as answering some of our original questions. Just as the stars and the planets in the heavens are guided by natural laws that hold them in orbit and assure their harmonious movement, man's right relationships in the social and political universe are said to be guided by similar sets of natural law. Just as science has penetrated the mysteries of the physical universe and broken through the veil of ignorance, so human reason can discover and explain the natural laws of the social universe for the guidance of men. Justice requires that human relationships be conducted in accordance with the precepts of nature independent of time and place. Natural laws once discovered can provide universal and immutable guides to action. The higher law undergirding the American constitutional system rests on a modern approximation of natural law as do certain metacodal principles in international relations, such as fair dealing among nations and faithful adherence to international treaties.

The reactions against natural law, however imposing its sacred and secular defenses, were foreshadowed in the doubts of the ancient thinker Cicero: "It has been observed that the laws of nature were either too general to offer much help in concrete cases or too specific to claim universal and absolute authority." In their application, natural law precepts have not infrequently become the property of the privileged and the strong, leading the seventeenth-century philosopher Blaise Pascal to argue: "Justice is subject to dispute; might is easily recognized and is not disputed. So we cannot give might to justice, because might has gainsaid justice. . . . And thus being unable to make what is just strong, we have made what is strong just."[2]

Both the classical and the Christian versions of natural law were criticized by modern philosophers and theologians. The critics of the classical view maintained that the Platonic, Aristotelian, and Stoic outlooks all contributed to substantial misunderstandings about the nature of man because of their emphasis on the uniqueness of man's rational faculties. What is unique in man is his *noús*. Although this can be translated as spirit, and for Plato the highest element of the soul, the primary emphasis has been on man's capacity for reason and thought. Mind is sharply distinguished from body. From the time of Parmenides, Greek philosophy assumed an identity between being and reason on the one hand and presupposed reason's influence on unformed and formless matter (which resists reason and is never fully responsive) on the other hand. In Aristotle, matter is "a remnant non-existent in itself unknowable and alien to reason, that remains after the process of clarifying the thing into form and conception." Plato and Aristotle share a common rationalism and, along with it, a dualism that equates reason with the creative principle, immortal and identified with God. Comparing the classical and Christian versions of natural law, Reinhold Niebuhr wrote:

> While the classical view of human virtue is optimistic when
> compared with the Christian view (for it finds no defect in the
> center of human personality) and while it has perfect confidence
> in the virtue of the rational man, it does not share the confidence
> of the moderns in the ability of all men to be either virtuous or
> happy. Thus an air of melancholy hangs over Greek life which
> stands in sharpest contrast to the all pervasive optimism of . . .
> bourgeois culture, despite the assumption of the latter that it had
> merely restored the classical world view. . . . Primarily, it was the
> brevity of life and the mortality of man which tempted the Greeks
> to melancholy.[3]

Greek tragedy, compared with Greek philosophy, finds that human life in its effort to be creative is also destructive. Despite the counsel of

Greek philosophers calling for restraint and moderation, Greek tragedy tends to confirm Friedrich Nietzsche's observation: "Every doer loves his deed more than it deserves to be loved."[4] Thus there is no resolution, or at most a tragic resolution, between the vitalities of life and the principle of measure; the various vitalities in life remain permanently in conflict not only with Zeus but with one another. This profound problem posed so persistently in Greek tragedy has tended to be largely ignored or passed over by the group of modern writers who have revived classical Greek political thought.

The consequences of a too-narrow and rigid use of natural law became apparent in the era of medieval Catholicism, particularly in the union of classical and Christian thought provided in the Thomistic synthesis of Aristotelian and Augustinian thought. This synthesis looked back to man's original righteousness lost in the Fall and his sense of natural justice uncorrupted by the Fall. This distinction concealed the complex relation of human freedom to all man's natural functions, including the use of human reason and the consequent involvement of every natural or rational standard and norm in man's essential weakness. Natural law itself cannot claim to be above mankind's frailties and limitations.

> Undue confidence in human reason, as the seat and source of natural law, makes this very concept of law into a vehicle of human sin. It gives the peculiar conditions and unique circumstances in which reason operates in a particular historical moment the sanctity of universality. The confidence of medieval Catholicism in the ability of an unspoiled reason to arrive at definitive standards of natural justice thus became the very vehicle of the sinful pretensions of the age. The social ethics of Thomas Aquinas embody the peculiarities and the contingent factors of a feudal-agrarian economy into a system of fixed socioethical principles.[5]

Critics from that day to the present have pointed to the tendency of Catholic natural law to build the contingent factors of social relations into a final normative code universally defined. Their criticism has focused particularly on the realms of family relations and international relations. Natural law historically has forbidden birth control and enjoined the dominance of the husband over the wife. Sexual relations are seen as limited by nature to the need for procreation with little account taken of the perils of human bondage or the complex relations set in motion, with possibilities for both creativity and evil, when animal relations are touched by human freedom. Turning to male supremacy, the concept finds support both in the Bible and in classical thought. Its authors overlook, however, the role of male arrogance in defining and applying such a standard. The relation to the sexes is a product of sex differentiation but also of human freedom, and "any premature fixation of certain historical standards . . . will inevitably tend to reenforce male arrogance and to retard justified efforts on the part of the female to achieve such freedom as is not incompatible with the primary function of motherhood."[6] Freedom in human relations makes the setting of guides and standards to last for all time extraordinarily difficult. And man's desire for power makes almost inescapable the tendency of any dominant group, class, or sex to seek to guarantee its continued dominance through permanent normative standards.

In international relations—the other sphere in which natural law has offered broad guidance—the Catholic theory of a just war, however superior to Lutheran relativism or cynical realism, is deficient. For the most part, natural law writings on war have tended to overlook the immense intellectual and political difficulties in making universal distinctions between justice and injustice and aggression. Obviously, not all wars are equally just, nor all combatants equally right. But judgments of their conduct are influenced by passions and interests so that "even the most obvious case of aggression can be made to appear a necessity of defense; and even a war which is judged by neutral opinion to be wholly defensive cannot be waged with completely good conscience because the situations out of which wars arise are charged with memories of previous acts of aggression on the part of those now in defense." To the members of the Grand Alliance, World War II was an example of unquestioned justice, yet for many months the leaders of Germany were successful in stopping resisters by claiming that their aggression was merely intended to correct the injustices of the Treaty of Versailles. The question of justice and aggression was never resolved in Vietnam. Americans who, in the beginning, had agreed to force North Vietnam to leave its neighbors alone felt growing moral revulsion to the war. Judgments of right and wrong in war are relativized by historical geographic and political circumstances. Disputes have seldom if ever been resolved by invoking the guides to just war offered by Francisco Suárez: "In order that a war may be justly waged, certain conditions must be observed. . . . First, it must be waged by a legitimate power. Secondly, its cause must be just and right. Thirdly, just methods should be used, that is equity in the beginning of war, in the prosecution of it and in victory." But wars have been waged in which the issue of justice, in Suárez's terms, remained in doubt whereas the life and death of nations and whole civilizations were involved. Decisions in such circumstances have to be made on the basis of norms that fall short of absolute justice. To sum up the criticism of natural law theories in Niebuhr's words: "The perennial mistake of rationalists, whether Stoic, Catholic or modern, is to exempt reason from either finiteness or sin or both and to derive universal rational norms from this confidence in reason." [7]

Nevertheless, if natural law's guides to action are too fixed and absolute, contemporary relativism and modern-day positivism are plauged by the opposite danger. Young people complain that the end of sexual repression, the breakdown of the family, and less permanent living arrangements have led to the destruction of guides to action and predictable expectations (what lawyers describe in contracts as performance implying counterperformance). How can anyone do what is expected when no understanding has been reached on what can normally be expected? When there are no rules of the game, everyone becomes his own rule maker, confronted with all the attendant problems of human arrogance from which past philosophers have suffered. In relationships within the more intimate human communities, when responsibility and moral commitment are gone or dismissed as remnants of an old-fashioned and puritanical age, the will of the stronger prevails. The only distinction between the present and the earlier social orders would seem to be that female arrogance has become at least as prevalent as male arrogance.

The breakdown of accepted guides to action is, if anything, more extreme in international relations than in family relations. One of the pathetic sides of the war in Vietnam was the relative indifference of a majority of Americans to the bloodshed and carnage of war as it affected the Vietnamese. A favorite inside code word of policy makers in Washington was to call for a little more "bloodletting." Although much of the criticism of the United States for its conduct of the war was overstated—especially singling out individual policy makers as war criminals—the plain fact is that such criticism aroused little if any public response. It was as if the spirit that had inspired Supreme Court Justice Robert Jackson and Professor Quincy Wright during the Nuremberg judgments had vanished overnight from the American scene. As far as public opinion was concerned (and we need to remind ourselves that majority opinion reflected in the Gallup and Harris polls showed substantial support for the war until the final year or two of the conflict), theories of just warfare or principles of proportionality had little mass appeal despite the sustained and visible efforts of the major groups who opposed the war. One possible explanation for the widespread malaise and public indifference must be the absence of accepted guides to action. In the 1940s, almost every American university and college offered at least two courses in international law, one in the law of peace and the other in the law of warfare. By the late 1960s, most established departments of political science and many law schools had dropped such courses, due no doubt to the far-reaching decline of viable guides to action in the conduct of war.

The Standards of Ethical Theories

The question of standards is by logic and past practice closely allied with guides to action. The distinction is made, however, in international law and in some branches of political theory that standards depend for their credibility less on whether they are universally observed than on whether they provide signposts and pointers to what is right and just. According to leading jurists, nations weigh other principles of politics and economics. Policy makers must decide which principles to follow in weighing putative costs and advantages. The validity of a standard in law or politics does not necessarily depend on its observance. In law, the writings of jurists and publicists help to define a standard, as do the common experiences of civilized nations. Positivists and natural law theorists may differ on whether standards come primarily from the experience of states or derive from certain a priori principles, but both appear to accept a similar definition of the nature, use, and limitations of standards.

To hold this view is not to argue that the meaning or content of legal and political standards is fixed once for all time. Paul Freund, Harvard University's great legal scholar, has written: "It is no disparagement of a work of art or of its interpreters that it takes on new relevance, yields new insights, answers to new concerns, as the generations pass. Nor is it a reproach to a Constitution intended to endure for ages to come, and to meet the various crises in human affairs or to its interpreters that it too responds to changing concerns of the society to which it ministers." Continuing this line of reasoning, Freund shows that *Hamlet* has in successive historical periods been interpreted as a story of revenge, an inquiry into sanity, a study of mother-fixation, or an example of the death wish. None of these perspectives is necessarily wrong; each possesses some validity. In the same way, "it need not be a cause of despair that to one gerneration the Constitution was primarily a means of cementing the Union, to another a safeguard of property, to another a shield of access to political participation and equality before the law." In scholarship, the standard for the historian is objectivity. But, as Stuart Hughes of Harvard has shown, objectivity "is to be valued only if it is hard-won —only if it is the end result of a desperate and conscious battle to rise above partisan passion." Quoting E. H. Carr, an Oxford University historian, "Man's capacity to rise above his social and historical situation seems to be conditioned by the sensitivity with which he recognizes the extent of his involvement in it."[8]

Therefore, the interpretation of *Hamlet*, the Constitution, and historical objectivity all involve standards, but standards whose application and expression are relativized by circumstances. Or in the language of Freund: "New vistas in constitutional law are not, in my judgment, boundless. . . . They are not free of shadows and even treacherous turns." These turns are made *more* treacherous, we might add, when practice departs too far from standards. However, law and politics in practice resemble art more than science. New vistas open as experience broadens needs and perspective. "In neither discipline will the craftsman succeed unless he sees that proportion and balance are essential, that order and disorder are both virtues when held in proper tension," Freund continues. The student of law and politics must seek both light and cross-lights. "There are," Freund concludes in words that cause the sycophant to despair, "no absolutes in law or art except intelligence."[9] And intelligence has greater resources than reason, the student of morality should add.

The Ordering of Ethical and Political Principles

At this stage of our inquiry, we must make clear that what Freund suggests about the value of order and disorder must be contrasted with another view of the statesman or jurist as instructor in justice and truth. The leaders of the second approach have chosen to negate the idea that leaders in the executive or judicial branch of government follow the election returns. The task of such leaders is not to be educated by the people but to educate the people. On the contrary, Freund observes a process of interaction through which the right ordering of principles emerges and "new vistas" are discovered.

The difference between the two approaches, however, is less one of conflicting views regarding the democratic process, although this point has been persistently argued by social theorists such as Karl Popper. It centers more on the extent to which the search for the good, the true, and the just is an unending process given the inevitable pluralism of prevailing ethical and political principles. One school of thought, following the traditions of natural law, insists that one overarching moral or political end is capable of ordering all the rest. Virtue for the good man transcends other ends, and it can be approached through reason. The idea of man as master of his destiny is based on the classical tradition mediated by the Renaissance—in part, an aspect of the Christian inheritance. Yet its latter-day expression, bourgeois individualism, has been threatened from the moment of its creation by the destruction of medieval solidarities. No one can be as "completely and discretely an individual as bourgeois individualism supposes, whether in the organic forms of an agrarian or the more mechanical forms of a technical society." From the very beginning, bourgeois individualism had insecure foundations, first in Platonism and Neoplatonism and later in the naturalism of the eighteenth and nineteenth centuries. In the words of a leading American social critic: "There is no place for individuality in either pure mind or pure nature. As the idealists lose individuality in the absolute mind, so the naturalists lose it in streams of consciousness when dealing with the matter psychologically." [10]

Modern culture, to the extent it rests on either rationalism or naturalism, fails to deal openly with the problem of evil: "The idea that man is sinful at the very centre [sic] of his personality, that is in his will, is universally rejected by the two traditions." For "if modern culture conceives man primarily in terms of the uniqueness of his rational faculties, it finds the root of his evil in his involvement in natural impulses and natural necessities from which it hopes to free him by the increase of his rational faculties." On the other hand, "if it conceives of man primarily in terms of his relation to nature, it hopes to rescue man from the daemonic chaos in which his spiritual life is involved by beguiling him back to the harmony, sanity and [the] harmless unity of nature." [11] Rationalism and naturalism stand on common ground in assuming that rational man or natural man is essentially good. Opposed to these views is the belief that man is both a creature of nature subject to all its pressures and vicissitudes and also a child of God.

The difficulty in ordering priorities among ethical principles within any tradition is that ethical choice involves arbitrating not only between good and evil but between *rights* and *rights*. Moral principles compete, often clashing and colliding with one another. We want to do what is right—but what is right? Choice involves moral dilemmas that confront men every time they seek to be virtuous. The devoted father seeks to do right for his family and children. Until recently, at least, he has been the main source of their support. Will he choose success in business to the neglect of the solidarity of family and the ever-present emotional needs of his children? Or will he strive to be a loving father at the price of business advancement? To sharpen the issue, how will he resolve his dilemma working, not beside his children each day in the fields of the family farm, but far from his home, commuting sometimes long distances? How will the national leader resolve his dilemma of promoting the nation's economic health and general welfare at home while safeguarding its security and helping the poor around the world whose worsening condition can only increase the chances of global conflict? In every sector of personal, national, and international life, dilemmas multiply, expressed in the inevitable tension between freedom and order, justice and power, or security and change.

These dilemmas are made the more poignant and perplexing because of man's fragmentary grasp of realities and the consequences of his deeds. A vast network of factors limits the course he can follow and his wisdom as he confronts his choices. He is caught at the juncture of necessity and freedom. He is both a creature of nature bound by his circumstances and a creator of much that he surveys. He stands within history and momentarily outside of it, both object and subject in the world he describes. His little pictures of reality reflect that reality but are also images in his mind. He is an American, a child of his family, a product of his environment, afloat at a brief moment in time on a tiny speck in the universe subject to all the hopes and despair his immediate circumstances warrant. At best he can take hold of a small part of reality. His vision of the future is bounded by past and present. He knows all too well that as generals fight the last war or as statesmen negotiate again the last peace, he sees at best only a few years ahead in gauging the consequences of his deeds. Even when they seek more for their nation or have a different vision of the future, that vision is limited by historical perspective. At most he can say with Lincoln: "I do the best I can and hope history will bring me out all right." Withal he views reality through the prism of self-interest. Even when he claims to speak for a higher purpose—the good of his children or the well-being of the world —his words betray his own anxiety over a self-centeredness that he cannot escape or transcend. However imposing the structure of rationalization with which he surrounds himself, he remains a self whose hopes and fears, interests and goals take precedence.

Yet at the same moment that he presses forward, he stands in judgment on himself, accusing and excusing himself as only mankind can do. This capacity for self-judgment, alternating between self-justification and self-guilt, is proof that man is more than a creature of nature. History too is proof of man's freedom and his self-determining nature. As creator, man seeks to make himself God or pure reason or lord of the universe. If other living beings have an inborn sense of their limits, man does not. As free spirit, he is only a little lower than the angels. He struggles to find himself somewhere between heaven and earth. Because his capacities are not preordained, he lives out his life seeking to discover the limits of his being. His struggle is with himself, with his fellows, and with nature.

The ever-present prospect of life's ending and the tension man feels because he is both creature and creator makes for profound anxiety. Man is anxious because he is caught by the pull of nature and the push of his dreams, his identity and his drive for self-fulfillment. He seeks security by an assertion of will and the exercise of his power lest his creation be strangled at birth. His struggle to find himself and to attain security and power brings him into conflict, rivalry, and contention with others embarked on a similar quest. The more he strives to be creator, gain security, and master his future, the more certain are his conflicts with others—parents, rivals in love, or nations reaching out for security and hegemony. And nowhere is the security-power dilemma as fateful or as inevitable as in the struggle for power among nation-states.

Where can men look for the resolution of the drama of the self and of nations, for an ordering principle or "an ethic beyond ethical principles" (Nikolai Berdyaev). The best-known and most available answers are found in certain present-day movements. Popular evangelical Christianity finds its standard or highest ordering principle in the evangelist's counsel: "Believe in God—and do as you please." Modern rationalism looks to the best of men, the philosopher of politics, seeking wisdom in contemplation far removed from all the ambiguities and contradictions of the human struggle. Present-day naturalism finds the highest good in accommodation with all the natural drives and appetites of man as a creature of nature unable to escape his creaturehood but unimpeded by guilt imposed by any higher nature. Marxism justifies by Marxist doctrine the tyrany and oppression of the state and the cruelty and barbarism of the pursuit of the Communist utopia. It anoints and defends the purging of six million kulaks with the promise of a classless society in which the domination of man by man will be replaced by the administration of things. Liberalism in its classical economic form sees raw competition of individuals and groups being guided by the interplay of the market and the beneficence of a hidden hand to the attainment of the general good. The interventionists at home and in the developing countries look to government to bring about economic and social justice in place of the exploitation of the weak by privileged landowners and a powerful political elite.

An Alternative View of Transcendence and Relativism

The question remains whether the prevailing viewpoints we have explored, taken alone or together, exhaust the search for transcendence in political thought. Or is there another view that more adequately reflects the complexities and problems of politics with fewer illusions? Is there another view that places in perspective the threefold relation of man with himself, the communities in which he lives, and an overarching moral and political order?

This study assumes that such a viewpoint exists and that politics viewed in such a light involves men seeking justice and order through methods designed to balance the good and evil in society by checks and balances and various forms of the separation of powers. Political reason looks not for abstract truths but rather for the means of adding and subtracting, multiplying and dividing true moral denominations viewed not in a mathematical or metaphysical but in a social and political context. Political realism is the main route to understanding and coping with politics as practiced. He who ignores or denies the political truths of realism does so at his peril. Despite all the brave talk of virtues and the self-sufficient man, politics goes on in an arena where virtues and vices coexist. Politics demands integrity and wholeness, exemplified by great statesmen, and a sense of the possible. The enduring chapters in political history have been written by men whose visions of past and future were balanced by prudence and an awareness of the limits of political action. An ethic of responsibility calls upon the political actor to consider the consequences of his acts, however vague and dim the outlines. Christopher Hobhouse, the British philosopher, wrote of those political thinkers bridging the gulf between the reactionary and the progressive, the empiricist and the doctrinaire. He might have added those who integrate individualism and collectivism or liberalism and conservatism. Such thinkers are the colossuses among political and moral philosophers. They point the way to the large ends of politics and the small steps by which men advance toward realization of these goals. No moral issue is ever an abstract question. What is right or wrong, morally speaking, is determined in relation to other considerations and consequences. Thus prudence is the master virtue in politics—a prudence that looks at relationships and practical effects. These questions must always be asked in any discourse on the morality of an act: What are its consequences? How well does this or that constellation of power and morality satisfy the requirements of justice and freedom?

Because of their unyielding faith in the uniqueness of reason, rationalists not only ignore the temptations of power (they speak of the ennobling effects of power but never its corrupting influences) but also ignore the use of moral principles as pretexts for self-interest and political intrigue. They are blind to the collective and historic wisdom of tradition, habit, and custom. They pass over the importance of such organic forces as loyalty and feeling or sentiment and prejudice that hold communities together from the family to the nation-state. They have comparatively little to say about the perennial sources of resistance to moral norms in human life and men's persistent recalcitrance in following principles of morality that lie outside their immediate spheres of concern.

Reinhold Niebuhr in his later years pointed to Edmund Burke as a political thinker who best understood that "the powers which are in cooperation and conflict in the human community are compounded of ethnic loyalties, common traditions, ancient sanctities, common fears, common hopes and endless other combinations of human motives." Those who recognize such factors tend toward a historical rather than a purely systematic discussion of politics. Man, the center of the study of politics, is best understood as a historical being rooted in time and place. A political or religious thinker who chooses to live in the world, who is free of the temptation of self-denial of which political rationalists themselves are guilty even when they accuse others of this fault, is ever conscious of the hazards of withdrawal to safe sanctuaries of abstractions and pure philosophy. "One of the most fruitful sources of self-deception," wrote Niebuhr in the 1920s, "is the proclamation of great ideals and principles without any clue to their relations to the controversial issues of the day." [12] The task of the political philosopher is to use concrete moral and political problems to illuminate general moral and political principles. Edmund Burke's letter to the electors of Bristol explaining to his constituents what he intended to do as their representative became a classic statement of the meaning of representative government. Niebuhr's examples of the different consequences of proximate and absolute moral good in the struggle between the partially realized goals of Western civilization and the tyranny of Nazism and communism provide a contemporary example of this approach.

Seen from the perspective of writers such as Niebuhr, the goal of politics is not the attainment of the higher values of religion or philosophy. It is not the realization of piety or pure virtue, although some statesmen exemplify these characteristics. The end of politics is justice. Justice means giving each person his due, taking into account individual and collective egoism. It seeks to balance and reconcile contending goals and interests. The realm of politics is the twilight zone in which moral principles and technical requirements merge and are ordered. Politics to the end of history will be a meeting place of conscience and power where ethical and coercive factors interpenetrate and where statesmen seek the basis for tentative and uneasy compromises. President Carter, who had been given a biography of Reinhold Niebuhr, underlined the following quotations from Niebuhr's writings:

> Man's capacity for justice makes democracy possible; man's inclination to injustice makes democracy necessary.
>
> Politicians are both tougher and more honest than the rest of us.
>
> We must never deify freedom. It is not God.
>
> Faith in God's forgiveness makes possible the risk of action.
>
> Justice must be the instrument of love.
>
> Man cannot love himself inordinately without pretending that it is not his, but a universal interest which he is supporting.
>
> Most of the evil is done by good people who do not know they are not good.
>
> How shall we judge the great statesman who gives a nation its victorious courage by articulating its only partly conscious and implicit resources of fortitude; and who mixes the most obvious forms of personal and collective pride and arrogance with this heroic fortitude? If [Churchill] had been a timid man, a more cautious soul, he would not have sinned so greatly, but neither would he have wrought so nobly.
>
> There must be a passion for justice.[13]

Those who ignore the relativities of justice as it exists in the living political world are incapable of proximate moral judgments. Pacifists and Socialists suffer as a group from utopian illusions about the historical possibilities of a moral life. Because of their tendencies toward perfectionism, they are unable to make discriminate judgments between the relative good and evil in political life. In an essay written in 1940, Niebuhr wrote: "The pacifists and socialists are one in believing that nothing is at stake in the present European struggle. The socialists take this position because they measure the evils of a capitalist society against the ideal possibilities of a social commonwealth of nations. The pacifists measure them against an ideal world in which there will be neither coercion nor resistance." Niebuhr and others who spoke out against this passive and self-denying view insisted that, if men could not express a moral preference for the relative justice of democratic societies measured against the gross injustice of the tyrannical states, no moral judgment would ever be possible. In June, 1940, Niebuhr resigned from the Socialist party because it could not bring itself to make such a judgment and confront Nazi expansionism. He saw the very existence of "open societies" as depending upon the outcome of the impending war with Hitler. Of the other threat to Western civilization, Niebuhr wrote with more caution. Following an early visit in 1930 to Russia, he explained:

> The Russian communists seem to believe it will be easy to create perfect social mutuality by destroying inequality of power. But can they destroy economic power without creating strong centers of political power? And how may they be certain that this political power will be either ethically or politically restrained? The abuse of power by communistic bureaucrats is very considerable and is bound to grow as the purer revolutionary idealists are supplanted by men who have consciously sought for the possession of power.[14]

Thus at the height of his Marxist period of thought, Niebuhr saw as a political realist that political life need not be ennobling, as his rationalist critics claimed it was, and that the worst crimes in politics may be committed in the name of utopian justice.

To continue, then, justice in society depends on an open society that rests on both a moral sense precedent to reason (which requires the individual to act at one and the same time on whatever judgments of good and evil he is able to form) and a political equilibrium among contending groups and forces. Burke had correlated the moral sense with a God-given "Enthusiasm to supply the want of Reason." The highest law of life is the law of love, which promises the perfection of man as an individual and a social being. The ideal possibility for man is a brotherly relation of life with life, but within every historical community this possibility was marred and impaired by competition and conflict and the coercive character of peace. Man's radical freedom—the true source of his creativity—is not, as the rationalists believe, synonymous with virtue. It remains true, as the editor of the London *Times* wrote: "The doctrine of original sin is the only empirically verifiable doctrine of the Christian faith." In Edmund Burke's classic phrase: "Enthusiasm often misleads us. So does reason too. Such is the Condition of our Nature; and we can't help it."[15] Because of the contradictions at the depths of man's freedom, he fails to fulfill the norm of his existence. Love and the perfect harmony of life with life are the "impossible possibilities" of man's nature—possibilities because they prescribe the essence of human nature and the perfection of that nature and impossibilities because man in his freedom seeks to overcome his finiteness and conquer his anxieties through self-assertion, which contradicts self-sacrificial love and introduces not harmony but conflicts of interest and power into the world.

If self-sacrificial love is an "impossible possibility" in history, mutual love and distributive justice are the highest good in history: "Only in mutual love, in which the concern of one person for another prompts and elicits a reciprocal affection, are the social demands of historical existence satisfied." Mutual love "seeks to relate life to life from the standpoint of self and for the sake of the self's own happiness." "From the perspective of society the highest moral ideal is justice," but "justice without love is merely the balance of power." However, although "the law of love is the basis of all moral life . . . it cannot be obeyed by a simple act of the will because the power of self-concern is too great."[16]

Justice in politics and life depends on the principle of the fence. Even the most loving partners must seek some kind of understanding on where the most vital interests of one begin and those of the other end. For political groups and nations, the need is more urgent still. The most demanding task of any diplomat is to be able to place himself in another's shoes. Whether we call it the development of mutual understanding, empathy, or justice, giving content to the mutuality of one another's interests becomes an unending challenge. Historians and moralists from Thucydides to the present have warned that there can be no justice among unequals. Classical and modern-day rationalists see little prospect that the sympathy and compassion which Americans have demonstrated for the weak and the downtrodden can long endure. The intellectual and moral foundations of sympathetic concern for the weak or underprivileged are too fragile and irrational. He who has achieved a certain level of excellence or virtue can neither understand nor respond to one who is not his equal. Sympathy is an emotional, not a rational, response. As such, it is destined to lose its force and to wither away in practice.

The Niebuhrian approach is at odds with the classical view on at least two important aspects of the problem of justice. First, history demonstrates that the strong may find in a practical morality combining self-interest and compassion the basis for giving help to the weak. The Marshall Plan was a judicious blending of magnanimity and American national interest. Its constituency included both churchmen and strategic thinkers who were concerned about Soviet expansion into the power vacuum created by a morally and materially devastated Europe. Within the United States, help to minority and disadvantaged groups has rested on similar foundations, particularly when business leaders concerned for a stagnating economy have taken the lead to assist the underprivileged.

Second, the strong find a further basis for helping the suffering and the deprived in a transcendent ethic of justice motivated by love. Within the family, no purely rational basis can be found for forgiveness and mutual understanding. The crushing weight of recurrent encroachments of will upon will by parents upon children, children upon parents, or spouse upon spouse is so continuous, unrelenting, and inescapable that the Biblical injunction "You must forgive seventy times seven" lies beyond all rational possibility. Yet for men or nations who, with or without premeditation, wreak havoc in each other's lives, no other prescription is prudent or realistic. Official religion when linked with politics has every bit as much need for the law of love. As a British historian and the former vice-chancellor of Cambridge University has written: "The truth is: that a religion, and particularly a supernatural religion, can be a very dangerous thing in the world, unless accompanied by (and rooted in) a super-abundant charity."[17] Most religions are political in the course of their development. The Koran regulates all aspects of life. The Orthodox Catholic Church was part of the state administration throughout centuries of its history. In some states a Protestant church was the official religion. The separation of church and state in the United States from the founding of the republic was an exception to developments in Europe and the Middle East. Yet the peril of merging religion and politics has been present in every culture including primitive societies.

Political Reason and Christian Morality

Nowhere is the essential role of charity and compassion more apparent than as expressed in the two mediating principles of justice—freedom and equality. Freedom rests on the belief in the dignity of man and the never-ending possibilities of man the creator. However, freedom is an instrument of justice, not an end in itself, as all its intemperate uses by the strong to impose their will on the weak plainly attest. Equality (the second regulative principle of justice) is at war with the inevitable disparity in individual talents. However, political history proves the unwillingness of men in almost every society to accept permanently the superiority of one group over others or the subordination of the many by the few solely because of wealth or position, vocation or personal endowments, and ethnic or regional identity.

Political reason, for its part, has a role to play in giving content and meaning to freedom and equality. The great epic periods of political achievement coincide with the merging of religious and rational insights and their implementation in policies reflecting political morality. Taken alone, each set of insights has its limitations. This is true of religion, in Butterfield's outspoken judgment:

> It isn't the function of religion or the church to solve the problems of diplomacy or to tell governments how to balance their budgets. Even historians, coming long afterwards and able to spend years in studying a matter, will be baffled by the complexity of the forces and the multiplicity of the factors that happen to underlie a particular crisis, and the many people—who think they can solve the problem, generally turn out to have overlooked some particularly awkward aspect of the case, and ignored some inconvenient considerations. Real statesmanship, of course, requires the ability to hold in one's mind a whole jungle of relevant details, a whole forest of complicating inconsistencies.

This is one side of the equation justifying the role of political reason, though not of abstract rationalism, in balancing the "enthusiasm" of faith and religion. In seventeenth-century England, Lord Clarendon, Charles II's chief minister, warned that ecclesiastical leaders were not well suited for governing a country or carrying out political responsibility. Something more than worthy motives or noble purposes was needed. Butterfield goes even further than Clarendon in judging who may be qualified: "I have parallel misgivings about the capacity of academic people in political affairs; and I seem always to acquire an extra headache when I know that another university professor is being called to the White House or to No. 10 Downing Street." [18]

Yet if religion has its limits as a pathway to political justice, and especially to wise statesmanship, so too does every form of rationalistic or time-bound hierarchical thought. It is tempting to argue that freedom and equality would have emerged in Western civilization regardless of the influence of religious tradition. The Greeks after all were the architects of much of democratic thought manifested in the Greek city-states. But the idea of equality was preached in the early modern world by believers who quoted the Bible, wrote that Christ had made all men free, and had faith that all human beings were equal in the sight of God. In eighteenth-century England, society included at its lowest stratum "brutalised masses of people" and above them "more innocuous people entirely unfitted for intellectual pursuits—creatures who obeyed their masters like dumb animals" and looked the part. Writing of the changes in English society and history's judgment on these people, Butterfield reports:

> Their betters—the people higher up in society, saw (very rightly in fact) that there was no hope of giving these people the franchise and getting them to take part in politics; and indeed it was assumed that the same would be the case with their children and grandchildren—it was assumed that their breed was basically unfitted for mental pursuits. It was John Wesley who, precisely on religious grounds, saw the potentialities of these creatures— saw that . . . salvation . . . was intended for them too, and raised them to a higher consciousness of themselves. The sons of those whom he trained to be lay-preachers . . . became important in the development of political consciousness in England, and we find them among the political agitators and trade union leaders of a later age.

Individualism as a modern concept was rooted in this soil, though threatened in its earliest history by opposing forces. It owed a great deal at the dawn of the modern age to the Christian teaching that man was a creative spirit, "that every single person [was] of superlative value, born for eternity, and therefore incommensurate with anything else in the created universe." [19] The force of individualism has declined in mass technological society. Without a fresh injection of the religious doctrine of personality, it is not clear today how long it will hold its own.

A further question, however, must be asked. What influence have such religious principles exerted in the history of statecraft? Here the record is less clear and unambiguous. No one can ignore the crimes that were committed in the name of religion in religious wars, whether by the followers of Christianity or Islam. Not only did religion introduce a fanaticism that made warfare more cruel, but it added substantially to the difficulty of restoring peace. Religion is a matter of ultimate belief, but political religions are the inventions of men and are as arbitrary as their will. The business of diplomacy is accommodation, not the resolution of ideological disputes. Historians look back to the sixteenth and seventeenth centuries and see the wars between Protestants and Catholics as more brutal than all wars until those of the twentieth century. Throughout the eighteenth century and following World Wars I and II, writers and diplomatists warned that such conflicts must never again occur. The foreign policies proposed by religious people are all too likely to become entangled with patriotic fervor, and vested interests are sanctified as though they represented absolute truth. All too often, those who espouse a certain faith subordinate it in practice to some quite limited political end, which they invest with all the sanctities of their religious faith.

However, in addition to this rather grim and hopeless picture of religious warfare and strife, there is an often-overlooked, more positive chapter. The Spanish conquest of South America is the story of a religious people who came as conquerors, enslaving the native inhabitants. These conquests led to a historic religious and international law debate. A group of Spanish monks, who have been called the precursors of modern international law, asked whether Christian principles were being violated in the name of the advance of civilization. In the controversy thus provoked, the religious critics of the Spanish conquest sought to define the human rights of a conquered people. They asked for a definition of legitimate treatment for a strange and remote people who refused to accept the truth of Christianity. (See John Eppstein, *The Catholic Tradition of the Law of Nations*). In other words, what would have been their rights if their conquerors had been Mohammedans who sought to impose the will of Allah? The Spanish writers who posed the issue drew on the Bible, Aristotle, St. Thomas Aquinas, and common law. Depending on their sources, they came to rather divergent conclusions. Those who rested their arguments on Aristotle maintained that the "natives were more like animals . . . below the use of reason, and Aristotle had said that those who lacked the use of reason could be legitimately enslaved." An early sixteenth-century pope offered another argument: "God intended all men for salvation, and . . . the Indians must be regarded as having the use of reason—a sufficient share of it to understand the Gospel at any rate."[20] An ancient religious tradition thus provided a concept of moral and political reason that guided statesmen to different policies than Greek rationalism.

The Cold War and Transcendence

It would be claiming too much for the uses of the transcendent truths of religion to maintain that its central concepts are readily translatable in an era of the Cold War. Religious people are for one thing a minority voice in the advanced democracies. They have the same rights and opportunities of persuasion as any other group—but no more. Their knowledge and professional skills are usually far behind those of trained diplomats. "It may seem an odd thing to say," Butterfield acknowledges, "especially when one is speaking as a Christian, but I think you need somebody soaked in the whole science of what we call Power Politics to be responsible for the subtle acts of judgment required."[21] Saints for the most part have not been especially gifted in the conduct of great power negotiations. The clashes between nation-states are too bruising and power-laden to lend themselves to the gentle suasion of religion.

At the same time, too much impatience and anxiety in foreign policy is often the source of tragic misunderstanding, miscalculation, and error. The Old Testament offers a wise maxim, which men and nations ignore at their peril: "Fret not thyself because of evil-doers." Young and inexperienced democracies are endangered by neglect of this maxim. The Weimar Republic, for example, was delivered into the hand of a dictator because of anxiety and doubt generated by critics within and outside the state. But does the Biblical counsel lead to self-denial and inaction? Butterfield thinks not: "It doesn't mean that you must never try to right a wrong but I think it explicitly intends to remind you that you must not expect to win every time, you must not say you will make no peace with Heaven, until all evils are eradicated."[22] Through exercising too much impatience and self-righteousness, those who fret are likely to bring about a greater evil than those they oppose.

What, then, is the positive contribution of religion to foreign policy beyond its counsel of restraint? Butterfield and Morgenthau have warned that religion lies outside the realm of providing any kind of precise guidance in the choice of specific or concrete policies. However, religion can provide a perspective on human motivations and the persistence of selfishness and sin. It can free men of the belief that all our problems could be solved except for those caused by a handful of criminals, whereas "the really knotty problem is that of human nature generally—the moderate cupidities of all men play their part." There are limits even for religion, however, as Butterfield observes: "Because of the contradictions and paradoxes involved, the realm of international relations, more than any other field, is liable to suffer at one and the same time from the cupidities of the wicked, the fears and anxieties of the strong and the unwisdom of the idealists."[23]

Nowhere is the high price of fretting about evildoers as great as when very powerful nations stand on the precipice of war. History abounds with examples of terrible wars between mighty nations, each thinking itself in the right, each caught up in the same moral predicament, each believing it had made its share of concessions for peace. Looking back after a war to the outbreak of conflict, historians debate the issue of war guilt, revise their viewpoints, and try vainly to remember or reconstruct the deeper causes of the struggle. Most often they find that fear was a factor. As in personal relations, so in wars; aggression is often the result of anxieties and fears. The leaders of anxious nations try to dispose of their fears through bold imperialistic threats or deeds. Religion ought to check the rash acts of an anxious sovereign. It offers an alternative to the Hobbesian fear that brought on World War I—a war that historians today characterize as an unnecessary war, a war that might have been avoided with even a marginal reduction of national fears. Religionists would advocate that diplomats should strive for the "moral margins" that might break the cycle of fear and of insecurity leading to aggression.

Writing of the Cold War, Butterfield suggests: "Perhaps . . . the most Christian thing that could happen would be for one of the Great Powers (acting not out of weakness but out of strength) to risk something . . . involving a trust in human nature this time, even though we know how foolish it is to trust in human nature. Something of that sort might be required, just as a marginal experiment . . . because it happens to be the only way out of the worst of deadlocks, the tightest of predicaments." Lest this suggestion be considered "soft" or a form of unconditional surrender, Butterfield quickly adds: "Keep out the sentimentalists [in another place, he warns against "the parsons"] and those for whom giving way is easy—they will come forward bringing surrender to Russia in their outstretched hands."[24] Someone fairly hard-boiled, a modern Bismarck, would be needed to execute a policy involving such a risk, Butterfield insists; but the approach would seek a realistic way out of the present impasse based on political prudence and practical morality. Nations have shown magnanimity in the past, and sometimes a general peace has lasted for a long time—in 1815 after the Congress of Vienna, in 1866 thanks to Bismarck after the defeat of Austria, and following World War II when the United States took the lead in fashioning workable relationships with Germany and Japan. A spirit of political wisdom and magnanimity may offer the best hope today, whether in relations between Israel's Menachem Begin and Egypt's Anwar Sadat or Russia's Leonid Brezhnev and the United States' Jimmy Carter.

Butterfield's proposal not only illustrates the possibility of an alternative foreign policy for the Cold War but also presents in highly concrete terms a new relationship between transcendent religious truths and the relativities of contemporary international politics. Its author is modest and tentative in the claims he makes for such a policy. He asks only that we not pass judgment too quickly on its prospects. The same needs only to be said in conclusion about the more general alternative framework for thinking about normative foreign policy and politics that has been set forth in this discussion.

The Tragic Element in Politics and International Relations

Major systems of thought and leading political philosophies with little else in common seem to share a zeal to dispose of the tragic element in international relationships. Significantly, writers in interpersonal relations argue less often that tragedy can be eradicated, in part because such relationships are usually not open to a wholesale recasting in sweeping ideological terms. In politics, however, almost every regnant theory assigns to tragedy a largely accidental, transient, and unnecessary role.

The Theory of Progress

The theory of progress views tragedy as an archaic remnant of unreformed and irrational societies clinging to outmoded primitive institutions and practices. Conflicts and rivalries persisted when men remained in a premodern state. With the dawning of the modern era, man (to use Emile Coué's words) was becoming better and better in every way. Condorcet and Auguste Comte outlined the various routes to social improvement and human perfectibility and concluded that progress was ushering out misunderstanding and human tragedy. Every theory of progress in the eighteenth and nineteenth centuries, however modified and refined, carried with it an undisguised faith that history's most troublesome problems would disappear in a bright new future. By the mid–twentieth century, progress had been reversed for the advanced industrial states by the barbarism of Hitler and Stalin, to say nothing of the tragedies of Hiroshima and Nagasaki, but it was resurrected for the poor and neglected countries of the world. The guarantee of progress, which democracy and electoral politics had offered to strife-ridden industrial societies, was transferred to the less developed states through promises of national self-determination and modernization. By the mid-1970s, large technical assistance agencies announced that poverty and exploitation could be rooted out through a redirecting of outside assistance to the Third World from the privileged few to the majority poor. Ancient tribal rivalries, deep-seated social imbalances, and vast inequalities in political power were seen, not as intractable obstacles to social change likely to remain indefinitely, but as mere temporary obstacles to a new social order.

Marxism and Liberalism

Marxism, for its part, has viewed human tragedy and suffering as a product of bourgeois society wherein the moral and political superstructure based on a capitalist means of production has dictated oppression of the proletariat. Just as liberal rationalism became the principal moral, intellectual, and political weapon of the rising middle class in its struggle to overcome the feudal system, Marxism has served to justify the claims and alter the status of the downtrodden and self-conscious victims of the industrial system. Historical necessity reinforced the political justifications for the strategies proposed for advancing the interests of the lower classes and was reinforced in turn by the Marxist science of society. Historical necessity and Marxist science combined to give a powerful impetus to Marxist politics. As a legitimizing force, it equaled, if not surpassed, the impact of liberalism in the nineteenth century.

For liberal rationalism, the fundamental concept that men were governed by rational laws which human reason could understand and apply led to four inescapable conclusions: "First, that the rationally right and the ethically good are identical. Second, that the rationally right action is of necessity the successful one. Third, that education leads man to the rationally right, hence, good and successful action. Fourth, that the laws of reason, as applied to the social sphere, are universal in their application." Evil came into the world through failure of reason; good can be restored through the laws of reason. The human actor succeeds or fails in proportion to his commitment to the commands of reason. These rationalist tenets are an obstacle to political understanding because they ignore the truth: "Politics must be understood through reason, yet it is not in reason that it finds its model. The principles of scientific reason are always simple, consistent and abstract; the social world is always complicated, incongruous and concrete."[25] A persistent strain of thought often dominant in recent social theories holds that time will close the remaining gap between science and morals. Norman Angell wrote of war as being caused not by evil intention but by social stupidity. The educational psychologist E. L. Thorndike prophesied that man had the possibility of almost complete control of his fate. Jospeh de Maistre predicted that the eighteenth century, which distrusted itself in nothing, hesitated at nothing, would bring a perfect harmony and social order through education, law, and social reform.

Marxism went liberalism one better. It saw the social order as evolving toward utopia on a more certain and deterministic basis. Conflict and the state were products of the class struggle; with the ending of that struggle in the triumph of the proletariat, the state would wither away. In Marxist terminology, the domination of man by man would be replaced by the administration of things. What was historically inevitable dictated by dialectical materialism was morally right in accordance with the Communist ethic. Reason, which had been the regulator in liberalism, was replaced by the autonomy of socialist economics for Marxism. In turning to economics as the primary instrument of social justice, Marxism absorbed the utopianism of classical economics, raising it to a more deterministic level. For both liberal economics and Marxism, the foremost expression of the harmony of interests was sought not in government or politics but in economics. Not by accident, Adam Smith and David Ricardo discovered the perfect model of a harmonious world governed by a system of rational laws in the economic order. For eighteenth-century liberals, there was little if any difference between the law of gravity and the law of free competition. Actors in both spheres were guided by a "hidden hand." However, after forty years of communism in the Soviet Union, its treatment of dissidents has demonstrated the Marxist opposition to every form of free and open politics. To this day, the similarity of this point of view between the vanguard spokesmen of the classless society and the more reactionary ideologues of the free enterprise system is apparent ("what is good for General Motors is good for America"); that is, the good of society as a whole is equated with the good of a particular group. By contrast, politics is seen as a shoddy business dominated by the recurrent clashes of selfish interest groups. Fortunately, this hapless order will pass, for both Marxism and liberal rationalists forecast the dawn of a new era in which the essential goodness of economic behavior will triumph over the confusion and divisiveness of politics. In Marxism, the classical antinomy between the essential evil of politics and the essential good of economics attains quasi-religious proportions: "In the end, when the state, the political organization par excellence, has withered away, the laws of economics will reign supreme, social strife will disappear, and harmony will be permanently established."[26]

Adam Smith felt that a supernatural or nonrational element—the "invisible hand"—was needed to guide selfish men to the general good. By the nineteenth century, liberalism had rationalized and demythologized this harmonizing element. Baruch Spinoza argued that the one sure way to avert war was to give political leaders a stake in peace by paying senators a percentage on exports and imports. The Saint-Simonist Michel Chevalier prophesied that when the bankers had formed their own Holy Alliance all chance of war would have vanished. Pierre Proudhon turned to a liberal economic framework as the foundation of a universal republic. Herbert Spencer believed that war would become obsolete when men appease their greedy instincts by capitalist investment. Businessmen at home and abroad would find ways of uniting with one another and with their workers for, as John Stuart Mill could say, "commerce first taught nations to see with good will the wealth and prosperity of one another. Before, the patriot . . . wished all countries weak, poor and ill-governed but his own; he now sees in their wealth and progress a direct source of wealth and progress to his own country. It is commerce which is rapidly rendering war obsolete." Writing in 1927, some eighty years later, the liberal Ludwig von Mises could proclaim: "In a period of history where the nations are mutually dependent upon foreign products, wars can no longer be waged."[27]

It remained for the famed champions of free trade from Adam Smith to Richard Cobden to John Bright to Secretary of State Cordell Hull to identify the attainment of worldwide harmony with free trade. Cobden saw in commerce the grand panacea. "Not a bale of merchandise leaves our shores but it bears the seeds of intelligence and fruitful thought to the members of some less enlightened community; not a merchant visits our seats of manufacturing industry but he returns to his own country the missionary of freedom, peace and good government." Free trade for Cobden was the "international law of the almighty," and free trade and peace were "one and the same cause." He confidently predicted that "railroads, steamboats, cheap postage and . . . [Britain's] example in free trade" will "keep the world from actual war." The promised development of the airplane was heralded by Victor Hugo as an "instrument of universal peace." The authors of the Communist Manifesto joined hands with their liberal antagonists in affirming: "National differences and antagonisms between peoples are daily more and more vanishing, owing to the development of the bourgeoisie, to freedom of commerce, to the world's markets, to uniformity in the mode of production and in conditions of life corresponding thereto." For liberals, this state of affairs was seen as a blessed end point in history; for Marxists, a necessary stage in the unfolding of the Communist prophecy of history.[28]

What free trade failed to accomplish would be carried to fruition by worldwide communications, foreshadowing the founding proclamation in the charter of UNESCO that "wars begin in the minds of men and it is in the minds of men that peace must be achieved." Saint-Simon looked to congresses of scientific societies as a primary means of promoting international peace. Conflict was rooted in men's ignorance of one another; increased educational and scientific contacts would bring understanding and harmony. In the 1970s, American representatives may be found at more than a dozen international conferences every day of the year; in contrast with the 28 congresses held between 1840 and 1860. From 1901 to 1910, the number had increased to 790, and by the 1980s it seems likely the number will have increased to several thousands.

Evaluating these trends, no one would argue that free trade and international communications are in themselves harmful or without merit to international relations. Rather, the historian can point out that "this belief in the harmony of interests, economics, free trade and communications as alternatives to war has its origin in the struggle of the rising middle classes against the interference of the state. . . . Free competition in domestic and free trade in the international field were the two fundamental principles upon whose observance the welfare of nations depended." During a certain period in the nineteenth century, "it seemed possible for each nation to expand its sphere of domination—which was understood exclusively in domestic terms—without ever clashing with the also expanding interests of any other nation, in the same way in which free competition between individuals would never result in real conflict but, in the end, only a greater amount of welfare for all." Circumstances in the nineteenth century lent credibility to the doctrine of free trade, but philosophers then and today misled their people in casting such facts and principles in the mold of eternal verities. The German economist Friedrich List explained:

> It is a very common clever device that when anyone has attained the summit of greatness, he kicks away the ladder by which he has climbed up in order to deprive others of the means of climbing up after him. . . . Any nation which by means of protective duties and restrictions on navigation has raised her manufacturing powers and her navigation to such a degree of development that no other nation can sustain free competition with her, can do nothing wiser than to throw away these ladders of her greatness, to preach to other nations the benefits of free trade.[29]

If liberalism suffered from the illusion that war and human conflict would yield to economics and worldwide communication, Marxism promised mankind a deterministic structure that guaranteed these self-same ends through the assurances of history, religion, and science. Not the state, but the classless society was postulated as the end toward which all history was tending. The moral and quasi-religious basis on which the faithful were called upon to accept sacrifices, suffering, and oppression was salvation within, not outside of, history. The full force of Marxism as an ideology of transformation cannot be explained from its standing as history or political religion; its claim as a comprehensive science in the modern scientific era provided its ultimate appeal. It left nothing to chance. It offered the world the capacity to predict history with an exactness and objectivity denied earlier philosophies. In capitalist societies, the class struggle was inevitable, as was the proletarian revolution. Earlier societies might guess at their fate, but Marxism offered a blueprint of societies that was beyond questioning and dispute. Its appeal as a science was the greater because science, not religion, had become the highest end in life for modern man. Science, and in particular Marxist science, would save man from tragedy, suffering, and war.

The Tragic Sense

The tragic sense in religious and political thought has little in common with the dominant world views of the past three centuries. Apparently, men have lost the tragic sense especially in the late twentieth century, despite the fact that we live in an era dominated at almost every point by individual and collective tragedy. Sociologists and a handful of political writers point to at least four characteristics of the twentieth century that have been all-pervasive for at least some people. One is a sense of powerlessness. Living in a mass society in an impersonal technological world, the ordinary citizen feels powerless to shape events. What can he do about nuclear disarmament, the poverty of the cities, or race conflict at home or abroad? In the last years of his life, the world statesman and eminent black diplomatist Dr. Ralph Bunche turned to the problems of the cities and urged that the private foundations call on the nation's social scientists for help in designing a blueprint for what he called "the eradication of the ghetto." Dr. Bunche's call for action got no response from the nation's social scientists or his colleagues in the foundation world. Men such as John D. Rockefeller III, Thomas Watson, Jr., and Douglas Dillon were not persuaded and pointed out that America was powerless to bring about the elimination of a massive social disease, the urban ghetto.

Another characteristic attitude of the twentieth century has been a pervasive sense of hopelessness and despair. Compare the residual optimism in important public statements at the beginning of the second half of the twentieth century (members of President Eisenhower's Commission on National Goals in the 1950s and of the Rockefeller panels) with the valedictory of a leader such as the late Governor Nelson Rockefeller of New York, who frankly acknowledged by 1975 that, for almost every social program initiated by his administration, problems had outrun resources and solutions. C. L. Sulzberger, the foreign correspondent of the New York *Times*, on retirement on December 31, 1977, after forty-four years as a journalist wrote: "How has the world changed in these years? Well, its population has more than doubled, the number of its independent states has multiplied manyfold, and it has entered the nuclear missile age without yet discovering how to feed, house, warm or employ itself, thus reducing war's main causes." He quoted André Malraux: "If it is not a global revolution that we are experiencing, it is our agony that is beginning." Sulzberger asked what has become of the American century so boastfully vaunted less than thirty-five years ago. We had visited the moon at a cost of billions of dollars—and found surprisingly little of interest. Ever faster airplanes have almost done away with the steamship and railroad travel and, for men, time to think. (When I joined the staff of the Rockefeller Foundation in the mid-1950s, the then-president Dean Rusk required that officers traveling to Europe go by steamship at least one way in order "to collect their thoughts and to think.") Sulzberger suggested that, with more than two decades yet to run, the American century's great accomplishment so far had been the New Deal, "which at last began to give momentum to social implications of an eighteenth century revolution" and that "its worst accomplishment was the Vietnam War, which, although its initial goals were by no means so sordid as current history proclaims, was a compound of mismanaged drift, bad generalship, increasing lack of purpose and befuddled leadership at all levels." He concluded: "We learned one paramount thing from that traumatic experience whose ramifications on our soul and society were complex. The mission of the United States is no more one of saving the world by imposing its political system than it is one of retreating from the world into huddled isolationism. Both dreams are now gone."[30]

"Faded dreams" are a part of another increasingly self-evident set of attitudes. We are the victims of a sense of growing doubts about personal values and national goals. The second Rockefeller panel, organized in the late 1960s, completed its work by issuing a few largely technical reports that attracted less attention than the individual writings of some of the members of the specialized panels on food and population. At the end of the studies, hamstrung from the start by charges that they were little more than vehicles for Governor Rockefeller's abortive campaign for the presidency, there was no clarion call for Americans to rally to new or old national purposes. Most of the public opinion polls from that day to the present stress the loss of personal faith of most Americans; surveys show that there has been a decline in church attendance if not church membership. It has proven increasingly difficult for Americans to sustain their faith in religious principles laid down at a time of sheep and shepherds, rather than an age of computers, long unemployment lines, and growing fears and uncertainties abut their capacity to govern themselves.

Finally, a malaise has set in that coincides with the prolonging of human life in the twentieth century. For men, average life expectancy has increased to sixty-nine and for women, seventy-eight, but the beneficiaries ask one another: To what end? What if men have gained long lives and lost their souls? The aged who spend the last years of life awaiting the inevitable end in the hopelessness and often the squalor of nursing homes can hardly be expected to praise the scientists who have given them a few more years of life.

Yet this fourfold manifestation of the tragic dimension of life is largely ignored by the best of our political leaders, at least in their public statements. We face the persistence of human tragedy and are lectured on human well-being. Compare the homilies on religion and morality of a good and decent leader such as President Carter with the enduring truths enunciated by President Lincoln. At the conference on ethics and foreign policy conducted in mid-June, 1977, by the State Department and the faculty of the University of Virginia at Charlottesville (see pages 72–95), the one dimension never mentioned was the tragic element. (This author was one of the organizers and must share responsibility with official Washington.) Our sensitivity to the needs of the weak, the suffering, and the powerless seldom goes beyond a feeling of pity; and even pity is in short supply. (For example, consider the rather callous statements of a Christian president, Jimmy Carter, on abortion and the needs of lower-class women who cannot afford abortions.)

These signs of the times, reflected in the statements not of evil but of good men, may reflect the triumph of materialism over morality. They also show how difficult it is to be compassionate in a realistic age. In possibly his only work on tragedy and politics, the theologian Niebuhr wrote: "Pity is curiously mixed with both love and reverence. Love for equals is difficult. We love what is weak and suffers. It appeals to our strength without challenging it. . . . If their strength is triumphant our reverence may turn into fear or even into hatred. Triumphant strength is usually mixed with force or guile. Therefore our greatest reverence is reserved for the strength which we can pity because it is too pure to be triumphant." When we feel pity, it arises because we discern meanings in the human drama not comprehended by the actors. In Niebuhr's words: "In actual life pathos overwhelms tragedy and the spectator feels only pity without reverence. . . . If there was a greater degree of comprehension by the participants of the drama of the forces which determine their action, they might be aroused to some heroic defiance of the forces and fates which enthrall them and hurl them to destruction."[31] This is true of the victims of warfare in our times. They have loyalty and courage. However, they do not often struggle against the anarchic forces that bring war, often because they cannot comprehend them and are powerless to do anything about them.

On the other hand, it is too simple to reserve pure tragedy for the occasional hero of nobility and strength. The genuinely tragic is curiously compounded with the pitiful. Victims of fate and of history's forces become enmeshed by both their strengths and their weaknesses, by moral purposes and moral blindness. In pure tragedy the suffering is self-inflicted; the hero brings suffering upon himself. Promethean tragedy exemplifies the perennial self-destruction of man caused, not by others, but by his over-reaching himself. It is manifest in Christianity by man's imagining himself to be God. Will historians of diplomacy say that the United States experienced this form of tragedy in Vietnam?

Pity, irony, and tragedy represent differing dimensions of and reactions to the human condition, each calling for separate definitions. Tragedy is distinguished by its realization of the unbridgeable gulf between human aspirations and attainments. Such an awareness points to the necessity to live in an imperfect world with fear and uncertainty. The human drama never reaches a wholly successful conclusion or a single triumphal ending. Its little acts and scenes go on with unending trials and the need for testing, each full of despair as well as momentary exaltation. Learning to live with fear and uncertainity is another facet of the tragic sense. There is an inevitable tension between the viability of righteousness and the viability of one's own moral base. It requires the morally sensitive to ask the timeless question: How do we reduce the immense human costs of social and political change? How do we limit the effects of tragedy while accepting their inevitability? How can we act courageously knowing our actions may bring a tragic ending?

In summary, an acceptance of the tragic element in politics and international relations demands an understanding of a single persistent and stubborn truth. Tragedy is not an accidental turn of events that human reason or social engineering can once and for all overcome. From birth to death, in every dimension of life, pain and suffering are inseparable from man's gratifications. Human anguish is greater because tragedy not infrequently occurs when a person reaches out for goals and rewards denied him by his nature and the recalcitrance of external reality. We feel pity for someone struck down by forces over which he has no control. We see tragedy in the endless and fateful struggle of strong men and women to conquer adversity or limitations that they cannot or will not accept. Yet, in the end, the distinction between those who are pitied and those who are victims of tragedy is less than complete, is not absolute. For weak and strong alike, history has its tragic cycle in life and death.

Man is anxious, feels insecurity, demands an end to anxiety, and seeks to dominate his environment and his fellows. However inadvertently, the quest for security and dominance adds to personal or national anxiety, conflict and insecurity. One man's quest for security breeds fear and insecurity in others. An absolute predicament or irreducible dilemma results which lies at the core of human conflict. It is illusory to suppose, in so insecure a world, that fear, anxiety, and uncertainty, or the resulting conflict and tragedy, can be permanently eliminated. So long as the geometry of human conflict remains at this fundamental level, so long as contemporaries refuse to recognize its sources, and so long as its forms and character represent a terrible knot beyond the ingenuity of man to untie, all history's panaceas and utopias will be irrelevant. In such times, interpreters who would claim a hearing must come to terms with the tragic element in international politics.

Science, Morality, and Transnationalism

Historians have for centuries debated the purpose of history. Some agree that the study of history should focus on objective reality; its aim should be to report on people, institutions, and material factors in the life of a group or society. Others insist that historians must not ignore the life of the mind, what people believed, thought, and felt and how this influenced the social forces and human tendencies at work in civilization. To distinguish between these two approaches, we can compare historical writing and the philosophy of history. Historians generally seek to report and describe past events. Philosophers of history ordinarily undertake one additional task; they ask *why* events took place as they did, attempting to fathom the meaning and to formulate principles of history. It is not always possible to draw a sharp line between the two approaches, but the standards of a historian are unlikely to correspond at all points with those of a philosopher. Although both Thucydides and Augustine formulated principles of history, only the former wrote narrative history. The historian is judged by the accuracy with which he portrays the past; the philosopher will be judged by the value and significance of his world view for understanding the present.

Religious Universalism

Augustine of Hippo wrote as a philosopher of history and a religious thinker of the age that still bears his name. According to the historian Christopher Dawson, "he was, to a far greater degree than any emperor or general or barbarian war-lord, a maker of history and a builder of the bridge which was to lead him from the old world to the new."[32] He was born in a Roman province in North Africa in 354 of a Christian mother and a pagan father. For nine years a follower of Manicheanism, he became a Catholic and was consecrated bishop of Hippo, North Africa, in 395. He wrote 118 treatises including the most celebrated spiritual autobiography of all times, *The Confessions*, depicting his personal and religious struggles. His most comprehensive work was *City of God*, a profound account of the life, thought, and strivings of ancient and early Christian man.

The world of Augustine was shaken by the invasion of Rome by Alaric the Goth on August 24, 410. For the first time in its long history, Rome was conquered and ravished. There followed a stream of polemics in which pagan writers charged that the conquest had occurred under a Christian emperor and demonstrated the debilitating effects of Christianity on the security of the Roman Empire. Christianity, by propounding an ethic of self-denial and renunciation of worldly concerns, had weakened the citizens' loyalty and commitment to the state. Also, Rome had once seen its destiny as bound up with the worship of pagan gods. When Christianity supplanted paganism, the latter's gods prophesied vengeance. The disaster that befell the Empire was due to the enfeeblement by Christianity of the civic spirit and the angering of the pagan gods.

Augustine answered one of his critics, Volusianus, by pointing out that the pagans had taught the same virtues, such as not repaying injury with injury, for which Christians were being condemned. Moreover, Christian citizen-soldiers were not enjoined to lay down their arms or to refuse service to the state. Internal decay, not the Christianity of the emperors, had brought ruin to the empire; pagan writers, including Sallust and Juvenal, had themselves written of the far-reaching effects of immorality and society's other vices. The task confronting Rome was to arrest its internal corruption and instill in its citizens a regard for virtue. Augustine did not deny the existence of a once-prosperous, though pagan, Rome but saw its achievements as part of God's providential plan. Because of the civic virtues of the pagans, Rome attained a certain temporal efficiency. On a broader canvas, Augustine wrote about the history of the two cities—the City of God and the city of this world. His classic work details the two histories and the tension existing between them. The whole world from its beginnings has as its unique end a holy society for which everything has been made and from which the smallest event and humblest individual takes meaning and intelligibility. The City of God is ruled by love of God; the city of men, by a distorted love of self.

> There are two loves, the one of which is holy, the other unholy; one social, the other individualist; one takes heed of the common utility because of the heavenly society, the others reduces even the

commonweal to its own ends, because of a proud lust of domination; the one is subject to God, the other sets itself up as a rival to
God; the one is serene, the other tempestuous; the one peaceful,
the other quarrelsome; the one prefers truthfulness to deceitful
praises, the other is avid of praise; the one is friendly, the other
jealous; the one desires for its neighbor what it would for itself,
the other is desirous of lording it over its neighbor; the one directs its efforts to the neighbor's good, the other to its own.

If love was the law of the City of God, however, the law of the republic
was justice. However, "there could be no city of injustice if there were
no City of true justice. Every society worthy of the name is, therefore,
either the City of God or defined in relation to the City of God." Illus-
trating the inescapable tension between the two cities, Augustine wrote:
"Rome never was a republic because true justice never had a place in it.
. . . But accepting the more probable definition of a republic, I admit
there was a republic of a kind." [33]

It was the question of Rome's status as a city, a republic, and an au-
thentic society that preoccupied Augustine. Primitive religion had dominated, not a potential earthly universal society, but the family and the
ancient city. The family was founded on the religious worship of the
hearth (the household fire), and each family was a spiritually closed society. Brotherhood was not extended to strangers who did not worship
at the same sacred fire or honor the same dead ancestors. Families
were united by more than necessity, security, or affection; a man loved
his home as he now loves his church. Moving toward a universal society
meant overcoming the separation of families, first through grouping
them into *gentes* or associations, then into tribes, and lastly into cities.
Other gods, such as Zeus and Heracles, reigned above household gods.
Societies originated and developed as religion expanded its sphere. A
universal society and true unity existed only in the City of God and on
earth when there was only a single God-created man. Physically, all men
who have sprung from this single ancestor are related; morally, all men
recognize their common origins and their membership in one family.
"None of the faithful," Etienne Gilson writes, "could doubt that all men,
regardless of race, color or appearance, have their origin in the first
man created by God and that this first man was alone of his kind. There
was no doubt in St. Augustine's mind that God himself had created the
human race . . . so that men might understand how pleasing unity, even
in diversity, was to God; nor could they doubt that their unity was a
family unity." [34]

Such unity embraced all men, even the pygmies (although Augustine speculated about their existence) and the Sciopodes who protected themselves from the rays of the sun by the shadow of one foot and the Cynocephali who had heads like dogs and barked. God, Augustine explained, beautified the world through many diverse mortal beings all descended from the stock of Adam. Augustine's universalism rested on Christian brotherhood born of a common ancestor but realized ultimately not in a world society but in the City of God. Or in Gilson's words: "St. Augustine did not bequeath to his successors the ideal of a universal human city united in view of purely temporal ends." [35] The City of God existed to inspire men with an unquenchable desire to organize the earth into a single society made in the image and likeness of a heavenly city. It mattered less that man's feeble attempts to build a universal society were frustrated. The light of universal brotherhood and of a perfect city would continue to illuminate man's search for concord, justice, and virtue.

Scientific Transnationalism

To reread Augustine's classic writings is to understand the difference between his time and ours in the quest for morality. In place of Augustine's universalism based on religion, large regions of the world have turned instead to science. They have answered yes to the question: Can science save us? Men are engaged in a conscious revolt against the historic restraints that religion and society have imposed on free inquiry. They see in the physical sciences the sole possibility for progress and growth. In the modern era, until quite recently at least, we have heard more about scientific breakthroughs than about imitations of Christ. From the industrial revolution to the present, societies have tended to pursue the good life through material advances made possible by science and technology. Equal opportunity for all peoples is linked with material advancement; for example, economists tell us that higher incomes and increased employment for women will draw them into the labor market, assure greater equality, and thus lower the birthrate in an overpopulated world. Even critics of science acknowledge that the strident debate between the spokesmen for extreme free enterprise and extreme collectivism can be moderated only through "the resources of an inductive rather than a deductive social science." [36] Based on such inquiries, important policy decisions by competing social and economic systems can be continuously reviewed and amended in the light of new evidence.

Yet science, particularly in its application to human and especially moral problems, is plagued by persistent illusions and misconceptions. The first illusion is the myth of the existence of a true science of human behavior free of all presuppositions. Objective social science today is given the wholly imaginary character of an approach to autonomous, incontrovertible, and self-evident facts. In practice, responsible and open-minded scholars have learned the impossibility of giving any form or meaning to social research without some sort of framework or rough outline for organizing their research. Ironically, underlying assumptions, such as the possibility of progress or the perfectibility of man, determine the focus of scientific inquiry and shape its conclusions. A second illusion results from the concealment of the failure of all those conclusions to conform to the facts. Modern culture, despite all its scientific progress, is caught up in egregious miscalculations. The brave new world of the twentieth century, proudly predicted by eighteenth-century rationalists if men would only disavow all their otherworldly illusions, scarcely resembles utopia. Such contradictions and errors inherent in a rationalist and scientific approach probably stem from the dual meaning of *scientific*. On the one hand, science as empiricism means humility before the facts; on the other hand, science as rationalism means invoking logical coherence as the test of truth. The two connotations may be in conflict because the test of rational coherence prompts men to deny obvious facts if they fall outside of a coherent scheme.

Another fallacy of present-day social science results from the position of the observer who is a participant as well. The natural scientist in his laboratory has no mission except uncovering the truth about his work; but the vision of the social scientist is beclouded by ideological taint, national loyalty, and his own individual social and economic status. He cannot be fully objective, for he grounds his observations on his place in history and his own individual membership in a given society and group. Not a detached mind, but the self with all its passions and interests and endless capacity for rationalization is the agent of the social scientific method. A fourth illusion arises from modern concepts of causation and prediction, which underestimate the complexity of causation and the play of contingent forces. Prediction is possible in terms of rough probabilities, but as Niebuhr has argued: "In both nature and history each new thing is only one of an infinite number of possibilities which might have emerged at that particular juncture. It is for this reason that, though we can trace a series of causes in retrospect, we can never predict the future with accuracy."[37] History has its recurrences and cyclical trends; but a particular leader, the effects of bad weather or an accident, or an unforeseen event may channel history in unexpected ways. Finally, the most persistent illusion holds that science is the profoundest fruit of culture because it is the latest. Auguste Comte's conception of history as moving from a religious to a metaphysical to a scientific age is partly true insofar as it describes a historical trend. Its value judgment that the latest attainments of the culture are wisest and best, however, is of doubtful validity, particularly its corollary that the human situation is ambiguous merely because of a scientific lag or a residual ignorance that science has not yet corrected. What may indeed be required is a movement from science to philosophy to correct the movement from philosophy to science, or a recovery of the wisdom of philosophy and the humility and magnanimity accompanying transcendent religion.

Science suffers most, however, from its curious mixture of a fatuous optimism about the future and a lack of concern for the urgencies of the day not yet susceptible to the scientific method. About the latter, Niebuhr once prophesied that, if we should ever fall into the abyss of an atomic war, we could be quite certain that on the eve of the conflict some psychological association would bestow a medal upon an outstanding scientist for having found the key to the problem of eliminating aggression from human life.[38] Regarding science's optimism, Niebuhr expressed grave doubts that statesmen who were scientific could consider such problems as the control of atomic energy from the standpoint of a universal mind freed of all national bias. Statesmen pay heed to the national interest more consistently than do the scientists, not because they are less intelligent but because they carry responsibilities to those they serve.

Yet science—whatever its illusions, its false optimism, and its lack of concern for immediate problems that lie beyond scientific control—has transformed the globe and man's understanding of it. Thanks to science, we live in a shrinking world. Worldwide revolutions in transportation, communications, and war have depended on science. Presidents and secretaries of state on global missions conduct diplomacy in successive foreign capitals, not because they are wiser or more resourceful but because jet travel has made nations close neighbors. Early warning and peace enforcement systems rest on science. Science is the catalyst for bringing one world into being—a world united not by moral consensus or a universal sense of brotherhood or an awareness of man's common origins (as discussed by St. Augustine) but by an extensive network of interdependent relationships around the world. More than that, science, which is rational and objective, offers a firmer basis for universalism than does morality, which is dominated by subjectivity and emotions. Even moral principles will eventually be brought under scientific control, for to the scientist in the postbehavioral era of social sciences, values constitute nothing more than special kinds of facts. American social scientists proceed not on the basis of hunches or intuition but through methodologies and paraphernalia of scientific investigation that provide "powerful insights," which earlier studies and writings had lacked. Present-day scholars are not armchair thinkers but men and women who refuse to accept what cannot be tested and proven in the laboratory of life.

Transnationalism Reconsidered

Leading American scholars explain transnational relations by saying that the world of foreign policy has been transformed by "frontier crossers," whether diplomats or tourists, financiers or multinational corporation executives, airline pilots or students. While the number of "frontier crossers" merely illustrate what is happening to change the world, their increase is quantifiable and measurable by scientific techniques. Interdependence need no longer be based on speculative thought but can be tested by the number of telephone calls or letters passing between Great Britain and Poland or Nigeria and Ghana. Social scientists tell us that the explosion of worldwide communications testifies to the lessening importance of the nation-state—if not to its demise. Moreover, transnational associations, which are for the most part nongovernmental international bodies, are bringing about the erosion of national loyalties. Citizens who formerly thought of themselves as Englishmen or Nigerians now see themselves as part of a worldwide community of interlocking groups and peoples. In the educational world, the flow of ideas has become worldwide. Students choose holiday study programs in foreign countries, and professors intermingle in conferences with other professors, one year in Boston, the next in Tokyo, and thereafter in Nairobi, Santiago, or Montreal. Finally, foreign policy problems that once could be considered wholly within a national or regional context now are present around the globe. Secretaries of state describe this phenomenon by noting that issues on the periphery of a nation's sphere of interest have a way of moving to the center; for example, Korea, Vietnam, and Iran. Apparently, it is no longer possible to think strategically in the language of vital interests when the threat to international security crops up everywhere in the world, given the realities of the Cold War. Problems are interconnected and linkages are required if lasting solutions are to be found. Transnationalism, not rationalism, has come to dominate foreign policy concerns.

The critics of this pervasive and controlling viewpoint of international relations question all three of the premises and assumptions of the transnational approach. First, they ask whether the hunger for measurement of the quantifiers and their conclusions about the facts of international contacts are not quite obviously self-evident and visible on the surface and whether, through indifference to meanings less subject to quantification, some scientific interpretations may not be more misleading than helpful. No one can doubt that certain peoples in a growing number of countries have more contact with one another than they did fifty or one hundred years ago. The factors responsible are increasing population, greater incomes and wealth, and undoubted improvements in the technical means of sending communications. Quantifiers, who tend to see what is important as what can be counted and measured, point to such technical and material changes and their immediate consequences without examining nonmaterial and intangible attachments to persistent national loyalties and the intensity of values and beliefs. Because more Canadians and Americans in business and education talk more often by phone hardly proves that anti-Americanism is dead in Canada or that Americans as a whole are any less suspicious of their neighbors to the north than in the past. If interdependence is to be viewed realistically, the political and foreign policy context within which communications take place ought not be ignored. It is possible to demonstrate that contacts often increase during periods of the most intense national rivalry; for example, communications between Soviet and American leaders by hot line increase at moments of deepening crisis. Transnationalism is not always a concomitant of peace and order; it generates conflict as often as harmony.

Critics of transnationalism note further that the debate over the decline of nationalism is a repetition of a historic controversy and raises issues that were debated in the first three decades of the twentieth century in the liberal democratic world. The new social scientists, with their undisguised contempt for history, ignore the fact that certain transnational practices were, if anything, more in evidence before 1914. During the Napoleonic Wars, British scientists such as Michael Faraday attended international congresses in Paris, the capital of the enemy.

Travel by train without passports or visas was possible anywhere in Europe, except in Russia, Spain, Portugal and the Ottoman Empire. (Their use in the Iberian Peninsula was limited, however, to certain periods.) European diplomats served the foreign offices of successive European countries, and Swiss mercenaries fought for various national armies. A plethora of books and studies written in the period between the two World Wars were intended to show that nationalism was on the wane, prompting Hitler to write: "Other people's illusions about power were my great opportunity." The academician's illusion then and now rests in part on the belief that a few limited and segmental relations between specialized national groups across national boundaries are representative of political and social relations as a whole.

Yet the majority of the world's peoples do not partake in such relations but live out their lives, not within nation-states, but in tribal and village groups. Frequently their mind-set is shaped by such a factor as the limitation of reading material; for example, 95 percent of the Chinese people were restricted to a daily reading diet of the writings of former Chairman Mao. Within such a state, mental restrictions have increased not diminished. Similar mental prohibitions exist throughout the world Communist movement, and Communist leaders in countries such as Italy probably support NATO only because they fear for their security with the passing of Tito in neighboring Yugoslavia. The Communist International, a long-standing example of transnationalism, has lost much of its force because men such as Marshal Tito and Nicolae Ceausescu depend for their power more on national constituencies than on Moscow. Moreover, the world's crises involving interdependence are triggered not by the multinational corporations that symbolize transnationalism but by national governments. The global oil crisis beginning in 1973 was brought about by the demands of the oil-producing nations, working through intergovernmental bodies such as OPEC, for higher rates of return on the sale of national resources to the industrial countries. Consumer states have tried to counter these demands through opposing intergovernmental coalitions except when countries such as France, Japan, and England have decided to go it alone. National policies by national governments motivated by national reasons on both the consumer and producer sides have constituted the main source of the energy problem. Multinational corporations have been thrust aside when vital national interests are involved.[39]

Finally, critics ask whether the most costly blunders in foreign policy have not occurred when national interests have been subordinated.

America may have suffered its greatest defeat in Vietnam because it imagined that the Indochina problem could be explained as an international conspiracy controlled by Moscow or Peking rather than as a long-standing nationalist conflict and a revolt against all foreign domination. Transnationalism and the ending of national rivalries, some European commentators say, has affected American thought in the mid–twentieth century, much as the hope of the Second Coming affected medieval Europe. Woodrow Wilson went empty-handed to the Paris Peace Conference without a well-thought-out plan to protect American national interests, leading Lloyd George to say that he "tried to apply the straight footrule of his ideals to the gnarled and knotty trunks of European nationalism." American leaders after World War II believed that a new international organization of all nations would eliminate the traditional means of controlling national expansionism. Such failures of the transnational outlook to provide guidance for wise foreign policy decisions should at least give prophets and pundits pause.

The fatal flaw, however, of transnationalism as a guide to immediate policy choices, ironically enough given its scientific pretensions, is its disregard of facts and realities. Riding what they consider the wave of the future, the transnational social scientists apparently feel no need to attend to visible and stubborn facts. I. L. Claude, of the University of Virginia faculty, reviewing one of the innumerable publications of the Council on Foreign Relations in its multimillion-dollar foundation-financed project on the 1980s, observes: "The author, starting from the premise that international relations have been fundamentally transformed, makes no effort to balance his analysis by considering continuities along with changes; one is simply invited to assume the overpowering significance of the latter."[40] For example, the commonsense knowledge that force has not been eradicated in wars of national liberation is conveniently overlooked, and the stigma of being out-of-date is imputed to those who analyze national rivalries by characterizing their approach as Westphalian thinking. Apparently it is better—and more scientific—to count letters and weigh parcels passing between any two countries than to analyze political relationships.

Concealing or obscuring facts is nowhere more conspicuous than in discussions of transnational groupings or political and economic communities of nation-states. (One critic has observed that transnationalism is limited to the unimportant aspects of international relations). Integration theory in world politics, which has a strong social scientific bias, has demonstrated a surprising disregard for facts. What remains a genuine puzzle both to "integrationists" and their critics is how theories can be constructed when the viable examples are so sparse. When integration is approached as a fact rather than an aspiration, case studies dwindle to the one significant if quite limited example of the European community. Integration in Eastern Europe hardly corresponds to the model of free and voluntary associations; it would appear in practice merely to be another name for Soviet imperialism. Even within Western Europe, given the slow pace and stubborn roadblocks thrown up by the founding states (France is but one example), true integration remains more a hope for the future than a present all-determining reality. Outside Europe, nationalism in Africa and Asia—leading to the multiplication of so many new states that the world's number has tripled since 1945—points to the opposite conclusion of that propounded by the "integrationists." Nationhood there, long delayed by the dominance of the colonial powers, has assumed a more passionate and emotional character than in most other parts of the world. Nor are there any significant signs of nationalism's being on the wane. In the early 1950s, Americans, Englishmen, and Canadians who participated in institution building in higher education in Africa and Asia were comparatively free to function visibly as educational advisers and even as heads of departments or deans of important faculties. Today the most experienced educationists from the developed countries have found that they could be effective only by working behind the scene, making themselves available for counsel and advice but rarely occupying official positions. What is true of higher education is true *a fortiori* in agriculture and in population and environmental assistance. Outsiders at best, in the favorite words of the public administrators, can remain on tap, not on top.

Given the persistence of extreme nationalism, it is difficult to understand the stubborn resistance of transnational thinkers to facts. One explanation may be that the study of international politics has proceeded by starts and stops from one approach to another, each designed to hold out fresh hope for the grim and conflict-ridden world. The harsh and bitter struggles of nations-in-arms have so appalled and revolted men of conscience that they have joined in a headlong rush to substitute a more peaceful international order. In recent years scientists, remembering their role in discovering the know-how for producing weapons of mutual annihilation, have felt a particular responsibility. Those physical scientists who have turned from the slow and painful discipline of their laboratories have infused efforts to understand the word *politics* with a frenzied reformist zeal. Social scientists, intrigued by the power of science to propel men to the moon, have joined the crusade, adopting techniques they belived were responsible for physical science's success stories. Along the way they have lost sight of realities that common-sense observation should have taught them were problems to be faced. The immense prestige of the physical sciences, coupled with the march of self-conscious social science reformers, has prevented their seeing the world as it is. Transnationalism is a premature form of universalism because the prevailing forces of international politics are still moving along other paths. Its impact is confined to aspects of international politics which exclude in large measure the vital interests of states. However popular as a concept, its significance awaits authoritative study by realists as well as idealists.

The Moral Problem Again

The search for viable concepts of morality and foreign policy, therefore, has not ended with the scientific revolution nor the first faint signs of a transnational community. The task of the moralist has become if anything more perplexing, given the state of world politics. Gone are the moral certainties of St. Augustine and the convictions about universal brotherhood. The late Roscoe Pound wrote: "We are told that observation shows us social interdependence through similarity of interest and through division of labor as the central fact in human existence."[41] For Pound, however, philosophy—not science—promised new theories and conceptions for understanding interdependence and its application and meaning for discrete areas of the law. A similar note has been struck in more recent times by the Indonesian cultural historian and diplomat Soedjatmoko. To an Asian, what is missing from most present-day American debates about morality and foreign policy is concern with a philosophy of history or the destination of mankind. Every previous historical era had such perspectives, but for our times all controlling world views have been shattered. Not only have the millenial ideas of Christianity come under question, but the promised Communist utopia has been replaced by Soviet and Chinese authoritarianism and oppression. Man's loss of faith and his growing incapacity for deeply rooted beliefs have some connection with his passion to crowd as much as possible into the present. We live within shifting time frames; when we can no longer accept the hope of life after death, the time frame of peace and justice changes. (It is worth noting that some Moslems continue to believe in the certainty of life after death with effects on political fanaticism and wars of conquest).

If there is a way back to a more coherent and defensible view of morality, it is through awareness that the present world scene has elements of both continuity and change. We remain perilously suspended between a once-healthy but forgotten religious universalism and a too-pretentious definition of the unities of modern-day transnationalism. Whether we like it or not, morality continues to work itself out in a world populated by nation-states whose needs call for an unending search for recognition of the needs of others. A too narrow nationalism imperils civilization as it has in the past, but exhortations and scientific declarations show little prospect of bringing about its demise. One of the most poignant examples of the moral predicament that we face in moving from nationalism to universalism is the present position of UNESCO. That international (transnational) organization founded on the assumed universalism of scientific humanism has become a fierce battleground in the struggle between developed and underdeveloped nation-states. Basically, the problem of transnationalism is rooted in differences in perception of the role and character of the nation-state. To scientists, whether natural or social scientists, and no less to the great corporations, the present nation-state is outmoded. The logic of the situation in the developed world requires that men transcend national loyalties. In the Third World, the problem is almost the direct opposite. There the nation-state limited by the unstable character of states that do not reflect ethnic realities but ancient colonial boundaries has emerged as a necessary instrument for the development of particular freedoms, social justice, and national unity. It is also the negotiating unit toward the attainment of a better world. This negotiating process goes on day after day even within so-called transnational organizations.

It will not do, therefore, to claim that the "blind groping" and endless process of adapting moral principles to complex and intractable realities are ancient tasks from which science and transnationalism have liberated us. The demands for political and moral wisdom are greater than ever before. Man needs all the resources at his command: wise statecraft, diplomatic insight, moral maxims, moral reasoning, technical understanding, science, and practical morality. To claim that all these taken together would solve the moral problem is a counsel of perfection. To believe that science alone has all the answers is nothing short of a crippling illusion.

❖ Conclusions

Practical Morality and Prudence

The search for norms and values that can provide practical standards for evaluating American foreign policy, or any nation's foreign policy, is primarily a quest for viable and coherent guides to action. Those who seek moral answers must find their way through the twisted wreckage of a multitude of earlier endeavors that have failed from an excess of either cynicism or too lofty idealism. Thinkers who wrestle with the ambiguities and contradictions of the moral problem, moreover, do so within a concrete historical and political context. Attitudes and policies by governments toward international morality create an intellectual climate, and the response of national and international publics reinforces or conflicts with these pronouncements and policies. A regime may come to power proclaiming certain goals and purposes; popular opinions are shaped by its declarations. The climate for thinking and writing about political morality in the administrations of Woodrow Wilson, Franklin D. Roosevelt, Richard M. Nixon, or Jimmy Carter has differed. At one time, the student of morality may be disposed to counter one set of attitudes or illusions (or to defend them); at another time, changing circumstances may lead him to see the moral problem in a different light. The social observer stands within history; he is fated to be a creature of the national and political environment about which he writes. The physical or biological scientist in his laboratory, by contrast, is to a considerable degree free of these constraints. His position in the political order or his judgments of political attitudes or approaches usually are not a determining factor in his basic research, whether on cancer or on the physical properties of an object in space.

Fortunately, the moral philosopher or social scientist is not bereft of supporting resources possessing objective and lasting value. Practical legal and political philosophy provides signposts of recurrent concerns in ethics and politics. Although this approach may offend the pure theorists of political thought, it focuses the observer on the central issues. From ancient and modern legal and political writings, the student of morality may glean new insights; from society and past political practice, he may gain an awareness of the political problem and the moral predicament, thus enabling him to say: "This predicament I have truly known; I have not merely understood it in my mind, I have felt it in my bones, it belongs to me; through it I have acquired a wiser moral insight." [1]

Legal theorists such as Edmond Cahn and Paul Freund challenge the nihilism which contends that any talk of right and wrong drives man beyond practical reason to flights of fancy, speculation, and dreams. They do not assert that moral decisions are matters of simple choice or that the ends and means involved are readily clarified. On the contrary, they point to the manifold factors that breed confusion and moral uncertainty. For example, Cahn states: "Dazzling economic and social transformations, the popularization of scientific method and the cynicism bred of world wars, the observation of foreign societies and exotic customs, the growth of relativism and hedonism in philosophy, and the development of a sophisticated semantics—all have challenged the established landmarks and eradicated the familiar lines between moral and immoral." [2] As Cahn suggests, the obliteration of moral landmarks has led not to the healthy doubts of the inquiring mind but to the sickening and panicky doubts that come as man loses his bearings. The legal theorists further ask, if moral uncertainty prevails and if the words of once-authoritative moral spokesmen such as the clergy have lost much of their authority, what are we to say of those who commit heinous crimes without the capacity of judging right from wrong. In law, we are told, he who cannot distinguish right from wrong is held to be not guilty by reason of insanity. If such is the legal test and the perplexities of present-day moral choice have left men floundering in a state approaching incapacity, does this suggest that a judgment of mental and moral incompetence must be rendered upon us all?

Law provides certain resources, however, and a moral and intellectual framework for resolving this paradox. Legally, the test of sanity in criminal courts is not whether a man has the capacity for distinguishing between right and wrong in general. Such a test, we are told, "would be enough to perplex the brain of an Aristotle; certainly no judge or jury would be able to administer it with any hope of obtaining intelligent results." In practice, the actual test is whether, in the particular case, the mental incompetence of the person disabled him from knowing that what he was doing was wrong. If so disabled, he is considered insane; if not, he is held to be sane and responsible. For the judge, "although the rule has its faults, it does not require the impossible." To put the question of moral competence in a more general context:

> So far as the moral experience is comparable to the judicial process, the American lawyer would applaud our concentrating on what is unique, immediate and apprehensible in each specific moral crisis. He would say that for too many centuries men have looked up to the distant and immutable stars as ensigns of the moral law; that though such heaven-gazing may be useful to inculcate sentiments of reverence and humility, it furnishes little or no understanding of the concrete values that collide at any human crossroads.[3]

One underlying thesis of the present study (which lies outside the field of jurisprudence and legal theory) rests on the assumption that the viability of an approach to political morality can be measured by the help it offers for understanding and action when "concrete values collide at any human crossroads." Most of the landmarks in general philosophy tend to concentrate on overall values, not concrete values that collide and compete. The goal of moral conduct has been defined as the attainment of the good or virtuous life. Over the course of three millenia of political writing, the good has frequently been defined either as happiness or righteousness. One group of thinkers has viewed happiness as something attainable by man through a discovery of the points of equilibrium and harmony for the intellectual, emotional, and instructive aspects of personality. Another group has seen it as at best a temporary condition, more likely to occur with "the cure of some disease, the lifting of some yoke, the reconciliation of some conflict or the satisfaction of some appetite."[4] If the former state of happiness is one reserved for the aristocratic few who can attain such inner harmony, the latter is seen as democratic in scope because it deals with the suffering, the anxiety, and the continual succession of problems that have always filled so large a part of human life. If happiness as inner harmony and order was a characteristic of Greek thought, happiness as the limitation of suffering and pain for the greatest number has been a first principle of utilitarianism.

Those who define the good as righteousness follow yet another and more unitary course of thought.

> Since the good is equivalent to the right—morality has no concern with other values; the conscience may perhaps consult an advisory cabinet of world advantages and utilities, but it must finally arrive at and live by its own determinations. At its conceived best, this view may be called monarchic; it not only establishes a single internal ruler of the individual's moral commonwealth but also annoints him, the individual man, as sovereign of the good in his own life.[5]

The strength of this view lies in its stress on individual moral responsibility. Its risks lie in a certain ethical perfectionism and history's lesson that nothing can be crueler than righteousness, that the corruption of the best all too often becomes the worst.

Most philosophical discussions of happiness and righteousness have limited utility for politics, and more particularly for international politics, because of their generality and abstractness and their remoteness from fundamental human problems. A leading contributor to the philosophy of international politics writes: "I entered the University of Frankfurt in 1923. I decided to study philosophy; for philosophy, so I thought, would answer my quest for the meaning of human existence and unravel the mysteries of the universe. I was to be profoundly disappointed."[6] Having listened impatiently to a lengthy discourse on the minute differences between Bishop Berkeley's and David Hume's philosophy of knowledge, the young Morgenthau asked if the sense of "great wonderment" that Aristotle considered the crux of philosophy was not the irrational element that drove philosophic inquiry forward. The professor, a specialist on epistemology, dismissed the question as irrelevant because philosophy was essentially a rationalistic endeavor.

The generality of philosophic writings poses the most serious problem for ethics and foreign policy. We know, looking back to primitive religious and animistic rites, that the "good was generally set down in commands too terse and dogmatic . . . for exceptions of time, place, and circumstance, and, since the commands came from an assumedly unchanging source, they were themselves unchangeable." The debate over contextual ethics and the charge by present-day critics that recognizing differences in moral standards will lead inevitably to their demise obscure the ancient character of the discussion. Throughout the history of moral discourse, moral standards have had their own peculiar textures and degrees of pliability. Thus moral excellence is impossible for anyone who deals with a standard without taking its context and setting into account. "Some standards can be bent without injury and some will not bend at all; some standards allow for the urgency of passing needs; some standards will become peremptory only in a precise and rather specialized social setting and will yield everywhere else to the demands of custom or convenience."[7] Then too there are the merely transient, ceremonial, or ritualistic standards which intertwine with the ethical, leading the unthoughtful observer to see in the fall of the one the fateful destruction of the other.

In international politics, these distinctions take on special importance because of the sanctionless nature of much international law and the precariousness of national security. Discussions that ignore the peculiar texture of ethics and foreign policy are more likely to be harmful than constructive. Principles of international law pay tribute to this fact by balancing two principles: *pacta sunt servanda* (treaties ought to be observed) and *rebus sic stantibus* (circumstances change obligations). Compulsory jurisdiction provisions of adherence by nation-states to the judgments of the International Court of Justice are hedged with "reservations." Through their application of the historic concept of "reason of state," nations define international morality to coincide with the demands of national survival. Legal rules and standards are peremptory only when national interest is not endangered. The merely ceremonial in foreign policy may appear to its high priests to be inextricably bound up with enduring moral and legal precepts. To the practitioners of statecraft, however, adherence to pacts outlawing all warfare (such as the Kellogg-Briand Treaty or the Pact of Paris) partakes more of ritual than of serious foreign policy commitments.

Nevertheless, however much foreign policy practitioners emphasize the importance of the concrete in moral choices, separating the particular case from the general principle or set of principles is not in itself sufficient for a theory of international morality. The playful barbs of the lawyers that commend the isolation of moral or legal issues from excessive generalizations divorced from reality are useful in delimiting legal judgments. In T. R. Powell's tart phrase: "If you can think of a thing, inextricably attached to something else, without thinking about the thing it is attached to, then you have a legal mind."[8] Such reminders help the judge to remember that he is not God, or for that matter the legislature. They follow the broad contours of the law; but they exclude that remote, collateral, and prejudicial evidence which is precisely the ethicist's focus in seeking to fix moral responsibility.

Morality, as distinct from legal analysis, cannot escape issues of interconnectedness; its spectrum both vertically and horizontally is broader than the law's. Even the law, however—while limiting itself to the case, the reception of rules, and the trial, to say nothing of the judgment or the decree which in common law involves categorical sanctions (the defendant is liable to pay the plaintiff's damages or not)—must seek for new connections and new statements more satisfying than the old. Law, which emphasizes continuity, also needs to be creative; and creativity, in Jerome Bruner's view, involves a tension between vitality and technique, between passion and decorum, between the "frenzy of a mathematical insight and the decorum of an equation." Because of its inherent discipline, the law may obscure or minimize innovation. In this, it is in many ways reminiscent of the remark of a Latin American visitor: "In my country we boast of being socialist, but we are not; in your country, you boast that you are not, but you are." If creativity in the law is too upsetting to those who require the maintenance of certain dependable and legitimate expectations, creative ambiguity provides another channel for bringing about change. The criticism of particular judicial decisions as merely reflecting unprincipled or unarticulated trends tends to overlook the value of decisions that "moved in a certain direction but left open the turns that might be taken." An illustration from American legal history is the long series of civil rights decisions. Judge Philip C. Jessup has argued that the same pattern may be unfolding with human rights on the international scene. The British political philosopher Michael Oakeshott expresses the validity of this tradition when he writes: "Those who look with suspicion on an achievement because it was not part of the design will, in the end, find themselves having to be suspicious of all the greatest human achievements."[9]

What is basic to the legal approach and central to its view of the interconnectedness of things is an underlying modesty about the direct application of general principles and the manner in which they evolve. In his early writings, Justice Holmes observed:

> It is the merit of the common law that it decides the case first and determines the principle afterwards. Looking at the forms of logic it might be inferred that when you have a minor premise and a conclusion, there must be a major, which you are also prepared then and there to assert. But in fact lawyers, like other men,

frequently see well enough how they ought to decide on a given state of facts without being very clear as to the *ratio decidendi*. In cases of first impression Lord Mansfield's often-quoted advice to the business man who was suddenly appointed judge, that he should state his conclusions and not give his reasons, as his judgment would probably be right and the reasons certainly wrong, is not without its application to more educated courts.

Holmes reasoned that only with a series of determinations on the same subject matter and the process of "reconciling cases" could the principle be firmly stated which until then had been at best obscurely sensed or felt. Of the process he wrote: "A well-settled legal doctrine embodies the work of many minds, and has been tested in form as well as substance by trained critics whose practical interest it is to resist it at every stage." In the determination of legal norms in the common law, there is a process at work that is half based on specifics and the case at hand, half determined by the realm of creative ambiguity. Assessing that process, Paul Freund can write: "This is not to exalt blind groping or mystical intuition . . . but to suggest that insight may not outrun foresight . . . that the advancement of doctrine need not await an exposition of its full reach."[10] Looking back on the decisions of a lifetime in all the diverse spheres of human experience, who can say that this process is restricted to the law?

Morality in politics and foreign policy takes its cue from the law in this matter. Its highest realizable form of judgment is prudence. For the working diplomat, as compared with the cloistered scholar, practical morality is generally the highest moral attainment. Diplomacy, like law, has its share of "blind groping" and "intuition." It operates within limits set by accidents and contingencies. "Prudence," wrote Niebuhr, "is a civic virtue because it is necessary not only to strive for justice, but to take cognizance of all contingencies in preserving the stability and health of a community." Prudence is the wise application of the principles of justice to the contingencies of interest and power in political life. "Political tasks," Niebuhr insisted, "require a shrewd admixture of principle and expediency, of loyalty to general standards of justice and adjustment to actual power."[11]

Niebuhr's practical morality has not commended itself to most moralists and rationalists. Utopian idealists would put an end to the role of self-interest and power in political life. Expediency more often is given a pejorative rather than a positive meaning. Talk of the limitations of morality leads some of the followers of the late Leo Strauss to condemn such an approach as being an ethic of self-denial. The poet laments the tendency of man to do the right thing for the wrong reason. Pragmatism is denounced for its negative view of man and politics. And the cynic finds fault with the practical moralist for claiming too much for morality in politics even as the abstract moralist questions any compromise of principle with expediency.

Moralists and rationalists, for their part, are open to a no less outspoken criticism. Hans J. Morgenthau writes in "Fragment of an Intellectual Autobiography": "This aversion to a dogmatism that sacrifices pragmatic effectiveness for logical or ideological consistency has remained a persistent element of my intellectual attitude." On the necessity for blind groping and intuition condemned by the rationalists, Morgenthau writes:

> Our aspirations, molding our expectations, take account of what we would like the empirical world to look like rather than what it actually is. Thus endlessly, empirical reality denies the validity of our aspirations and expectations. I aspired to understand the riddle of human existence, and I expected academic philosophy to show me the way; but academic philosophy did not do what I expected it to do. We expect the oracle to give us a clearcut answer. What we get is an enigma compounding the riddle. What remains is a searching mind, conscious of itself and the world, seeing, hearing, feeling, thinking, and speaking—seeking ultimate reality beyond illusion.[12]

Practical morality rests on the assumption that in domestic politics and international politics prudence can supply concrete reasons where abstract principles are insufficient. Edmund Burke placed prudence first in the rank of virtues in politics and morality. Its rules are seldom exact, never universal (although it makes reference to ideals that are universal). We can never be sure of its judgments as they forecast the future. Its failures rest on the fact that every political strategy falls short of its goals or bears only the most remote relationship to what was intended. Democracy from one perspective represents an institutionalized form of prudence with its balancing of power and its methods of finding proximate solutions to apparently insoluble problems. In one sense, democracy represents the ironic triumph of common sense over the foolishness of wise men. "Wise men are inevitably tempted to follow either one or the other line of 'rational' advance of which the bourgeois and the Marxist ideologues are perfect types. The one form of thought regards all social and historic processes as self-regulating. The alternative type of thought conceives a social or historical goal, presumably desired for all humanity and seeks to 'plan' for its achievement." Edmund Burke states the problem even more forcefully: "I have known, and . . . cooperated with great men; and I have never yet seen any plan which has not been mended by the observations of those who were much inferior in understanding to the person who took the lead." [13]

Thus political morality, or practical morality, remains close to the people, to politics, and to the moral problem. It is unashamed of the need in politics to settle for the best possible solution. It strives to prevent the destruction of higher moral principles by claims for their immediacy, knowing full well that they are too far removed to offer concrete guides for every foreign policy problem. The precepts that do offer guidance are not in themselves the final ends of society but coexist with other precepts and guidelines.

Practical morality, because it asks less of moral principles, leaves more to their continuing influence. It is built not on fixed codes or universal standards but on a persistent and continuing process of moral as well as political valuation. If this more modest conception of the role of morality is needed in domestic politics, its value is even greater on the international scene where the force of nationalism gives the clash of interests and power an intensity and ferocity not known in other spheres. Internationally, "the claim to universality which inspires the moral code of one particular group is incompatible with the identical claim of another group; the world has room for only one, and the other must yield or be destroyed." In international politics, as we have seen, "the nationalistic masses of our time meet in the international arena, each group convinced that it executes the mandate of history, that it does for humanity what it seems to do for itself, and that it fulfills a sacred mission ordained by providence, however defined." It may well be that in such an international order rivals "meet under an empty sky from which the gods have departed." [14] It is also possible, however, that practical morality, as in the harsh conflicts that lead to the division of families and the rancorous clashes of hostile political movements, can still exercise a gentle civilizing effect.

Practical morality knows that zeal for a cause may be one of the strongest and most dangerous irritants to which human passion is subject. It strives, therefore, to limit the crusading spirit. Practical morality recognizes the ubiquity of both self-interest and national interests. Hence it seeks ways of identifying convergent interests, not denying their existence. Practical morality observes that neither men nor nations can escape moral valuations. Thus it rejects moral cynicism. Practical morality understands the reality of power without sanctifying it as man's final end in life. It warns of the perils of power, mitigates the struggle and channels power to constructive aims, civilizes the means of power, and protects the individual in his private pursuit of ultimate ends. Practical morality operates at the intersection of politics and morality, not promising utopia or accepting the "war of each against all." It draws on the thought of great minds and the lessons of experience while looking creatively for new turns; it serves men where they are in the present without abandoning hope; it is in the process of *becoming* and is not confined to tablets of stone. Practical morality serves us now and for the future. Its legacy has undergirded and inspired the beginning and the end of this study. On it rest the prospects and potential for morality in foreign policy.

Notes

❖ Chapter I

1. Morton A. Kaplan, *Justice, Human Nature and Political Obligation* (New York: Free Press, 1976), ix, 6.
2. June Bingham, *Courage to Change: An Introduction to the Life and Thought of Reinhold Niebuhr* (New York: Charles Scribner's Sons, 1961), 62.
3. Sir Harold Nicolson, *Diplomacy* (London: Oxford University Press, 1939), 50.
4. Niccolo Machiavelli, *The Prince and the Discourses* (New York: Random House, 1940), 63–64.
5. Nicolson, *Diplomacy*, 45–46.
6. *Ibid.*, 76.
7. Kenneth W. Thompson, *Masters of International Thought* (Baton Rouge: Louisiana State University Press, 1980).
8. Sir Harold Nicolson, *Portrait of a Diplomatist* (Boston: Houghton Mifflin, 1930), 312, 314.
9. *Ibid.*, 316.
10. Tribute by the author to Agnes R. Thompson, August 25, 1976.

❖ Chapter II

1. Karl Popper, *The Open Society and Its Enemies* (4th ed.; Princeton, N.J.: Princeton University Press, 1963); William M. McGovern, *From Luther to Hitler: The History of Fascist-Nazi Political Philosophy* (Boston: Houghton Mifflin, 1941).
2. Worthington C. Ford (ed.), *The Writings of George Washington* (New York: G. P. Putnam's Sons, 1892), XIII, 316.
3. From his speech in the United States Senate, January 9, 1900, in Ruhl J. Bartlett, *The Record of American Diplomacy* (4th ed.; New York: Alfred A. Knopf, 1964), 385.
4. Julius W. Pratt, "The Ideology of American Expansion," in Avery Craven (ed.), *Essays in Honor of W. E. Dodd* (Chicago: University of Chicago Press, 1935), 345.
5. Quoted in Robert Ferrell, *American Diplomacy: A History* (3rd ed.; New York: W. W. Norton, 1975), 181.
6. *Ibid.*, 304.

7. Albert Bushnell Hart (ed.), *Selected Addresses and Public Papers of Woodrow Wilson* (New York: Boni & Leveright, 1918), 247–48; Clark M. Eichelberger, *Organizing for Peace: A Personal History of the Founding of the United Nations* (New York: Harper & Row, 1977), 203.

8. Eichelberger, *Organizing for Peace*, 203.

9. William Graham Sumner, "Democracy and Responsible Government," in his *The Challenge of Facts and Other Essays* (New Haven, Conn.: Yale University Press, 1914), 245–46.

10. Reinhold Niebuhr, *Christian Realism and Political Problems* (New York: Charles Scribner's Sons, 1953), 99.

11. Alexis de Tocqueville, *Democracy in America* (New York: Vintage Books, 1954), II, vi; Michel de Crèvecoeur, *Letters from an American Farmer* (New York: E. P. Dutton, 1912), 41; Thomas Jefferson to John Adams, October 28, 1813, in Thomas Jefferson, *Writings* (Washington, D.C.: Thomas Jefferson Memorial Association, 1904), XIII, 401.

12. De Tocqueville, *Democracy in America*, II, 11.

13. *Ibid.*, 18.

14. *Ibid.*, 236.

15. Daniel P. Moynihan, "The United States in Opposition," *Commentary*, March, 1975, p. 33.

16. *Ibid.*, 43.

17. *Ibid.*

18. *Ibid.*, 44.

19. De Tocqueville, *Democracy in America*, II, v.

20. Lord John Edward Dalberg-Acton, *Essays on Freedom and Power* (Glencoe, Ill.: Free Press, 1948), 364.

21. De Tocqueville, *Democracy in America*, II, 44.

22. John Stuart Mill, *Utilitarianism, Liberty and Representative Government* (London: J. M. Dent, 1910), 178; Abraham Lincoln to Horace Greeley, August 22, 1862, in Roy P. Basler (ed.), *Abraham Lincoln: His Speeches and Writings* (New York: World Publishing Co., 1946), 652.

23. Albert Shaw (ed.), *The Messages and Papers of Woodrow Wilson* (New York: Review of Reviews Corp., 1924), I, 356.

24. James Madison, *Letters and Other Writings, 1829–1836* (Philadelphia: J. B. Lippincott, 1865), 20.

25. Reinhold Niebuhr, "Power and Ideology," in William T. R. Fox (ed.), *Theoretical Aspects of International Relations* (Notre Dame, Ind.: University of Notre Dame Press, 1959), 107–108.

26. *Ibid.*, 115.

27. De Tocqueville, *Democracy in America*, II, 236.

28. Kenneth W. Thompson and Barbara R. Fogel, *Higher Education and Social Change: Promising Experiments in Developing Countries* (2 vols.; New York: Praeger, 1976, 1977).

29. De Tocqueville, *Democracy in America*, II, 44.

❖ Chapter III

1. Elizabeth Drew, "Human Rights," *New Yorker*, July 18, 1977, pp. 41, 42.

Of all the writings on the origins of the Carter human rights campaign, this article remains the most lucid, best-informed appraisal of the politics of human rights and the evolution of a policy.

2. Reinhold Niebuhr, *The Irony of American History* (New York: Charles Scribner's Sons, 1952), 23.

3. Reinhold Niebuhr, *The Structure of Nations and Empires* (New York: Charles Scribner's Sons, 1959), 299.

4. Reinhold Niebuhr and Alan Heimert, *A Nation So Conceived* (New York: Charles Scribner's Sons, 1963), 27.

5. Louis Halle, "The Application of Morality to Foreign Policy" (Conference on Ethics and Foreign Policy, University of Virginia at Charlottesville, June, 1977), 2.

6. George F. Kennan, Letter to the author on human rights (Conference on Ethics and Foreign Policy, University of Virginia at Charlottesville, June, 1977).

7. Philip C. Jessup, "Ethics and Foreign Policy" (Conference on Ethics and Foreign Policy, University of Virginia at Charlottesville, June, 1977), 1; Halle, "The Application of Morality to Foreign Policy," 7, 8.

8. Jessup, "Ethics and Foreign Policy," 2.

9. Quoted in Norman Graebner, "Humanitarianism and Foreign Policy" (Conference on Ethics and Foreign Policy, University of Virginia at Charlottesville, June, 1977), 1, 2.

10. *Ibid.*, 3, 5, 7.

11. Niebuhr, *The Irony of American History*, 130.

12. Hans J. Morgenthau, "Human Rights" (Conference on Ethics and Foreign Policy, University of Virginia at Charlottesville, June, 1977), 1.

13. Jessup, "Ethics and Foreign Policy," 3.

14. Kennan, Letter to the author.

15. See Hans J. Morgenthau, *Human Rights and Foreign Policy; First Distinguished CRIA Lecture on Morality and Foreign Policy* (New York: Council on Religion and International Affairs, 1979).

16. Karl von Clausewitz, quoted in Michael Howard, "Ethics and Power in International Politics," Third Martin Wright Memorial Lecture, January 12, 1977, p. 372.

17. Howard, "Ethics and Power in International Politics," 373, 374.

18. Reinhold Niebuhr, *Moral Man and Immoral Society: A Study in Ethics and Politics* (New York: Charles Scribner's Sons, 1932), 4.

19. Frederick T. Gates, "An Address on the Tenth Anniversary of the [Rockefeller] Institute [for Medical Research], 1911" (Frederick T. Gates Collection, Rockefeller Foundation Archives, New York City); Raymond B. Fosdick, *The Story of the Rockefeller Foundation* (New York: Harper & Brothers, 1952), 290.

20. Raymond B. Fosdick, "President's Review," *Rockefeller Foundation Annual Report*, 1941, p. 10.

21. New York *Times*, August 1, 1976, Section IV, p. 1.

22. Hans J. Morgenthau, "The Pathology of American Power," *International Security*, I (Winter, 1977), 14.

23. *Ibid.*, 16.

24. London *Times*, September 28, 1938.
25. Morgenthau, "The Pathology of American Power," 18–19.
26. *Ibid.*, 20.
27. Kenneth W. Thompson, Soedjatmoko *et al.*, *Reconstituting the Human Community* (New Haven: The Hazen Foundation, 1972); Kenneth W. Thompson and Barbara R. Fogel, *Higher Education and Social Change: Promising Experiments in Developing Countries* (2 vols.; New York: Praeger, 1976, 1977); The Stanton Panel, *International Information, Education and Cultural Relations: Recommendations for the Future* (Washington: Georgetown University, 1975).
28. P. C. C. Evans, London *Times Higher Education Supplement*, June 3, 1977, p. 21a.
29. W. Arthur Lewis, "The University in Less Developed Countries," *International Council for Educational Development Occasional Paper No. 11*, pp. 6, 7.
30. *Ibid.*, 7–8, 8–9.
31. William James, London *Times Higher Education Supplement*, June 3, 1977.
32. Theodore Hesburgh, comment to the author concerning the twelve-donor agency study of higher education and social change, September, 1975.
33. Fosdick, "President's Review."
34. New York *Times*, March 15, 1965, p. 30.
35. Lester B. Pearson *et al.*, *Partners in Development: Report of the Commission on International Development* (New York: Praeger, 1969), 8.

❖ Chapter IV

1. Edmond Cahn, *The Sense of Injustice* (Bloomington: Indiana University Press, 1949), 2.
2. *Ibid.*, 6; Blaise Pascal, *Pensées* (New York: Modern Library, 1941), 103.
3. Werner Jaeger, *Aristotle* (London: Oxford University Press, 1934), 337–45; Reinhold Niebuhr, *The Nature and Destiny of Man: A Christian Interpretation* (New York: Charles Scribner's Sons, 1945), I, 9.
4. Friedrich Nietzsche, *Kritik und Zukunft der Kultur* (Zurich: Rascher & Cie, 1935).
5. Niebuhr, *The Nature and Destiny of Man*, I, 281.
6. *Ibid.*, 282.
7. *Ibid.*, 283; Francisco Suárez, *Tractatus de Legibus* (Madrid: Consejo Superior de Ivestigations Cientificas, Instituto Francisco de Vitoria, 1971), I, 9; Niebuhr, *The Nature and Destiny of Man*, I, 284.
8. Paul Freund, *On Law and Justice* (Cambridge, Mass.: Harvard University Press, 1968), 8; Stuart Hughes, "Is Contemporary History Real History?" *American Scholar*, XXXII (1963), 520.
9. Freund, *On Law and Justice*, 20.
10. Niebuhr, *The Nature and Destiny of Man*, I, 22, 23.
11. *Ibid.*, 23–24.
12. Reinhold Niebuhr, *The Structure of Nations and Empires* (New York:

Charles Scribner's Sons, 1959), 72; Reinhold Niebuhr, *Leaves from the Notebook of a Tamed Cynic* (New York: Willett, Clark & Colby, 1929), 191.

13. June Bingham, *Courage to Change* (New York: Charles Scribner's Sons, 1961).

14. Reinhold Niebuhr, *Christianity and Power Politics* (New York: Charles Scribner's Sons, 1940), 70; Reinhold Niebuhr, *Moral Man and Immoral Society* (New York: Charles Scribner's Sons, 1932), 192–93.

15. H. V. F. Somerset, *A Note-Book of Edmund Burke* (London: Cambridge University Press, 1957), 68; quoted in Reinhold Niebuhr, *Man's Nature and His Communities* (New York: Charles Scribner's Sons, 1965), 24.

16. Niebuhr, *The Nature and Destiny of Man*, I, 68, 82; Reinhold Niebuhr, "Moralists and Politics," *Christian Century*, XLIX (July 6, 1932), 858; Niebuhr, *Man's Nature and His Communities*, 125.

17. Herbert Butterfield, "Religion and Politics" (an unpublished paper made available to the author).

18. *Ibid.*, 2, 4.

19. *Ibid.*, 2, 7.

20. *Ibid.*, 9.

21. *Ibid.*, 11.

22. *Ibid.*, 11–12.

23. *Ibid.*, 12.

24. *Ibid.*, 10.

25. Hans J. Morgenthau, *Scientific Man vs. Power Politics* (Chicago: University of Chicago Press, 1946), 10, 13.

26. *Ibid.*, 77.

27. *Ibid.*, 80. (The quotations and examples of utopian thought are all drawn from Morgenthau's first great work, *Scientific Man*, a treatise which has lost none of its relevance in the 1980s.)

28. *Ibid.*, 81, 82, 83.

29. *Ibid.*, 83–85.

30. C. L. Sulzberger, "Memories I: Faded Dreams," Charlottesville (Va.) *Daily Progress*, December 18, 1977, p. 5.

31. Reinhold Niebuhr, *Beyond Tragedy* (New York: Charles Scribner's Sons, 1937), 155, 158.

32. Quoted in St. Augustine, *City of God*, ed. Vernon J. Bourke (Garden City, N.Y.: Image Books, 1958), 1.

33. *Ibid.*, 23, 24, 27.

34. *Ibid.*, 25.

35. *Ibid.*, 32.

36. Reinhold Niebuhr, *Christian Realism and Political Problems* (New York: Charles Scribner's Sons, 1953), 3.

37. Reinhold Niebuhr, "Editorial," *Christianity and Society*, X (Spring, 1945), 4.

38. Reinhold Niebuhr, "The Blind Leaders," *Christianity and Society*, XIV (Spring, 1949), 6.

39. See the writings of F. S. Northedge of the London School of Economics in the *Journal of International Studies*.

40. I. L. Claude, review of Edward L. Morse's *Modernization and Transformation in International Relations*, in *Political Science Quarterly*, XCII (Winter, 1977–1978), 716.

41. Roscoe Pound, *An Introduction to the Philosophy of Law* (New Haven, Conn.: Yale University Press, 1922), 23.

❖ Conclusions

1. Edmond Cahn, *The Moral Decision* (Bloomington: Indiana University Press, 1955), 4.

2. *Ibid.*, 9.

3. *Ibid.*, 10, 11.

4. *Ibid.*, 11.

5. *Ibid.*, 14.

6. Kenneth W. Thompson and Robert J. Myers (eds.), *Truth and Tragedy: A Tribute to Hans Morgenthau* (Washington, D.C.: New Republic Book Co., 1977), 4.

7. Cahn, *The Moral Decision*, 21, 22.

8. Quoted in Paul Freund, *On Law and Justice* (Cambridge, Mass.: Harvard University Press, 1968), 71.

9. Jerome Bruner, *On Knowing: Essays for the Left Hand* (Cambridge, Mass.: Belknapp Press of Harvard University Press, 1962), 24–25; Freund, *On Law and Justice*, 72; Michael Oakeshott, "The Universities," *Cambridge Journal*, II (1949), 532.

10. Oliver Wendell Holmes, "Codes and the Arrangement of the Law," *American Law Review*, V (1870), 1, reprinted in *Harvard Law Review*, XLIV (1931), 725; Freund, *On Law and Justice*, 76.

11. Reinhold Niebuhr, "School Aid, the President and the Hierarchy," *New Leader*, XLIV (March 20, 1961), 9; Reinhold Niebuhr, "Realistic Internationalism," *Christianity and Society*, IX (Fall, 1944), 4.

12. Quoted in Thompson and Myers, *Truth and Tragedy*, 14, 16–17.

13. Reinhold Niebuhr, *The Irony of American History* (New York: Charles Scribner's Sons, 1952), 106; Edmund Burke, "Reflections," *Works* (8 vols.; London: Henry G. Bohn, 1855–1864), III, 456–57.

14. Hans J. Morgenthau, *Politics Among Nations: The Struggle for Power and Peace* (5th ed.; New York: Alfred A. Knopf, 1978), 263.

Index